DYNAM

ADMINISTRATION

The Collected Papers of Mary Parker Follett

Edited by

HENRY C. METCALF, Ph.D.

Director of The Bureau of Personnel Administration, New York
Co-Author of "Personnel Administration: Its Principles and Practice"
and "Labor Relations under the Recovery Act"

and

L. URWICK, O.B.E., M.C., M.A., F.I.I.A.

Chairman, Urwick, Orr & Partners Ltd., London (Consulting Specialists
in Organization and Management)
Sometime Director of the International Management Institute, Geneva
Author of "The Meaning of Rationalisation," "Management of To-morrow"
Co-Author of "Papers in the Science of Administration," etc.

Martino Publishing
Mansfield Centre, CT
2013

Martino Publishing
P.O. Box 373,
Mansfield Centre, CT 06250 USA

ISBN 978-1-61427-477-3

© *2013 Martino Publishing*

Cover design by T. Matarazzo

Printed in the United States of America On 100% Acid-Free Paper

DYNAMIC ADMINISTRATION

The Collected Papers of Mary Parker Follett

Edited by

HENRY C. METCALF, Ph.D.

Director of The Bureau of Personnel Administration, New York
Co-Author of "Personnel Administration: Its Principles and Practice"
and "Labor Relations under the Recovery Act"

and

L. URWICK, O.B.E., M.C., M.A., F.I.I.A.

Chairman, Urwick, Orr & Partners Ltd., London (Consulting Specialists
in Organization and Management)
Sometime Director of the International Management Institute, Geneva
Author of "The Meaning of Rationalisation," "Management of To-morrow"
Co-Author of "Papers in the Science of Administration," etc.

HARPER & BROTHERS PUBLISHERS

NEW YORK AND LONDON

Printed in the United States of America

CONTENTS

FOREWORD

MAJOR URWICK and Dr. Metcalf have rendered a conspicuous service by editing this collection of Mary Follett's lectures on business management. They contain teaching which was of importance when the lectures were delivered, and which many people felt should be preserved in a collated form and given a wider public. The circumstances of to-day have increased that importance. Many people are being called upon to fill new administrative posts, and these lectures teach the principles which should underly all administrative method.

As the Editors point out in their Introduction, Mary Follett devoted a lifetime to searching for the true principles of organization which would ensure a stable foundation for the steady, ordered progress of human well-being. That her search was not in vain will be evident to all who read the lectures. Her teaching is not theoretical, but is based on a close study of the practice of a large number of business undertakings. She chose this field of enquiry to supplement her work on local and national government because she realized that the principles which should determine organization are identical, no matter what the purpose which that organization is designed to serve. As she said in one of her lectures, "I am studying business management because it is among business men, not all, but a few, that I find the greatest vitality of thinking to-day, and I like to do my thinking where it is most alive."

I have often listened to Mary Follett's lectures, and I enjoyed her friendship for many years. As one who, as a business administrator and in other spheres, has tried to act on the principles she enunciates, I can say with confidence that there is not a single administrator who, if he has an open mind (and all others are hopeless!), would not benefit by reading this collection of her papers. They are not abstruse, nor overloaded and difficult to read; on the contrary, they are simple, straightforward and easily understandable. Yet the teaching they contain is so profound as to merit study by even the most successful of practical administrators.

The Editors have very wisely provided an introductory chapter in which Mary Follett's work is outlined against the background of her active life. The principles which she outlined are fundamental to all human progress. They should be widely known and acted upon, particularly at the present time, when good organization is a matter of supreme importance to national survival. They will be found more necessary when the war is over and humanity is faced with the almost superhuman task of fashioning a new and better world.

It is with every confidence that I commend this book not only to every administrator in England and in the United States, whether great or small, whether in business or in Government, but also to those whose duty it is to select and train men who will hold responsible positions in the future governance of society.

B. S. ROWNTREE.

HIGH WYCOMBE.
December, 1940.

INTRODUCTION

THIS volume pays tribute to a political and business philosopher of the first rank, Mary Parker Follett—a truly creative, intensely vital mind, which found its way to the fundamental problems first of the community and State, and later of industrial organization and administration, through a keen insight into human nature and tireless devotion to the task of arriving at a practical application of the social sciences in government and in industry.

Miss Follett was not a "business woman," in the sense of having actually managed any sort of business. But her lucid and illuminating ideas about organization were of priceless interest and value to the many industrial leaders and students of human relations problems, organization and politics with whom she came in contact. Her conceptions were in advance of her time. They are still in advance of current thinking. But they are a gold-mine of suggestion for anyone who is interested in the problems of establishing and maintaining human co-operation in the conduct of an enterprise. They have the added advantage of being presented with remarkable simplicity and clarity.

Briefly stated, the Follett philosophy is that any enduring society, any continuously productive industrial organization, must be grounded upon a recognition of the motivating desires of the individual and of the group. Consistently, Miss Follett sought to force home a realization of the fact that the democratic way of life, implemented by intelligent organization and administration of government and of industry, is to work toward an honest integration of all points of view, to the end that every individuality may be mobilized and made to count both as a person and as an effective part of his group and of society as a whole.

Before she died, Miss Follett felt that she had at last

9

arrived at some definite principles underlying human organization, and present wherever good organization is found. In the final paper in this volume she endeavoured to summarize these principles. But they are best studied in the light of the prolonged intellectual exploration which led up to them, as revealed in the earlier papers.

．　　　．　　　．　　　．　　　．

Born in Boston in 1868, Mary Follett was much influenced in her early school days by one of the mistresses at the Thayer Academy. This teacher and friend impressed upon her the significance of scientific methods of study and awakened an interest in philosophy. From her, too, Mary must have derived immense intellectual stimulation, as well as a leaning towards simplicity of life.

She continued her studies at Radcliffe College (then known as "The Annexe"). Her work there and her later accomplishments gave her a place among the College's fifty most distinguished graduates, memorialized in the *Radcliffe Quarterly* for April, 1934. "Mary Parker Follett, An Appreciation" was written by Professor Richard Cabot of Harvard University, who was one of the group of intimate friends in Cambridge, Mass., with whom she associated most closely. His "Appreciation" began:

"One of the most distinguished of Radcliffe's graduates ended in December, 1933, a life unique in the quality of its service to the community.

"Her graduation with the class of 1898, *summa cum laude*, followed a course devoted to economics, government and philosophy, and led up to graduate study in Paris. . . ."

Her six years at Radcliffe were broken by one year at Newnham (Cambridge, England), 1890–1, where she read history, law and political science, laid the foundations of her interests in English life, customs and conditions, and formed the first of many deep and lasting friendships which proved to be the backbone of her close bond with English life. It is recorded that Newnham exercised considerable influence on her, and she returned to America no longer an inexperienced girl, but a developed and assured woman. It is worth adding that her first book *The Speaker of the House of Representatives*, grew out of a paper read to the Newnham Historical Society.

Mary Follett's outstanding characteristic was a facility for winning the confidence and esteem of those with whom she came in contact; she established a deeply-rooted understanding and friendship with a wide circle of eminent men and women on both sides of the Atlantic. The root of this social gift was her vivid interest in life. Every individual's experience, his relations with others and with the social groups—large or small—of which he was a part, were the food for her thought. She listened with alert and kindly attention; she discussed problems in a temper which drew the best out of the individual with whom she was talking. The strength of the personal associations she thus built up was remarkable. For thirty years she shared a home with her friend, Miss Isobel L. Briggs, in Boston. For more than five years after Miss Briggs' death, she lived in Chelsea (London) with Dame Katherine Furze.

As the years passed, Miss Follett began gradually to translate the knowledge she had acquired throughout her earlier life into valuable service to the community. She began her public work in 1900 with the formation of the Roxbury Debating Club in the Roxbury Neighbourhood House of Boston, which later expanded into the "Highland Union" and the "Roxbury League." This was to be the scene of her active work for many years. It was a locality of poor families, with boys and girls going early to work in its factories and shops and sorely in need of the social, recreational and educational facilities provided by the Roxbury Centres. Here she began to work out in practical form the principles which were later to appear in *The New State*, with the local group serving as the basis of a new and more realistic conception of democracy.

As far back as 1900 also, Miss Follett conceived the idea of opening up the schoolhouses of Boston after school hours for educational and social activities. By 1909 she was Chairman of the School House Sub-Committee of the Women's Municipal League of Boston. This League aimed at legislation which would make the school buildings available for evening community activities. The value of such work had not to be proved, but only the soundness of the claim for public use of the idle buildings. To have to provide special buildings for the evening activities seemed, as Mary Follett herself put it, "bad business management on our part." In 1911, the Committee, now renamed "The Committee on the Extended Use of School Buildings," secured the experimental use of one building for the winter. By the following winter, the success of the experiment had encouraged legislation providing facilities in four schools. This proved the foundation of a widespread social movement. For many people came to see the Boston School Centres and went away inspired to work for the same objectives in their own cities.

In tribute to her work, James T. Mulroy, Director of Extended Use of the Public Schools of Boston, writes:[1]

"Miss Follett can be truly called the founder of the Boston School Centers—originally termed Evening Centers. . . .

"From the very beginning of the school center movement in this city, Miss Follett served as chairman of the department advisory committee; even up to her sudden and unexpected death she exerted a guiding hand and influence in maintaining the high standards and ideals set by her for the work at its inception, and in shaping and formulating the policies of the department. Her alert, keen mind, civic consciousness and vision made a deep imprint on the social and educational life of Boston. The staff and friends of the Boston School Centers feel the loss of Miss Follett and will ever revere her memory."

.   .   .   .   .

Miss Follett's interest next centred on the possibilities of vocational guidance. During a visit to Edinburgh in 1902,

[1] Letter dated September 15th, 1935, in Bureau of Personnel Administration files.

she was much impressed by some pioneer vocational guidance work there, and she had long cherished a desire to develop guidance activities in connection with evening schools. She was about to undertake this work privately when, in the autumn of 1912, the directors of the Boston School System decided to set up a Placement Bureau in connection with certain day schools and the Girls' Trade Union League. Miss Follett readily accepted membership on the first Placement Bureau Committee and shared the expenses of the five years' work. It then became an official municipal "Department of Vocational Guidance," in which Miss Follett maintained an active interest almost until her death.

The work of the Placement Bureau afforded her an even more valuable contact with industry. Under her guidance, files of information about working conditions in different industries were gradually built up. It was at this time, in fact, that her main interest shifted from political and social issues to problems of industrial relations.

Miss Follett's vital interest in the human problems of industry did not, however, detract her attention altogether from her study of the wider issues, for she was still at work on the interpretation of her studies of society and her experience in communal activity. Her first publication was the pamphlet on *The Speaker of the House of Representatives*, (1909), but her main work, *The New State*, did not appear till 1920, to be closely followed (1924) by a masterly treatise in a parallel field under the title *Creative Experience*.

Miss Follett had now reached the front rank of political scientists. *The Speaker of the House of Representatives* had carried an Introduction by the well-known Professor Albert Bushnell Hart. *The New State* was reviewed in learned journals the world over, and brought her national and international recognition. It led to her friendship with Lord Haldane, the English statesman and philosopher, and with other distinguished philosophers and political scientists. The higher the intellectual calibre of the men who came in contact with her thought, the more impressed were they by her intellectual originality. Her aim was quite simple: she wanted a better ordered society in which the individual could live a fuller and more satisfactory life, and she endeavoured by her own pioneering to contribute to all the social experiments which were being made in an attempt to find the real avenue to this fuller life.

Always a realist, the study of the legal forms and the machinery of government only served to bring home the more fully to Mary Follett the fact that authority, sovereignty, power, and basic concepts of government are, in the final analysis, psychological issues. Without going into the question of democratic *versus* autocratic forms, it is clear that government—the direction of the many by the few in the interest of common order and unified action—must, in the long run, rest on consent. It may be a passive consent; it may be an acquiescence dictated by fear; but consent must be there. The alternative is revolution. And the psychological analysis of the nature of that consent and the conditions under which it can be made spontaneous and effective were Miss Follett's approach to the problems of government, whether of business or of society.

Her second book, *Creative Experience*, which is mainly psychological in interest and content, marks a definite advance both in the crystallization of thought and in style and phraseology. Its thesis is the reciprocal character—the interpenetration—of all psychological phenomena, from the simplest to the most complex: Human relationships—the warp and woof of society and of industry—are at their best when difference is solved through conference and co-operation, when the parties at interest (1) evoke each other's latent ideas based upon the facts of the situation, (2) come to see each other's viewpoints and to understand each other better, and (3) integrate those viewpoints and become united in the pursuit of their common goal.

Miss Follett makes it clear that there is never in real life, as there is in some laboratory experiments, a stimulus followed by a reaction as a distinct unit of study. The reaction releases further stimuli, and so on, *ad infinitum*.

Life is a continuous process. While a moment may be caught in a net of words as though it were unrelated to the past and its future, it escapes in the very act. Every human activity is inevitably "bound upon the wheel of change." It is not a thing in itself, but merely a moment in a process. To pretend otherwise is merely a convention, a convenience. And it is largely because men allow themselves to be blindfolded by these conventions that they fail so pitifully to understand the nature of the social phenomena with which they are dealing.

Creative Experience indicated, further, the trend of her ultimate interest. Many of her illustrations, even at this stage, were drawn from business situations, which from this time on occupied more and more of her time and thought. The book brought an immediate response from business men, many of whom called upon her to assist them with their own problems. "Often," she is reported to have said, "they could only spare time for luncheon, but I never had such interesting meals. One of these men gave me in a nutshell the threads of a tangle he had with his employees. He wanted me to straighten it out. I answered him straight from Fichte; he didn't know that, of course, but I did, and it seemed to meet the case."[2]

A sequel to her work with the Placement Bureau and the Vocational Guidance Bureau was membership on the Massachusetts Minimum Wage Board, where she (representing the public) met for years with representatives of the employers and of the employees. Furthermore, through her books she was brought into close touch with men who were responsible for the organization and management of industry, so that she learned at first hand their problems and their outlook. In a gradual transition, involving no abrupt changes of viewpoint nor severing of old connections, Mary Follett had passed naturally and logically from political science and the problems of government to social administration and the solution of social problems, and thence smoothly

[2] Quoted by F. M. Stawell in her Memoir in the *Newnham College Letter* for January, 1935.

into the realm of industrial organization and administration.
As Professor Cabot put it in the article quoted above:

"Her industrial experiences combined with her interests in
psychology because it was the psychology of business relations
that interested her. Psychologists and philosophers are swayed
in our time by the currents of biological opinion. Economics, her
leading study in college, is of course interwoven both in business
and in government. Ethics and sociology are aspects of the
human relations with which in all the other undertakings she
had been dealing. She saw one principle running through all
these social sciences, and wondered why they should be so
parochial, so departmentalized, in their behaviour. 'I do wish,'
she once said, 'that when a principle has been worked out, say
in ethics, it didn't have to be discovered all over again in psychology, in economics, in government, in business, in biology, and
in sociology. It's such a waste of time!' "

That viewpoint, together with the idea of reciprocal
reaction, of continuous process, were among Mary Follett's
chief contributions to the study of organization.

.   .   .   .   .

As explained later, it was in the annual conference
series on *Business Management as a Profession,* conducted
in New York for business executives by the Bureau
of Personnel Administration, that Miss Follett made her
first public contributions to the art of business administration. Beginning with the course entitled "Scientific Foundations of Business Administration,"[3] given in the year 1924–5,
she was a regular Bureau conference leader for four con-
secutive years, with a final paper contributed to the course
on "Economic and Social Planning," given in 1931–2.[4]
On visits to England in 1926 and 1928, she spoke at the
Rowntree Lecture Conferences (Oxford) and at a meeting
of the National Institute of Industrial Psychology. The
papers which she read were in the main adaptations of those

[3] Reprinted in this volume as Nos. I, II, III, and IV.
[4] Reprinted in this volume as No. XIV.

given in New York.[5] Although she displayed to English executives her full understanding of industry and its problems and her sound analysis of industrial organization, it was perhaps characteristic of English scepticism towards the scientific approach to management that her teaching roused but little enthusiasm outside of a small circle.

From 1929 to 1933 she lived in England. While she made no further public contributions until 1932, during this entire period she was studying English industrial conditions, chiefly by frequent personal meetings with industrialists and business men, by attending group discussions, and by the incessant application of her own method of thorough-going analysis of the problems she met. She was finding that the vital issues and original experiment in new forms of government, which were necessary for the establishment and maintenance of a truly democratic order, were more widespread in business than in any other form of human activity. Her own testimony, from two separate occasions, is worth quoting:[6]

1. "Since I have been in England I have been asked several times why I am studying business management. I will try to tell you. Free to choose between different paths of study, I have chosen this for a number of reasons. First of all, it is among business men (not all, but a few) that I find the greatest vitality of thinking to-day, and I like to do my thinking where it is most alive. I said last winter to a Professor of Philosophy: 'Do you realize that you philosophers have got to look to your laurels, that business men are doing some very valuable thinking and may get ahead of you?' And he acknowledged this, which I think was a very significant concession. Moreover, I find the thinking of business men to-day in line with the deepest and best thinking we have ever had. The last word in science—in biology—is the principle of unifying. The most profound philosophers have always given us unifying as the fundamental principle of life. And now business men are finding it is the way to run a successful

[5] See "Notes on English Papers," Appendix II, p. 318.
[6] The first quotation is from the paper given to the Rowntree Lecture Conference at Oxford in 1926. The second is taken from the first paper in the series given at the London School of Economics in 1933. (Neither appears in the earlier American texts from which the papers in question were adapted.)

business. Here the ideal and the practical have joined hands. That is why I am working at business management, because, while I care for the ideal, it is only because I want to help bring it into our everyday affairs.

"Another reason is because industry is the most important field of human activity, and management is the fundamental element in industry. It is now generally recognized that not bankers, not stockholders, but management is the pivot of business success. It is good management that draws credit, that draws workers, that draws customers. Moreover, whatever changes should come, whether industry is owned by individual capitalists, or by the State, or by the workers, it will always have to be managed. Management is a permanent function of business.

"The third reason why I am working at business management is because I believe in *control*, and so do our most progressive business men. I believe in the individual not trusting to fate or chance or inheritance or environment, but learning how to control his own life. And nowhere do I see such a complete acceptance of this as in business thinking, the thinking of more progressive business men. They are taking the mysticism out of business. They do not believe that there is anything fatalistic about the business cycle that is wholly beyond the comprehension of men; they believe that it can be studied and to some extent controlled."

2. "One of the most interesting things about business to me is that I find so many business men who are willing to try experiments. I should like to tell you about two evenings I spent last winter and the contrast between them. I went one evening to a drawing-room meeting where economists and M.Ps. talked of current affairs, of our present difficulties. It all seemed a little vague to me, did not seem really to come to grips with our problem. The next evening it happened that I went to a dinner of twenty business men who were discussing the question of centralization and decentralization. Each one had something to add from his own experience of the relation of branch firms to the central office, and the other problems included in the subject. *There* I found hope for the future. *There* men were not theorizing or dogmatizing; they were thinking of what they had actually done and they were willing to try new ways the next morning, so to speak. Business, because it gives us the opportunity of trying new roads, of blazing new trails, because, in short, it is pioneer work, pioneer work in the organized relations of human beings,

seems to me to offer as thrilling an experience as going into a new country and building railroads over new mountains. For whatever problems we solve in business management may help towards the solution of world problems, since the principles of organization and administration which are discovered as best for business can be applied to government or international relations. Indeed, the solution of world problems must eventually be built up from all the little bits of experience wherever people are consciously trying to solve problems of relation. And this attempt is being made more consciously and deliberately in industry than anywhere else."

During these later years also Mary Follett first became intimately acquainted with the organization and activities of the League of Nations. On her visits to Geneva, she was much impressed by all that she saw and learned, all the more so because she was made acutely aware of the difficulties that beset the League's administrative organization in its everyday work. She saw in the League of Nations a grand opportunity for the development in international relations of her fundamental principle of co-ordination as the basis of all well-organized human activity. She saw in it, too, further illustration of the many problems that she had found in the course of her studies of industrial organization, and made frequent allusions to it in her papers. In the League of Nations, she said, there is to be found "a striking example of the emergence of a leadership of function."[7]

On one of her visits to Geneva, she made the acquaintance of Dame Katherine Furze, then actively engaged in the Girl Guide movement, a movement which had much in common with the doctrines that Mary Follett herself had long been propounding for the better development of society. Close friendship developed, and Dame Katherine became Mary Follett's English hostess for the remaining years of her residence in London.

Mary Follett's last contribution in England to the subject of organization and management was the group of lectures

[7] Paper on "Leadership" read to the Rowntree Oxford Conference, October, 1928 (see "Notes on the English Papers," Appendix II, p. 318).

given in January–February, 1933, for the newly formed Department of Business Administration at the London School of Economics (University of London).[8] Several months earlier, however, she had visited America and given her final paper, entitled "Individualism in a Planned Society," for the Bureau of Personnel Administration.

On her return to England, she stayed well into the autumn of 1933, and then, in order to attend to some personal affairs, she hurriedly went off again to America. For some time her health had been giving cause for anxiety. But almost to her last breath she was mentally alert and absorbed in human relations problems. She died on December 18th, 1933.

.   .   .   .   .

Some day, it is to be hoped, a complete volume will be devoted to an honest and sympathetic interpretation of the life and works of Mary Parker Follett. In this brief account we cannot begin to give an adequate portrayal of this remarkably genuine, unique personality, whose warm friendship and stimulating presence were cherished by all who were privileged to know her, who was in herself an example of the principle which she found basic for every form of human organization, from each individual life to world relations—co-ordination. For she was a person of universal mind and viewpoint, rounded culture, combining an interest in religion, music, painting, nature, history and travel with her consuming lifetime absorption in discovering the basic principles which, put into operation in the government of city, state and nation, as well as of industry, would result in a socio-economic-political order in which every man would have the opportunity to give expression to his God-given right to live and grow and develop to the utmost of his capacity.

Comparison of her last papers with those given even in the earliest years reveals a remarkable consistency of thought. She had, by the soundness of her earliest analytical approach,

[8] See "Notes on English Papers," Appendix II, p. 318.

struck the true principles, and nothing that she found in her extensive later contact with business organization and management gave cause for changing them. She had built her structure upon the individual, his instincts and habits and desires, as a result of her insight during the early years, when she was engaged in social work. She saw that on the job, both as an individual and as part of a working group and of the total work force, he was activated by the same habits and desires as he was in his more personal life. Consequently she saw the individual and human relationships as the bedrock foundation of business organization, and business organization as simply a part of the whole human organization which makes up society. She knew that the fundamental organizational problem of any enterprise—be it national government, local government, business management, an educational system or Church administration—is the building and maintenance of dynamic, yet harmonious, human relations for joint effort in the most effective conduct of that enterprise. In her papers she consistently sought to make this point clear, as indicated by the following illustration:[9]

"You may wonder why I have talked of government, and of the League of Nations, instead of spending all my hour on leadership in industry. I have done it deliberately, because it seems to me a fact of very great significance that we are finding the same trend in all these different fields. It reinforces us in our conviction that we are moving in harmony with the deeper and more vital forces of human progress."

She showed her belief in this view, too, by the illustrations that she used in her exposition of the principles of industrial organization—illustrations that were drawn from the home, from social activities, from state councils, as well as from the affairs of many fields of industry and business. But perhaps the clearest evidence lies in the three papers that she gave in her later years to specialist groups, teaching them her basic

[9] From "Leadership," given at the Rowntree Oxford Conference, October, 1928.

doctrine of the leadership of function, of authority founded on the facts of the situation and on recognition of the fundamental personal and emotional factors that are part of both the leader and the led. These three papers were:

1. "The Opportunities for Leadership for the Nurse in Industry." (Annual Conference of the American Association of Industrial Nurses, May, 1928.)

2. "The Psychiatrist in Industry." (Occasion and place of reading not known, but probably about 1928 and certainly in America.)

3. "The Teacher-Student Relationship." (Occasion and place of reading not known, but probably 1928, and may have been given in England.)

Simply put, Mary Follett's universal principle means that business management is not something which is of significance only to those who seek a competence in the conduct of some competitive, profit-making enterprise. It is a part, and a significant part, of the wider field of human government. Business men have a great deal to learn from organized activities outside their own firms and industries, and other branches of human organization can learn much from what is best in business. The world of to-day needs new relationships among its groups.

One of the most heartening aspects of her philosophy is that it enables those whose lot is cast in business to see their work, not merely as a means of livelihood, not only as an honourable occupation with a large content of professional interest, but as a definite and vital contribution towards the building of that new social order which is the legitimate preoccupation of every thinking citizen. It is because her philosophy of organization and management opens up the possibility of the identification of business administrators, not only with the essential interests of their stockholders, the desires of their consumers and the best interests of their workers, but also with the deep, flowing currents of opinion which are shaping the society of the future, that it is the most important contribution to the business literature of our time.

Mary Follett was always preoccupied with the dynamic view of organization, with the thing in process, so to speak. Authority, Power, Leadership, the Giving of Orders, Conflict, Conciliation—all her key words are active words. There is a static or structural approach to the problem of organization which has its value; but those who are most convinced of the importance of such structural analysis would be the first to admit that it is only a step on the journey, an instrument of thought; it is not and cannot be complete in itself; it is only the anatomy of the subject. As in medicine, the study of anatomy may be an essential discipline, but it is in the physiology and psychology of the individual patient that that discipline finds its working justification.

Thus the four principles which she finally arrived at to express her view of organization were all active principles. In her own words, they are:

"1. Co-ordination by direct contact of the responsible people concerned.

2. Co-ordination in the early stages.

3. Co-ordination as a reciprocal relating of all the features in a situation.

4. Co-ordination as a continuing process."

Since these principles are carefully explained and illustrated by Miss Follett herself in the final paper in this volume, we must content ourselves here with merely this concise statement of them. These principles epitomize her teaching. She makes clear that, rightly understood and interpreted, they form the basis—the psychological foundations—upon which any enduring, smoothly-operating organization must rest.

.   .   .   .   .

The history of industry and business in the past twenty years is, in considerable part, a record of progress in the technique of management, in the methods by which the activities of business are organized and controlled. There has been some degree of development in the consideration given to the human and personal aspects of organization, but in the acceptance of a philosophy of management little headway has been made. Fifteen years ago Mary Follett expounded a philosophy of management that even to-day is a generation ahead of practice, and one can find therein a significant parallel with the pioneering work of Frederick W. Taylor. In his teaching, the adoption of a new philosophy of management—"the mental revolution" as he put it—was a fundamental part of his new technique; but, as knowledge of his methods spread, the practice of scientific management was allowed to develop and expand shorn from its underlying philosophy. Mary Follett was not concerned merely with the technique, the methods of management; her contacts with business and its leaders gave her ample chance of seeing the new technique emerge and grow. But with deeper insight she could see what too many business leaders missed, that the philosophy of management and its psychological foundations were still unheeded, perhaps even unknown. In this lies the greatness of her contribution. It is as modern and applicable to-day as it was when first she spoke; it will be as modern and applicable to-morrow.

Though she was concerned with principles rather than technique, she must not be thought of as theoretical. She was always insistent on the need "to get behind both academic abstractions and traditional conceptions and to try for a thoroughly realistic treatment of authority, power, leadership and control."

She was interested in problems of government, of organization and administration. Being an extremely large-minded person and wholly unimpressed by conventional categories, she was convinced of three things: first, that all such problems, whenever they occur, are fundamentally problems in human relations; secondly, while every human being is different, there is a sufficiently large common factor in human reactions to similar situations to permit the development of principles of administration; thirdly, and in

24

consequence, those principles must be sought and applied wherever the organization of human endeavours is required in the pursuit of a common objective. Her study of business management, brilliant and stimulating though her lectures are in and of themselves, was in her mind just a normal development—part of her general research into the theory and practice of the orderly control of human affairs. She found that in studying the management or government of business enterprises, she had a source of information and suggestions far richer than that afforded by the more conventional subject matter of political science.

In the same way, she found it natural that developments in the field of business administration should provide an avenue to progress in other branches of administration. Speaking of the processes of control and organization in business, she once remarked:[10]

"Certain changes have been going on in *business practice* which are destined, I believe, to alter our thinking fundamentally. I think this is a contribution which business is going to make to the world, and not only to the business world, but eventually to government and international relations. Men may be making useful products, but beyond this, by helping to solve the problems of human relations, they are perhaps destined to lead the world in the solution of those great problems of co-ordination and control upon which our future progress must depend."

Note on Mary Follett's Contributions to the Conferences of the Bureau of Personnal Administration

"Dr. Metcalf is deserving well of his countrymen, and of those all over the world, who are interested in the basic problem of economic control. If he had only 'discovered' Miss Follett and nothing else, he would have made a notable contribution to the philosophy of business."[11] The

[10] From the introductory and concluding remarks of her first lecture in the series given at the London School of Economics, 1933.
[11] *Bulletin of the International Management Institute*, Geneva, June, 1929.

"discovery" of Miss Follett, her "debut" in the business world, came about in this manner.

Dr. Metcalf had worked with Miss Follett in a number of forward-looking activities in Boston before the first World War. This relationship grew out of their common interest in vocational guidance. Along with her vocational guidance work in connection with the Boston school system, Miss Follett was actively interested in the work of the Vocation Bureau of Boston—set up by a group of business executives, educational and social leaders—because she was coming to realize that the real roots and the benefits of the vocational guidance movement were to be found in the work relations rather than in the school environment.

In 1918, Dr. Metcalf left full-time academic work to aid in setting up training programmes for employment managers for the Federal Government shipyards and munitions plants during the first World War. This was followed, in 1920, by the establishment of the Bureau of Personnel Administration, dedicated to the furtherance of sound employer-employee relations, whether in industry or any other form of organization.

All this is apropos the inception of one of the regular activities of the Bureau of Personnel Administration—a carefully prepared annual conference series on the general theme, "Business Management as an Evolving Profession," in which leading industrialists, Government officials, labour leaders, economists, psychologists, educators, lawyers, doctors, theologians and other oustanding leaders discuss, in the light of their own particular study and experience, some aspect of sound industrial management and human relationships. The aim and objective always have been to enable the executives, personnel workers and students of human relations problems in attendance to come to see industry as a whole and in its widely ramifying inter-relationships.

Certainly in those early years none was better qualified than Miss Follett to take a prominent part in this work, in which she maintained a vital interest throughout her life. Of her unique and fundamental contributions to the Bureau's conference series, previously included in four of the volumes resulting therefrom, all but one are reprinted in this volume, as well as her final paper, available hitherto only in mimeographed form. Together they give in a developmental way her philosophy of business administration.

It was in the winter of 1924-5 that Miss Follett made her first public contribution to the philosophy of business management. In the conference series entitled "Scientific Foundations of Business Administration" she presented the first four papers reprinted in this volume: "Constructive Conflict," "The Giving of Orders," "Business as an Integrative Unity" and "Power." They evidenced her interest in two basic questions: (1) "What do you want men to do?" and (2) "How will you scientifically control and guide men's conduct in work and social relations?"

In subsequent years she gave the further series of papers which gradually unfolded the fullness of her philosophy. It was perhaps in the second group—the papers on "Business Management as a Profession"—that there appeared some of her most original contributions, founded on the slowly emerging trend toward a new science in business, involving a broader concept of the reaction of industrial life to economic, social, political, legal and ethical tendencies. She found the signs of the new scientific basis for business management in the application of so-called "scientific management" to managerial technique; in the increasing tendency toward functionalized management; in the decrease of arbitrary authority; in the vitality of business men's thinking.

Her next contributions were concerned more specifically with the psychological bases of management, with the exposition of what she herself put as the summary of most of her philosophy—"functional relation is the continuing process of self-creating coherence." This idea appears as her foundation of business leadership; the interweaving and interpenetrating of the best ideas of both the leader and the led is continuously creating new situations. The real leader, then, will have sufficient insight not only to *meet* the next situation, but to *make* the next situation. And a system of organization which will allow men to create the next situation will be based, not on the idea of equality or arbitrary authority, but on functional unity.

In her final paper at a Bureau Conference, "Individualism in a Planned Society," given in 1932—a paper which carried her thinking into the national and world arena—she summarized her life study and thinking in four basic principles of sound organization and administration. The heart of these principles is *co-ordination*, and their goal is *control*, based upon the foundation of (1) "fact-control" rather than "man-control," and (2) central control as meaning "the correlation of many controls" rather than "a super-imposed control."

In the conclusion of this paper she made an appeal that is strikingly apposite to the world conditions of to-day: "We have talked of our rights," she said. "We have guarded our freedom. Our highest virtues have been service and sacrifice. Are we not now thinking of these virtues somewhat differently? The spirit of a new age is fast gripping every one of us. The appeal which life makes to us to-day is to the socially constructive passion in every man. This is something to which the whole of me can respond. This is a great affirmative. Sacrifice sometimes seems too negative, dwells on what I give up. Service sometimes seems to emphasise the *fact* of service rather than the *value* of the service. Yet service and sacrifice are noble ideals. We cannot do without them. Let them, however, be the handmaids of the great purpose of our life—namely, our contributions to that new world we wish to see rise out of our present chaos, that age which shall bring us individual freedom through collective control."

The reader will inevitably be struck by some repetition of an argument in the papers here reprinted, sometimes even a repetition of detail and illustration. It must be remembered, however, that the papers were originally produced over several years, and we felt that they should not be edited in any way that would spoil their individual original form. The repetition is, in itself, a tribute to Mary Follett's consistency of thought, to the simplicity and unity of the principles she evolved. As shown earlier, these flowed naturally on from what she developed in her earlier writings in the field of political science. This continuous development from *The New State* and *Creative Experience* to the papers on the Scientific and Psychological Foundations of Business Management is so striking that it has been thought helpful to annotate the papers here reproduced in some measure in order to point out the parallel.

The body of thought built up by Mary Follett was not massive, not formidable; rather, it is strikingly simple. But it goes the deeper, and its fundamental significance and value in the solution of industrial as well of national and international problems to-day are beyond estimate.

.   .   .   .   .

To Mary Follett's many friends and former associates we wish to express our sincere appreciation for their helpfulness in contributing personal data and for their unanimous encouragement in our efforts to bring together in one volume her invaluable contribution to the philosophy of organization and management.

HENRY C. METCALF.
L. URWICK.

NEW YORK AND LONDON.
December, 1940.

I

CONSTRUCTIVE CONFLICT

THE subject I have been given for these lectures is *The Psychological Foundations of Business Administration*,[1] but as it is obvious that we cannot in four papers consider all the contributions which contemporary psychology is making to business administration—to the methods of hiring, promoting and discharging, to the consideration of incentives, the relation of output to motive, to group organization, etc.— I have chosen certain subjects which seem to me to go to the heart of personnel relations in industry. I wish to consider in this paper the most fruitful way of dealing with conflict. At the outset I should like to ask you to agree for the moment to think of conflict as neither good nor bad; to consider it without ethical pre-judgment; to think of it not as warfare, but as the appearance of difference, difference of opinions, of interests. For that is what conflict means—difference. We shall not consider merely the differences between employer and employee, but those between managers, between the directors at the Board meetings, or wherever difference appears.

As conflict—difference—is here in the world, as we cannot avoid it, we should, I think, use it. Instead of condemning it, we should set it to work for us. Why not? What does the mechanical engineer do with friction? Of course his chief job is to eliminate friction, but it is true that he also capitalizes friction. The transmission of power by belts depends on friction between the belt and the pulley. The friction

[1] This and the three succeeding papers reprinted from *Scientific Foundations of Business Administration*, Henry C. Metcalf, *Editor*, The Williams and Wilkins Company, Baltimore, 1926. Miss Follett's main theme in these four contributions to this series of conferences was "The *Psychological* Foundations." This paper was first presented before a Bureau of Personnel Administration conference group in January, 1925.

between the driving wheel of the locomotive and the track is necessary to haul the train. All polishing is done by friction. The music of the violin we get by friction. We left the savage state when we discovered fire by friction. We talk of the friction of mind on mind as a good thing. So in business, too, we have to know when to try to eliminate friction and when to try to capitalize it, when to see what work we can make it do. That is what I wish to consider here, whether we can set conflict to work and make it *do* something for us.[2]

Methods of Dealing with Conflict

There are three main ways of dealing with conflict: domination, compromise and integration. Domination, obviously, is a victory of one side over the other. This is the easiest way of dealing with conflict, the easiest for the moment but not usually successful in the long run, as we can see from what has happened since the War.

The second way of dealing with conflict, that of compromise, we understand well, for it is the way we settle most of our controversies; each side gives up a little in order to have peace, or, to speak more accurately, in order that the activity which has been interrupted by the conflict may go on. Compromise is the basis of trade union tactics.[3] In collective bargaining, the trade unionist asks for more than he expects to get, allows for what is going to be lopped off in the conference. Thus we often do not know what he really thinks he should have, and this ignorance is a great barrier to dealing with conflict fruitfully. At the time of a certain wage controversy in Massachusetts, the lowest paid girls in

[2] *Cf. Creative Experience*, p. 300: "What people often mean by getting rid of conflict is getting rid of diversity, and it is of the utmost importance that these should not be considered the same. We may wish to abolish conflict, but we cannot get rid of diversity. We must face life as it is and understand that diversity is its most essential feature. . . . Fear of difference is dread of life itself. It is possible to conceive conflict as not necessarily a wasteful outbreak of incompatibilities, but a *normal* process by which socially valuable differences register themselves for the enrichment of all concerned."

[3] *Cf. The New State*, Chapter XIV, for a discussion of the relations of capital and labour. "The weakness of arbitration and conciliation boards, with their 'impartial' member, is that they tend to mere compromise even when they are not openly negotiations between two warring parties" (p. 115).

31

the industry were getting about $8.00 or $9.00 a week. The demand made by two of the representatives of the girls was for $22.40 (for a minimum wage, note), obviously too great an increase for anyone seriously to think of getting at one time. Thus the employers were as far as ever from knowing what the girls really thought they ought to have.

But I certainly ought not to imply that compromise is peculiarly a trade union method. It is the accepted, the approved, way of ending controversy. Yet no one really wants to compromise, because that means a giving up of something. Is there then any other method of ending conflict? There is a way beginning now to be recognized at least, and even occasionally followed: when two desires are *integrated*, that means that a solution has been found in which both desires have found a place, that neither side has had to sacrifice anything. Let us take some very simple illus tion. In the Harvard Library one day, in one of the smaller rooms, someone wanted the window open, I wanted it shut. We opened the window in the next room, where no one was sitting. This was not a compromise because there was no curtailing of desire; we both got what we really wanted. For I did not want a closed room, I simply did not want the north wind to blow directly on me; likewise the other occupant did not want that particular window open, he merely wanted more air in the room.

I have already given this illustration in print. I repeat it here because this instance, from its lack of any complications, shows my point at once I think. Let us take another illustration. A Dairymen's Co-operative League almost went to pieces last year on the question of precedence in unloading cans at a creamery platform. The men who came down the hill (the creamery was on a down grade) thought they should have precedence; the men who came up the hill thought they should unload first. The thinking of both sides in the controversy was thus confined within the walls of these two possibilities, and this prevented their even trying to find a way of settling the dispute which would avoid these alternatives. The solution was obviously to change the position of the platform so that both up-hillers and down-hillers could unload at the same time. But this solution was not found until they had asked the advice of a more or less professional integrator. When, however, it was pointed out to them, they were quite ready to accept it. Integration involves invention, and the clever thing is to recognize this, and not to let one's thinking stay within the boundaries of two alternatives which are mutually exclusive.[4]

Take another case. There is sometimes a question whether the meetings of works committees should be held in the plant or outside: the argument for meeting inside is the obvious advantage of being near one's work; the argument against, the fear of company influence. I know one factory that made what I consider an integration by having the meetings of the works committee held in the separate club building of the employees situated within the factory grounds. Here the men felt much freer than in any other part of the plant.

A friend gave me this example. He was called on jury service in a murder trial. The District Attorney asked him whether he had any objection to capital punishment. He replied, "Yes, definitely so." The "conflict" was then on, for the judge thought this opinion incapacitated him for service in a murder trial. My friend summed up the incident to me in these words: "After the judge had subjected me to a kind of cross-examination, I was put into the jury box, but neither the judge nor myself was left as victor; the experience had changed us both. We found the solution instead of vindicating the pre-judgment of either of us; the solution being that it is possible to render a verdict in accordance with evidence so that you need not evade your duties as a citizen whatever your opinion of capital punishment."

By far the most interesting examples of integration which have come to my attention recently were four sent to the London *Times* by Gilbert Murray, four integrations which

---

[4] For a fuller exposition of the principle of integration as the foundation of Mary Follett's thought on the subject of group psychology, see *Creative Experience*, Chapter IX, "Experience as Creating." *Cf.* p. 156: "Integration, the most suggestive word of contemporary psychology, is, I believe, the active principle of human intercourse scientifically lived."

he had found in the Report of the Dawes Committee.[5]

It is often difficult to decide whether a decision is a true integration or something of a compromise, and there is a flaw I think in one of the four cited by Gilbert Murray. But signs of even partial integration, signs even that people want integration rather than domination or compromise, are encouraging.

Some people tell me that they like what I have written on integration, but say that I am talking of what ought to be instead of what is. But indeed I am not; I am talking neither of what is, to any great extent, nor of what ought to be merely, but of what perhaps may be. This we can discover only by experiment. That is all I am urging, that we try experiments in methods of resolving differences; differences on the Board of Directors, with fellow managers or heads of departments, with employees, or in other relations. If we do this, we may take a different attitude toward conflict.

The key-word of psychology to-day is desire. If we wish to speak of conflict in the language of contemporary psychology, we might call it a moment in the interacting of desires. Thus we take from it any connotation of good or bad. Thus we shall not be afraid of conflict, but shall recognize that there is a destructive way of dealing with such moments and a constructive way. Conflict as the moment of the appearing and focusing of difference may be a sign of health, a prophecy of progress. If the Dairymen's League had not fought over the question of precedence, the improved method of unloading would not have been thought of. The conflict in this case was constructive. And this was because, instead of compromising, they sought a way of integrating.

[5] In a Letter to the Editor in *The Times*, June 6th, 1924, Professor Gilbert Murray writes to draw attention to the influence of previous decisions and methods of the League of Nations on the members of the Dawes Committee. He quotes four matters on which French and British opinion was widely divergent, but where agreement was reached by the mutual adoption of League solutions in previous comparable problems. These instances are illustrations of the method of "integration" that Mary Follett was so keen to expound. (The matters in dispute were: the currency of German reparations payments; the fixation of total German liability; the necessity of external control, or wisdom of trusting completely to German good faith; the relation of German capacity to pay to the problem of fixing the final total liability.)

Compromise does not create, it deals with what already exists; integration creates something new, in this case a different way of unloading. And because this not only settled the controversy but was actually better technique, saved time for both the farmers and the creamery, I call this: setting friction to work, making it *do* something.

Thus we see that while conflict as continued unintegrated difference is pathological, difference itself is not pathological. The fights in the Democratic convention were a hopeful sign for the Democratic party. What I think we should do in business organization is to try to find the machinery best suited for the normal appearing and uniting of diversity so that the difference does not stay too long crystallized, so that the pathological stage shall not be reached.

One advantage of integration over compromise I have not yet mentioned. If we get only compromise, the conflict will come up again and again in some other form, for in compromise we give up part of our desire, and because we shall not be content to rest there, sometime we shall try to get the whole of our desire. Watch industrial controversy, watch international controversy, and see how often this occurs. Only integration really stabilizes. But by stabilization I do not mean anything stationary. Nothing ever stays put. I mean only that that particular conflict is settled and the next occurs on a higher level.

Psychology has given us the phrase "progressive integratings"; we need also the phrase progressive differings. We can often measure our progress by watching the nature of our conflicts. Social progress is in this respect like individual progress; we become spiritually more and more developed as our conflicts rise to higher levels. If a man should tell you that his chief daily conflict within himself is —Shall I steal or not steal?—you would know what to think of his stage of development. As someone has said, "A man is known by the dilemmas he keeps." In the same way, one test of your business organization is not how many conflicts you have, for conflicts are the essence of life, but *what* are your conflicts? And how do you deal with them? It is to be hoped that we shall not always have strikes, but it is equally to be hoped that we shall always have conflict, the kind which leads to invention, to the emergence of new values.

Having suggested integration as perhaps the way by which we can deal most fruitfully with conflict, with difference, we should now consider the method by which integration can be obtained. But before we do that I want to say definitely that I do not think integration is possible in all cases. When two men want to marry the same woman, there can be no integration; when two sons both want the old family home, there can usually be no integration. And there are many such cases, some of little, some of great seriousness. I do not say that there is no tragedy in life. All that I say is that if we were alive to its advantages, we could often integrate instead of compromising. I have a friend who annoys me in this way. She makes a statement. I say, "I don't agree with that because . . ." and I intend to give my reasons, but before I have a chance she says, "Well, let's not fight about it." But I had no intention of fighting.

Bases of Integration

If, then, we do not think that differing necessarily means fighting, even when two desires both claim right of way, if we think that integration is more profitable than conquering or compromising, the first step toward this consummation is *to bring the differences into the open*. We cannot hope to integrate our differences unless we know what they are. I will give some illustrations of the opposite method—evading or suppressing the issue.

I know a factory where, after the War, the employees asked for a 5 per cent. increase in wages, but it was not clear to either side whether this meant a 5 per cent. raise over present wages or over pre-War wages. Moreover, it was seen that neither side wished to know! The employees naturally preferred to think the former, the managers the latter. It was some time before both sides were willing to face the exact issue; each, unconsciously, hoped to win by keeping the whole problem hazy.

One of the longest discussions I ever heard on a minimum wage board was in regard to the question of fares to and from work: first, whether this item should be included at all with board, lodging, etc., in a cost-of-living budget, that is, whether transportation to and from the plant should be a cost on production. When finally it was decided to leave the item in and allow 60 cents a week for it, instead of the $1.20 which the 10-cent Boston car fare would necessitate if this item were to be allowed for in full, it seemed to me a clear case of evasion or suppression. That is, the employers were not willing to face at that moment the question whether wages should include transportation. I sat on that board as a representative of the public, and I suggested more than once during the discussion that we should find out whether most of the girls in that particular industry did live near the plant or at a distance too great for walking. Also I suggested that we should find out whether, if they lived near the plant, the cost of board and lodging in that neighbourhood was so high that it would more than offset car fares. But the employers in this instance were not ready to face the issue, and therefore the clearly evasive decision of 60 cents was made.

Another interesting case of suppression occurred in a committee of which I was a member. The question was a disagreement concerning the pay of two stenographers who were working for us. Those who urged the higher amount persisted in speaking of the stenographers' day as an eight-hour day because the hours are from nine to five, although with the hour out for lunch that obviously makes a seven-hour day.

Wherever you have the fight-set, you are in danger of obscurities, conscious or unconscious. As long as trade unionism is a defensive movement, as long as employers' associations are defensive movements, we shall have obscurities. As long as internationalism is what it is, evasion will go on. Of course not to *appear* to evade is part of good diplomacy, for you don't want the other side to think you are trying to "get by" on anything. But we shall continue to evade or suppress as long as our real aim is not agreement, but domination. Lord Shaw, chairman of the Coal Commission, put it as one of the essentials in arbitration that both sides should genuinely desire agreement. Here we get a very direct lesson from psychology.

The psychiatrist tells his patient that he cannot help him unless he is honest in wanting his conflict to end. The "uncovering" which every book on psychology has rubbed into us for some years now as a process of the utmost importance for solving the conflicts which the individual has within himself is equally important for the relations between individuals, or between groups, classes, races, nations. In business, the employer, in dealing either with his associates or his employees, has to get underneath all the camouflage, has to find the real demand as against the demand put forward, distinguish declared motive from real motive, alleged cause from real cause, and to remember that sometimes the underlying motive is deliberately concealed and that sometimes it exists unconsciously.

The first rule, then, for obtaining integration is to put your cards on the table, face the real issue, uncover the conflict, bring the whole thing into the open.

One of the most important reasons for bringing the desires of each side to a place where they can be clearly examined and valued is that evaluation often leads to *revaluation*. We progress by a revaluation of desire, but usually we do not stop to examine a desire until another is disputing right of way with it. Watch the evolution of your desires from childhood, through youth, etc. The baby has many infantile desires which are not compatible with his wish for approbation; therefore he revalues his desires. We see this all through our life. We want to do so-and-so, but we do not estimate how much this really means to us until it comes into conflict with another desire. Revaluation is the flower of comparison.

This conception of the revaluation of desire it is necessary to keep in the foreground of our thinking in dealing with conflict, for neither side ever "gives in" really, it is hopeless to expect it, but there often comes a moment when there is a simultaneous revaluation of interests on both sides and unity precipitates itself. This, I think, happened in Europe at the London Conference last summer, or rather it happened before that and led to the Conference. Integration is often more a spontaneous flowing together of desire than one might think from what I have said; the revaluing of interests on both sides may lead the interests to fit into each other, so that all find some place in the final solution.

The bearing of all this on business administration is, I hope, obvious. A business should be so organized (this is one of the tests for us to apply to our organization) that full opportunity is given in any conflict, in any coming together of different desires, for the whole field of desire to be viewed. Our employees should be able to see, as we should be able ourselves to see, the whole field of desire. The *field of desire* is an important psychological and sociological conception; many conflicts could, I believe, be prevented from ending disastrously by getting the desires of each side into one field of vision where they could be viewed together and compared. We all believe to a certain extent in Freud's "sublimation," but I believe still more that various desires get orientated toward one another and take on different values in the process of orientation.

It will be understood, of course, that all this applies to ourselves as well as to the other side; we have to uncover our sub-articulate egoisms, and then, when we see them in relation to other facts and desires, we may estimate them differently. We often think it is a question of eliminating motives when it is only a question of subordinating them. We often, for instance, treat personal motives as more ignoble than we need. There is nothing necessarily discreditable in the politician "standing by" his friends. The only ethical question is how much that motive is weighing against others. The unethical thing is to persuade yourself that it is not weighing at all.

I have time barely to mention a very important point: the connection between the *realignment of groups* and a revaluation of interests. I have found this important in watching the realignments of political parties. We must in any conflict between groups watch every realignment to see how far it changes the confronting desires, for this means how far it changes the conflict.

I began this section by saying that the first step in integration is to bring the differences into the open. If the first step is to put clearly before ourselves what there is to integrate, there is something very important for us to note—namely, that the highest lights in a situation are not always those which are most indicative of the real issues involved. Many situations are decidedly complex, involve numerous and varied activities, overlapping activities. There is too great a tendency (perhaps encouraged by popular journalism) to deal with the dramatic moments, forgetting that these are not always the most significant moments. We should not follow literary analogies here. You may have a good curtain with, to quote Kipling, the lovers loving and the parents signing cheques. Yet, after all, this may not be the controlling moment in the lives of these people. To *find the significant rather than the dramatic features* of industrial controversy, of a disagreement in regard to policy on board of directors or between managers, is essential to integrative business policies.

Such search is part of what seems to me the second step in integration. If the first step is to uncover the real conflict, the next is to take the demands of both sides and break them up into their constituent parts.[6] Contemporary psychology shows how fatal it is to try to deal with conglomerates. I know a boy who wanted a college education. His father died and he had to go to work at once to support his mother. Had he then to give up his desire? No, for on analysis he found that what he wanted was not a college education, but an education, and there were still ways of his getting that. You remember the southern girl who said, "Why, I always thought damned Yankee was one word until I came north."

This method of *breaking up wholes* is the way you deal with

[6] *Cf. Creative Experience*, pp. 167–8: "Again, labour and capital can never be reconciled as long as labour persists in thinking that there is a capitalist point of view and capitalists that there is a labour point of view. There is not. These are imaginary wholes which must be broken up before capital and labour can co-operate."

business problems; it is the method which precedes business decisions. Take the case of inaugurating a system of approval shipment. A. W. Shaw, in his *Approach to Business Problems*, shows the sub-problems involved here:

1. What will be the effect on collections and on the cost of shipment?

2. What is to be the credit policy?

3. Will the stock in transit or in the hands of customers reduce the number of turnovers per year?

4. Will the risk of damage to returned goods be great enough to jeopardize the regular profit?

5. Will the increase in sales more than offset any added cost in the administrative department?

6. Also psychological factors, as customers' curiosity and caution.

I have given this illustration at length because it seems to me that this is the method which should be applied to controversy. I wish indeed that every controversy might be considered a problem.

You will notice that to break up a problem into its various parts involves the *examination of symbols*, involves, that is, the careful scrutiny of the language used to see what it really means. A friend of mine wanted to go to Europe, but also she did not want to spend the money it would cost. Was there any integration? Yes, she found one. In order to understand it, let us use the method I am advocating; let us ask, what did "going to Europe" symbolize to her? In order to do that, we have to break up this whole, "going to Europe." What does "going to Europe" stand for to different people? A sea voyage, seeing beautiful places, meeting new people, a rest or change from daily duties, and a dozen other things. Now, this woman had taught for a few years after leaving college and then had gone away and led a somewhat secluded life for a good many years. "Going to Europe" was to her a symbol, not of snow mountains, or cathedrals, or pictures, but of meeting people—that was what she wanted. When she was asked to teach in a summer school of young men and women where she would meet a rather interesting staff of teachers and a rather interesting group of students, she immediately accepted. This was her integration. This was not a substitution for her wish, it was her *real* wish fulfilled.

I have given other illustration of symbols in Chapter IX of my book, *Creative Experience*. There was an interesting one in the Loeb-Leopold case. I think there should have been taken into consideration in that case what life imprisonment symbolized. As there was no question of freeing the boys, the decision was to be made between death and life imprisonment. Therefore, when the latter sentence was given, that was a symbol, it seemed to me, of victory for the boys, especially since everyone thought that their detention would last only a few years. In many cases, on the other hand, life imprisonment is a symbol of defeat. I do not think that this was taken into account sufficiently in considering the effect of the sentence on the country.

It is, of course, unavoidable to use symbols; all language is symbolic; but we should be always on our guard as to what is symbolized. For instance, the marketing co-operatives say that they want their members to keep their pledges. That statement is a symbol for what they *really* want, which is to get enough of the commodity to control the market. Every day we use many more not-understood symbols, many more whole-words, unanalysed words, than we ought to. Much of what is written of the "consumer" is inaccurate because consumer is used as a whole-word, whereas it is quite obvious that the consumer of large wealth has different desires and motives from the consumer of small means.

We have been considering the breaking up of the whole-demand. On the other hand, one often has to do just the opposite; find the whole-demand, the real demand, which is being obscured by miscellaneous minor claims or by ineffective presentation. The man with a genius for leadership is the one who can make articulate the whole-demand, unless it is a matter of tactics deliberately to conceal it. I shall not stop to give instances of this, as I wish to have time for some consideration of a point which seems to me very important for business, both in dealings with employees and with competing firms, and that is the anticipation of demands, of difference, of conflict.

Mr. Earl Howard, labour manager for Hart, Schaffner and Marx, said to me once, "It isn't enough merely to study the actual reactions of your employees; you must anticipate their reactions, beat them to it." That—to beat them to it —is exactly what each firm does try to do with its competing firms, but I do not think many managers study and anticipate the reactions of their employees as carefully as they do those of competing firms. It would be just as useful.

You could probably give me many illustrations of the *anticipation of response*. We could find innumerable examples in our households. A man liked motoring, his wife walking; he anticipated what her response might be to a suggestion that they motor on Sunday afternoon by tiring her out playing tennis in the morning.

The middlemen are deliberately anticipating response on the part of the farmers. In their struggle with the marketing co-operatives, they are basing their calculations of the future on the assumption that the particularistic tendency of the farmer is such that he cannot be held in line permanently, that he has been carried off his feet by victory and promises; moreover, that the use of legal power in enforcing contracts will in the end defeat the movement, that the farmer will surely rebel against this sort of coercion.

The anticipation of conflict, it should be noted, does not mean necessarily the avoidance of conflict, but playing the game differently. That is, you integrate the different interests without making all the moves. A friend of mine says that my theory of integration is like a game of chess. I think it is something like that. The tyro has to find his solution by making his actual moves, by the crude method of changing the places of his chessmen. A good chess player does not need to do this, he sees the possibilities without playing them out. The business man in dealing with competitive firms is like the good chess player. As the real conflict between two

43

good chess players is a conflict of possibilities that would be realized if they played them out, so in business you do not have to make all the moves to make your integrations; you deal with antecedents, premonitory symptoms, etc. You do not avoid doing certain things, you have done them without doing them.

But assuming that in our business we do watch response and anticipate response, that still is not going far enough. It is not enough to ask to what our employee or our business confrère or business competitor is responding, nor even to what he is likely to respond. We have to prepare the way for response, we have to try to build up in him a certain attitude. Of course every good salesman does this, but its necessity is not so fully recognized in other departments, and we shall therefore consider this question further in a later paper.

Yet even *preparation for response* is only a small part of the matter; we shall have to go deeper than that. There is *circular* as well as *linear* response, and the exposition of that is I think the most interesting contribution of contemporary psychology to the social sciences.[7] A good example of circular response is a game of tennis. A serves. The way B returns the ball depends partly on the way it was served to him. A's next play will depend on his own original serve plus the return of B, and so on and so on. We see this in discussion. We see this in most activity between one and another. Mischievous or idle boys say, "Let's start something"; we must remember that whenever we act we have always "started something," behaviour precipitates behaviour in others. Every employer should remember this. One of the managers in a factory expressed it to me thus: "I am in command of a situation until I behave; when I act I have lost control of the situation." This does not mean that we should not act! It is, however, something to which it is very important that we give full consideration.

Circular response seems a simple matter, quite obvious,

---

[7] *Cf. Creative Experience*, Chapter III, "Experience in the Light of Recent Psychology: Circular Response."

something we must all accept. Yet every day we try to evade it, every day we act and hope to avoid the inescapable response. As someone has said in another connection, "We feed Cerberus raw meat and hope that when we lie between his paws, he will turn out to be a vegetarian."

The conception of circular behaviour throws much light on conflict, for I now realize that I can never fight you, I am always fighting you plus me. I have put it this way: that response is always to a relation. I respond, not only to you, but to the relation between you and me. Employees do not respond only to their employers, but to the relation between themselves and their employer. Trade unionism is responding, not only to capitalism, but to the relation between itself and capitalism. The Dawes plan, the London Conference, were obviously moments in circular behaviour. Circular behaviour as the basis of integration gives us the key to constructive conflict.

Obstacles to Integration

Finally, let us consider the chief *obstacles to integration*. It requires a high order of intelligence, keen perception and discrimination, more than all, a brilliant inventiveness; it is easier for the trade union to fight than to suggest a better way of running the factory. You remember that the Socialist Party in Italy had a majority before Mussolini came in. But they would not take responsibility; they preferred to stay fighting, to attack what others were doing rather than to do themselves. They do not, I think, compare favourably with the English Labour Party.

Another obstacle to integration is that our way of life has habituated many of us to enjoy domination. Integration seems to many a tamer affair; it leaves no "thrills" of conquest. I knew a dispute within a trade union where, by the skilful action of the chairman, a true integration was discovered and accepted, but instead of the satisfaction one might have expected from such a happy result, the evening seemed to end rather dully, flatly; there was no climax, there was no side left swelling its chest, no one had conquered,

45

no one had "won out." It is even true that to some people defeat, as well as conquest, is more interesting than integration. That is, the person with decided fight habits feels more at home, happier, in the fight movement. Moreover, it leaves the door open for further fighting, with the possibility of conquest the next time.

Another obstacle to integration is that the matter in dispute is often theorized over instead of being taken up as a proposed activity. I think this important in business administration. Intellectual agreement does not alone bring full integration. I know one factory which deliberately provides for this by the many activities of its many sub-committees, some of which seem rather trivial unless one sees just how these activities are a contribution to that functional unity which we shall consider in a later paper.

I have been interested to watch how often disagreement disappears when theorizing ends and the question is of some definite activity to be undertaken. At a trade union conference, someone brought up the question of waste: how could the workmen help to eliminate waste? But it was found that most of the union men did not think it the job of the workmen to eliminate waste; that belonged to the management. Moreover, they did not think it to their interest to eliminate waste; wages were fixed by the union, by collective bargaining; everything saved went to swell profits; no more went into their pockets. It was seen, however, that there was another side, and the argument went on, but without coming to any agreement. Finally, however, by some manœuvring on the part of the chairman, it was acknowledged that there were certain forms of waste which the unions could be got to take cognizance of. A machinist, a plumber and a carpenter undertook to take up with their unions the question of how far they could agree to take some responsibility for these particular types of waste. I hope the fact then emerged, when it was considered as a practical issue, that for some forms of waste the management is responsible, for some forms the employees, and for some forms the union.

A serious obstacle to integration which every business man should consider is the language used. We have noted the necessity of making preparation in the other man, and in ourselves too, for the attitude most favourable to reconciliation. A trade unionist said to me, "Our representatives didn't manage it right. If instead of a 15 per cent. increase they had asked for an adjustment of wages, the management would have been more willing to listen to us; it would have put them in a different frame of mind." I don't quite see why we are not more careful about our language in business, for in most delicate situations we quite consciously choose that which will not arouse antagonism. You say to your wife at breakfast, "Let's reconsider that decision we came to last night." You do not say, "I wish to give you my criticism of the decision you made last night."

I cannot refrain from mentioning a personal experience. I went into the Edison Electric Light Company and said to a young woman at a counter, "Where shall I go to speak about my bill?" "Room D for complaints," she replied. "But I don't wish to make a complaint," I said. "I thought there was a mistake in your bill." "I think there is," I said, "but I don't wish to complain about it; it was a very natural mistake." The girl looked nonplussed, and as she was obviously speechless a man came out from behind a desk and said: "You would prefer to ask for an adjustment, wouldn't you?" and we had a chat about it.

I think that the "grievance committees" which exist in most factories are a mistake. I do not like the "trouble specialists" of the Ford plant. I wish it were not so often stated that shop or department committees were formed to "settle disputes." If you will get lists of these so-called "disputes," you will find that often they have not so much of the fight element in them as this word implies. But much of the language expressing the relation between capital and labour is that of a fight: "traditional enemies," the "weapon of the union," etc.

I have left untouched one of the chief obstacles to integration —namely, the undue influence of leaders—the manipulation

47

of the unscrupulous on the one hand and the suggestibility of the crowd on the other. Moreover, even when the power of suggestion is not used deliberately, it exists in all meetings between people; the whole emotional field of human intercourse has to be taken fully into account in dealing with methods of reconciliation. I am deliberately omitting the consideration of this, not because I do not feel its importance as keenly as anyone, but because in these few papers we cannot cover everything.

Finally, perhaps the greatest of all obstacles to integration is our lack of training for it. In our college debates we try always to beat the other side. In the circular announcing the courses to be given at the Bryn Mawr Summer School for Workers, I find: "English Composition and Public Speaking; to develop the art of oral and written expression." I think that in addition to this there should be classes in discussion which should aim to teach the "art" of co-operative thinking, and I was disappointed that there was no such course in the programme of a school for workers. Managers need it just as much. I have found, in the case of the wage boards which I have been on, that many employers (I ought in fairness to say not the majority) came to these joint conferences of employers and employees with little notion of conferring, but to push through, to force through, plans *previously* arrived at, based on *preconceived* ideas of what employees are like. It seems as if the methods of genuine conference have yet to be learned. Even if there were not the barriers of an unenlightened self-interest, of prejudice, rigidity, dogmatism, routine, there would still be required training and practice for us to master the technique of integration. A friend of mine said to me, "Open-mindedness is the whole thing, isn't it?" No, it isn't; it needs just as great a respect for your own view as for that of others, and a firm upholding of it until you are convinced. Mushy people are no more good at this than stubborn people.

As an indirect summing up of this discussion, I should like to emphasize our responsibility for integration. We saw in our consideration of circular response that my behaviour helps create the situation to which I am responding. That implies (what we have daily to take into account) that my behaviour is helping to *develop* the situation to which I am responding. The standard of living goes up not only while, but partly because, it is being studied. This conception of the developing situation is of the utmost importance for business administration. It makes it impossible to construct a map of the future, yet all our maxims of foresight hold good; every business should reconcile these two statements. We should work always with the evolving situation, and note what part our own activities have in that evolving situation.

This is the most important word, not only for business relations, but for all human relations: not to adapt ourselves to a situation—we are all more necessary to the world than that; neither to mould a situation to *our* liking—we are all, or rather each, of too little importance to the world for that; but to take account of that reciprocal adjustment, that interactive behaviour between the situation and ourselves which means a change in both the situation and ourselves. One test of business administration should be: is the organization such that both employers. and employees, or co-managers, co-directors, are stimulated to a reciprocal activity which will give more than mere adjustment, more than an equilibrium? Our outlook is narrowed, our activity is restricted, our chances of business success largely diminished when our thinking is constrained within the limits of what has been called an either-or situation. We should never allow ourselves to be bullied by an "either-or." There is often the possibility of something better than either of two given alternatives. Every one of us interested in any form of constructive work is looking for the plus values of our activity. In a later paper, on *Business as an Integrative Unity*, we shall consider how we can find in business administration those plus values which alone mean progress, progress for the individual and for whatever business or service we have undertaken for ourselves and for our community.

II

THE GIVING OF ORDERS[1]

THE chief thing I have to say to you in this paper is that I wish we could all take a responsible attitude toward our experience—a conscious and responsible attitude.[2] Let us take one of the many activities of the business man, and see what it would mean to take a responsible attitude toward our experience in regard to that one thing. I am going to take the question of giving orders: what are the principles underlying the different ways of giving orders, which of these principles have you decided to follow? Most people have not decided, have not even thought out what the different principles are. Yet we all give orders every day. Surely this is a pity. To know what principles may underlie any given activity of ours is to take a conscious attitude toward our experience.

The second step is to take a responsible attitude, by deciding, after we have recognized the different principles, which ones we will follow. In the matter of giving orders, I wish we might all of us decide now, if we have not already done so, on the way we think orders should be given. We shall not arrive at the same conclusions, there may be a good deal of difference of opinion among us. What I urge is not that you adopt my principles, but that you stop to think what principles you are acting on or what principles you intend to act on in this matter, and then try giving orders in accordance with those principles as far as the methods of your firm permit.

And next I urge you to note results; for our first decision should be tentative. We should try experiments and note

1 See note, p. 30; this paper was presented in January, 1925.
2 *Cf. Creative Experience*, p. xi: "But we wish to do far more than observe our experience, we wish to make it yield up for us its riches."

whether they succeed or fail and, most important of all, why they succeed or fail. This is taking an experimental attitude toward experience.

We have then three steps: (1) a conscious attitude—realize the principles which it is possible to act on in this matter; (2) a responsible attitude—decide which we will act on; (3) an experimental attitude—try experiments and watch results. We might add a fourth step: pool our results.

In doing all this we should observe carefully what opportunities the methods of our particular firm afford for giving orders in the way we have decided provisionally is best, and come to some conclusion as to how far and in what way those methods would have to be changed if our principles were adopted. This will increase our consciousness in the matter.

Behaviour Patterns and Obedience to Orders

To some men the matter of giving orders seems a very simple affair; they expect to issue their orders and have them obeyed without question. Yet, on the other hand, the shrewd common sense of many a business executive has shown him that the issuing of orders is surrounded by many difficulties; that to demand an unquestioning obedience to orders not approved, not perhaps even understood, is bad business policy. Moreover, psychology, as well as our own observation, shows us not only that you cannot get people to do things most satisfactorily by ordering them or exhorting them; but also that even reasoning with them, even convincing them intellectually, may not be enough. Even the "consent of the governed" will not do all the work it is supposed to do, an important consideration for those who are advocating employee representation. For all our past life, our early training, our later experience, all our emotions, beliefs, prejudices, every desire that we have, have formed certain habits of mind, what the psychologists call habit-patterns, action-patterns, motor-sets.

Therefore it will do little good merely to get intellectual agreement; unless you change the habit-patterns of people, you have not really changed your people. Business administration, industrial organization, should build up certain habit-patterns, that is, certain mental attitudes. For instance, the farmer has a general disposition to "go it alone," and this is being changed by the activities of the co-operatives, that is, note, *by the farmer's own activities.* So the workman has often a general disposition of antagonism to his employers which cannot be changed by argument or exhortation, but only through certain activities which will create a different disposition. One of my trade union friends told me that he remembered when he was a quite small boy hearing his father, who worked in a shoe-shop, railing daily against his boss. So he grew up believing that it was inherent in the nature of things that the workman should be against his employer. I know many working men who have a prejudice against getting college men into factories. You could all give me examples of attitudes among your employees which you would like to change. We want, for instance, to create an attitude of respect for expert opinion.

If we analyse this matter a little further we shall see that we have to do three things, I am now going to use psychological language: (1) build up certain attitudes; (2) provide for the release of these attitudes; (3) augment the released response as it is being carried out. What does this mean in the language of business? A psychologist has given us the example of the salesman. The salesman first creates in you the attitude that you want his article; then, at just the "psychological" moment, he produces his contract blank which you may sign and thus release that attitude; then if, as you are preparing to sign, some one comes in and tells you how pleased he has been with his purchase of this article, that augments the response which is being released.

If we apply this to the subject of orders and obedience, we see that people can obey an order only if previous habit-patterns are appealed to or new ones created. When the employer is considering an order, he should also be thinking of the way to form the habits which will ensure its being carried out. We should first lead the salesmen selling shoes or the bank clerk cashing cheques to see the desirability of a different method. Then the rules of the store or bank should be so changed as to make it possible for salesman or cashier to adopt the new method. In the third place they could be made more ready to follow the new method by convincing in advance some one individual who will set an example to the others. You can usually convince one or two or three ahead of the rank and file. This last step you all know from your experience to be good tactics; it is what the psychologists call intensifying the attitude to be released. But we find that the released attitude is not by one release fixed as a habit; it takes a good many responses to do that.

This is an important consideration for us, for from one point of view business success depends largely on this— namely, whether our business is so organized and administered that it tends to form certain habits, certain mental attitudes. It has been hard for many old-fashioned employers to understand that *orders will not take the place of training.* I want to italicize that. Many a time an employer has been angry because, as he expressed it, a workman "wouldn't" do so and so, when the truth of the matter was that the workman couldn't, actually couldn't, do as ordered because he could not go contrary to life-long habits. This whole subject might be taken up under the heading of education, for there we could give many instances of the attempt to make arbitrary authority take the place of training. In history, the aftermath of all revolutions shows us the results of the lack of training.

In this matter of prepared-in-advance behaviour patterns —that is, in preparing the way for the reception of orders, psychology makes a contribution when it points out that the same words often rouse in us a quite different response when heard in certain places and on certain occasions. A boy may respond differently to the same suggestion when made by his teacher and when made by his schoolmate. Moreover, he may respond differently to the same suggestion made by the teacher in the schoolroom and made by the teacher when they are taking a walk together. Applying this to the giving of orders, we see that the place in which orders are given, the circumstances under which they are given, may make all the difference in the world as to the response which we get.[3] Hand them down a long way from President or Works Manager and the effect is weakened. One might say that the strength of favourable response to an order is in inverse ratio to the distance the order travels. Production efficiency is always in danger of being affected whenever the long-distance order is substituted for the face-to-face suggestion. There is, however, another reason for that which I shall consider in a moment.

All that we said in the foregoing paper of integration and circular behaviour applies directly to the anticipation of response in giving orders. We spoke then of what the psychologists call linear and circular behaviour. Linear behaviour would be, to quote from Dr. Cabot's review of my book, *Creative Experience*, when an order is accepted as passively as the woodshed accepts the wood. In circular behaviour you get a "come-back." But we all know that we get the come-back every day of our life, and we must certainly allow for it, or for what is more elegantly called circular behaviour, in the giving of orders. Following out the thought of the previous paper, I should say that the giving of orders and the receiving of orders ought to be a matter of integration through circular behaviour, and that we should seek methods to bring this about.[4] The rest of this lecture could profitably be spent on this point, with further explanation and with illustration, but I am trying to cover a good deal of ground

[3] *Cf. Creative Experience*, p. 65: ". . . we shall have to keep in mind—first, the objective situation as constituent part of the behaviour process; secondly, that internal conditioning is of equal importance with external conditioning. . . . Often for instance we see the head of an industrial plant trying to solve a situation by studying his men rather than by considering men and situation, and the reciprocal effect of one on the other."

[4] *Cf. Creative Experience*, p. 69: "We cannot study the 'psychology' of the workman, the 'psychology' of the employer, and then the 'facts' of the situation, as so often seems to be the process of the investigation. We must study the workman and the employer in their relation to the facts—and then the facts themselves become as active as any other part of the 'total situation.' We can never understand the total situation without taking into account the evolving situation. And when a situation changes we have not a new variation under the old fact, but a new fact."

in these talks by making suggestions for you to expand for yourselves.

Psychology has another important contribution to make on this subject of issuing orders or giving directions: before the integration can be made between order-giver and order-receiver, there is often an integration to be made within one or both of the individuals concerned. There are often two dissociated paths in the individual; if you are clever enough to recognize these, you can sometimes forestall a Freudian conflict, make the integration appear before there is an acute stage.

To explain what I mean, let me run over briefly a social worker's case. The girl's parents had been divorced and the girl placed with a jolly, easy-going, slack and untidy family, consisting of the father and mother and eleven children, sons and daughters. Gracie was very happy here, but when the social worker in charge of the case found that the living conditions involved a good deal of promiscuity, she thought the girl should be placed elsewhere. She therefore took her to call on an aunt who had a home with some refinement of living, where they had "high tastes," as one of the family said. This aunt wished to have Gracie live with her, and Gracie decided that she would like to do so. The social worker, however, in order to test her, said, "But I thought you were so happy where you are." "Can't I be happy and high, too?" the girl replied. There were two wishes here, you see. The social worker by removing the girl to the aunt may have forestalled a Freudian conflict, the dissociated paths may have been united. I do not know the outcome of this story, but it indicates a method of dealing with our co-directors—make them "happy and high, too."

Business administration has often to consider how to deal with the dissociated paths in individuals or groups, but the methods of doing this successfully have been developed much further in some departments than in others. We have as yet hardly recognized this as part of the technique of dealing with employees, yet the clever salesman knows that it is the chief part of his job. The prospective buyer wants the article and does not want it. The able salesman does not suppress the arguments in the mind of the purchaser against buying, for then the purchaser might be sorry afterwards for his purchase, and that would not be good salesmanship. Unless he can unite, integrate, in the purchaser's mind, the reasons for buying and the reasons for not buying, his future sales will be imperilled, he will not be the highest grade salesman.

Please note that this goes beyond what the psychologist whom I quoted at the beginning of this section told us. He said, "The salesman must create in you the attitude that you want his article." Yes, but only if he creates this attitude by integration not by suppression.

Apply all this to orders. An order often leaves the individual to whom it is given with two dissociated paths; an order should seek to unite, to integrate, dissociated paths. Court decisions often settle arbitrarily which of two ways is to be followed without showing a possible integration of the two, that is, the individual is often left with an internal conflict on his hands. This is what both courts and business administration should try to prevent, the internal conflicts of individuals or groups.

In discussing the preparation for giving orders, I have not spoken at all of the appeal to certain instincts made so important by many writers. Some writers, for instance, emphasize the instinct of self-assertion; this would be violated by too rigid orders or too clumsily-exercised authority. Other writers, of equal standing, tell us that there is an instinct of submission to authority. I cannot discuss this for we should first have to define instincts, too long an undertaking for us now. Moreover, the exaggerated interest in instincts of recent years, an interest which in many cases has received rather crude expression, is now subsiding. Or, rather, it is being replaced by the more fruitful interest in habits.

There is much more that we could learn from psychology about the forming of habits and the preparation for giving orders than I can even hint at now. But there is one point, already spoken of by implication, that I wish to consider more explicitly—namely, the manner of giving orders. Probably more industrial trouble has been caused by the manner in which orders are given than in any other way. In the *Report on Strikes and Lockouts*,[5] a British Government publication, the cause of a number of strikes is given as "alleged harassing conduct of the foreman," "alleged tyrannical conduct of an under-foreman," "alleged overbearing conduct of officials." The explicit statement, however, of the tyranny of superior officers as the direct cause of strikes is I should say, unusual, yet resentment smoulders and breaks out in other issues. And the demand for better treatment is often explicit enough. We find it made by the metal and woodworking trades in an aircraft factory, who declared that any treatment of men without regard to their feelings of self-respect would be answered by a stoppage of work. We find it put in certain agreements with employers that "the men must be treated with proper respect, and threats and abusive language must not be used."

What happens to a man, *in* a man, when an order is given in a disagreeable manner by foreman, head of department, his immediate superior in store, bank or factory? The man addressed feels that his self-respect is attacked, that one of his most inner sanctuaries is invaded. He loses his temper or becomes sullen or is on the defensive; he begins thinking of his "rights"—a fatal attitude for any of us. In the language we have been using, the wrong behaviour pattern is aroused, the wrong motor-set; that is, he is now "set" to act in a way which is not going to benefit the enterprise in which he is engaged.

There is a more subtle psychological point here, too; the more you are "bossed" the more your activity of thought will take place within the bossing-pattern, and your part in that pattern seems usually to be opposition to the bossing.

This complaint of the abusive language and the tyrannical treatment of the one just above the worker is an old story

[5] This is probably a reference to the *Annual Reports and Comparative Statistics of Strikes and Lockouts*, subsequently incorporated in the Annual Reports of the Ministry of Labour.

to us all, but there is an opposite extreme which is far too little considered. The immediate superior officer is often so close to the worker that he does not exercise the proper duties of his position. Far from taking on himself an aggressive authority, he has often evaded one of the chief problems of his job: how to do what is implied in the fact that he has been put in a position over others. The head of the woman's cloak department in a store will call out, "Say, Sadie, you're 36, aren't you? There's a woman down in the Back Bay kicking about something she says you promised yesterday." "Well, I like that," says Sadie. "Some of those Back Bay women would kick in Heaven." And that perhaps is about all that happens. Of course, the Back Bay lady has to be appeased, but there is often no study of what has taken place for the benefit of the store. I do not mean that a lack of connection between such incidents and the improvement of store technique is universal, but it certainly exists far too often and is one of the problems of those officials who are just above the heads of departments. Naturally, a woman does not want to get on bad terms with her fellow employees with whom she talks and works all day long. Consider the chief operator of the telephone exchanges, remembering that the chief operator is a member of the union, and that the manager is not.

Depersonalizing Orders—Obeying the Law of the Situation

Now what is our problem here? How can we avoid the two extremes: too great bossism in giving orders, and practically no orders given? I am going to ask how *you* are avoiding these extremes. My solution is to depersonalize the giving of orders, to unite all concerned in a study of the situation, to discover the law of the situation and obey that.[6] Until we do this I do not think we shall have the most successful business administration. This is what does take place, what has to take place, when there is a question

[6] *Cf. Creative Experience,* p. 122: "We should notice, too, what is sometimes forgotten, that in the social situation two processes always go on together: the adjustment of man and man, and the adjustment of man and the situation."

between two men in positions of equal authority. The head of the sales departments does not give orders to the head of the production department, or vice versa. Each studies the market and the final decision is made as the market demands. This is, ideally, what should take place between foremen and rank and file, between any head and his subordinates. One *person* should not give orders to another *person*, but both should agree to take their orders from the situation. If orders are simply part of the situation, the question of someone giving and someone receiving does not come up. Both accept the orders given by the situation. Employers accept the orders given by the situation; employees accept the orders given by the situation. This gives, does it not, a slightly different aspect to the whole of business administration through the entire plant?

We have here, I think, one of the largest contributions of scientific management: it tends to depersonalize orders. From one point of view, one might call the essence of scientific management the attempt to find the law of the situation. With scientific management the managers are as much under orders as the workers, for both obey the law of the situation. Our job is not how to get people to obey orders, but how to devise methods by which we can best *discover* the order integral to a particular situation. When that is found, the employee can issue it to the employer, as well as employer to employee. This often happens easily and naturally. My cook or my stenographer points out the law of the situation, and I, if I recognize it as such, accept it, even although it may reverse some "order" I have given.

If those in supervisory positions should depersonalize orders, then there would be no overbearing authority on the one hand, nor on the other that dangerous *laissez-aller* which comes from the fear of exercising authority. Of course we should exercise authority, but always the authority of the situation. I do not say that we have found the way to a frictionless existence, far from it, but we now understand the place which we mean to give to friction. We intend to set it to work for us as the engineer does when he puts the belt over the pulley. There will be just as much, probably more, room for disagreement in the method I am advocating. The situation will often be seen differently, often be interpreted differently. But we shall know what to do with it, we shall have found a method of dealing with it.

I call it depersonalizing because there is not time to go any further into the matter. I think it really is a matter of *repersonalizing*. We, persons, have relations with each other, but we should find them in and through the whole situation. We cannot have any sound relations with each other as long as we take them out of that setting which gives them their meaning and value. This divorcing of persons and the situation does a great deal of harm. I have just said that scientific management depersonalizes; the deeper philosophy of scientific management shows us personal relations within the whole setting of that thing of which they are a part.

There is much psychology, modern psychology particularly, which tends to divorce person and situation. What I am referring to is the present zest for "personality studies." When some difficulty arises we often hear the psychologist whose specialty is personality studies say, "Study the psychology of that man." And this is very good advice, but only if at the same time we study the entire situation. To leave out the whole situation, however, is so common a blunder in the studies of these psychologists that it constitutes a serious weakness in their work. And as those of you who are personnel directors have more to do, I suppose, with those psychologists who have taken personality for their specialty than with any others, I wish you would watch and see how often you find that this limitation detracts from the value of their conclusions.

I said above that we should substitute for the long-distance order the face-to-face suggestion. I think we can now see a more cogent reason for this than the one then given. It is not the face-to-face suggestion that we want so much as the joint study of the problem, and such joint study can be made best by the employee and his immediate superior or employee and special expert on that question.

I began this talk by emphasizing the advisability of preparing in advance the attitude necessary for the carrying out of orders, as in the previous paper we considered preparing the attitude for integration; but we have now, in our consideration of the joint study of situations, in our emphasis on obeying the law of the situation, perhaps got a little beyond that, or rather we have now to consider in what sense we wish to take the psychologist's doctrine of prepared-in-advance attitudes. By itself this would not take us far, for everyone is studying psychology nowadays, and our employees are going to be just as active in preparing us as we in preparing them! Indeed, a girl working in a factory said to me, "We had a course in psychology last winter, and I see now that you have to be pretty careful how you put things to the managers if you want them to consider favourably what you're asking for." If this prepared-in-advance idea were all that the psychologists think it, it would have to be printed privately as secret doctrine. But the truth is that the best preparation for integration in the matter of orders or in anything else, is a joint study of the situation. We should not try to create the attitude *we want*, although that is the usual phrase, but the attitude required for co-operative study and decision. This holds good even for the salesman. We said above that when the salesman is told that he should create in the prospective buyer the attitude that he wants the article, he ought also to be told that he should do this by integration rather than by suppression. We have now a hint of *how* he is to attain this integration.

I have spoken of the importance of changing some of the language of business personnel relations. We considered whether the words "grievances," "complaints," or Ford's "trouble specialists" did not arouse the wrong behaviour-patterns. I think "order" certainly does. If that word is not to mean any longer external authority, arbitrary authority, but the law of the situation, then we need a new word for it. It is often the order that people resent as much as the thing ordered. People do not like to be ordered even to take a holiday. I have often seen instances of this. The wish to govern one's own life is, of course, one of the most fundamental feelings in every human being. To call this "the instinct of self-assertion," "the instinct of initiative," does not express it wholly. I think it is told in the life of some famous American that when he was a boy and his mother said, "Go get a pail of water," he always replied, "I won't," before taking up the pail and fetching the water. This is significant; he resented the command, the command of a person; but he went and got the water, not, I believe, because he had to, but because he recognized the demand of the situation. *That*, he knew he had to obey; *that*, he was willing to obey. And this kind of obedience is not opposed to the wish to govern one's self, but each is involved in the other; both are part of the same fundamental urge at the root of one's being. We have here something far more profound than "the egoistic impulse" or "the instinct of self-assertion." We have the very essence of the human being.

This subject of orders has led us into the heart of the whole question of authority and consent. When we conceive of authority and consent as parts of an inclusive situation, does that not throw a flood of light on this question? The point of view here presented gets rid of several dilemmas which have seemed to puzzle people in dealing with consent. The feeling of being "under" someone, of "subordination," of "servility," of being "at the will of another," comes out again and again in the shop stewards movement and in the testimony before the Coal Commission. One man said before the Coal Commission, "It is all right to work *with* anyone; what is disagreeable is to feel too distinctly that you are working *under* anyone." *With* is a pretty good preposition, not because it connotes democracy, but because it connotes functional unity,[7] a much more profound conception than that of democracy as usually held. The study of the situation involves the *with* preposition. Then Sadie is not left alone by the head of the cloak department, nor does she

[7] If it is understood as indicating an interweaving, not mere addition (M. P. F.). *Note.* To distinguish between Miss Follett's own notations and the editorial notes, we are initialling the former, as here.

have to obey her. The head of the department says, "Let's see how such cases had better be handled, then we'll abide by that." Sadie is not under the head of the department, but both are *under* the situation.

Twice I have had a servant applying for a place ask me if she would be treated as a menial. When the first woman asked me that, I had no idea what she meant, I thought perhaps she did not want to do the roughest work, but later I came to the conclusion that to be treated as a menial meant to be obliged to be under someone, to follow orders without using one's own judgment. If we believe that what heightens self-respect increases efficiency, we shall be on our guard here.

Very closely connected with this is the matter of pride in one's work. If an order goes against what the craftsman or the clerk thinks is the way of doing his work which will bring the best results, he is justified in not wishing to obey that order. Could not that difficulty be met by a joint study of the situation? It is said that it is characteristic of the British workman to feel, "I know my job and won't be told how." The peculiarities of the British workman might be met by a joint study of the situation, it being understood that he probably has more to contribute to that study than anyone else.

(I should like to say incidentally here, that what I am talking about when I say joint study is entirely different from what is being advocated in England, and tried out in mine and factory, as "the independent investigation of the worker," "independent workers' control." I think they are on quite the wrong track in this matter, and this I shall try to show in a later paper.)

There is another dilemma which has to be met by everyone who is in what is called a position of authority: how can you expect people merely to obey orders and at the same time to take that degree of responsibility which they should take? Indeed, in my experience, the people who enjoy following orders blindly, without any thought on their own part, are those who like thus to get rid of responsibility. But the taking of responsibility, each according to his capacity, each according to his function in the whole (all that we shall take up in the next paper under the title of *Business as an Integrative Unity*), this taking of responsibility is usually the most vital matter in the life of every human being, just as the allotting of responsibility is the most important part of business administration.

A young trade unionist said to me, "How much dignity can I have as a mere employee?" He can have all the dignity in the world if he is allowed to make his fullest contribution to the plant *and to assume definitely the responsibility therefor.*

I think one of the gravest problems before us is how to make the reconciliation between receiving orders and taking responsibility. And I think the reconciliation can be made through our conception of the law of the situation.

Obedience and Liberty

I have spoken of several dilemmas: how to take orders and yet not to be "under" someone, how to take orders and yet to keep one's pride in one's work, how to take orders and yet to have a share in responsibility. There is still another dilemma troubling many people which our present point of view helps to solve—namely, whether you can have obedience *and* liberty.[8] That group of political scientists and guild socialists who are denying the power of the State, say that we cannot have obedience *and* liberty. I think they are wholly wrong, but I think we should ask ourselves to what we owe obedience. Surely only to a functional unity of which we are a part, to which we are contributing. I agree with the guild socialists that the State is not that now. Those who are concerned with the reorganization of industry should take warning from the failures of the state.

James Myers, author of *Representative Government in Industry*,[9] comes near involving himself in this dilemma of the political scientists when he tells us that men in industry have so long merely obeyed orders that we have there a real social danger.

[8] *Cf. The New State*, Chapters XXVIII–XXXII, on political pluralism.
[9] Doubleday-Doran, New York, 1924.

He says, "We must reawaken the instinct of self-assertion." While I think Myers recognizes a real problem here, I certainly do not think that the instinct of self-assertion needs to be reawakened in many of us.

We have considered the subject of symbols. It is often very apparent that an order is a symbol. The referee in the game stands watch in hand, and says, "Go." It is an order, but order only as symbol. I may say to an employee, "Do so and so," but I should say it only because we have both agreed, openly or tacitly, that that which I am ordering done is the best thing to be done. The order is then a symbol. And if it is a philosophical and psychological truth that we owe obedience only to a functional unity to which we are contributing, we should remember that a more accurate way of stating that would be to say that our obligation is to a unifying, to a process.

This brings us now to one of our most serious problems in this matter of orders. It is important, but we can touch on it only briefly; it is what we spoke of in the foregoing paper as the evolving situation. I am trying to show here that the order must be integral to the situation and must be recognized as such. But we saw that the situation was always developing. If the situation is never stationary, then the order should never be stationary, so to speak; how to prevent it from being so is our problem. The situation is changing while orders are being carried out, because, by and through orders being carried out. How is the order to keep up with the situation? External orders never can, only those drawn fresh from the situation.

Moreover, if taking a *responsible* attitude toward experience involves recognizing the evolving situation, a *conscious* attitude toward experience means that we note the change which the developing situation makes in ourselves; the situation does not change without changing us.

To summarize, what have we learned from these two papers on the subject of the giving of orders? That, integration being the basic law of life, orders should be the composite conclusion of those who give and those who receive them; more than this, that they should be the integration of the people concerned and the situation; more even than this, that they should be the integrations involved in the evolving situation. If you accept my three fundamental statements on this subject: (1) that the order should be the law of the situation; (2) that the situation is always evolving; (3) that orders should involve circular not linear behaviour —then we see that our old conception of orders has somewhat changed, and that there should therefore follow definite changes in business practice.

There is a problem so closely connected with the giving of orders that I want to put it before you for future discussion. After we have decided on our orders, we have to consider how much and what kind of supervision is necessary or advisable in order that they shall be carried out. We all know that many workers object to being watched. What does that mean, how far is it justifiable? How can the objectionable element be avoided and at the same time necessary supervision given? I do not think that this matter has been studied sufficiently. When I asked a very intelligent girl what she thought would be the result of profit-sharing and employee representation in the factory where she worked, she replied joyfully, "We shan't need foremen any more." While her entire ignoring of the fact that the foreman has other duties than keeping workers on their jobs was amusing, one wants to go beyond one's amusement and find out what this objection to being watched really means.

In a case in Scotland arising under the Minimum Wage Act, the overman was called in to testify whether or not a certain workman did his work properly. The examination was as follows:

Magistrate: "But isn't it your duty under the Mines Act to visit each working place twice a day?"

Overman: "Yes."

Magistrate: "Don't you do it?"

Overman: "Yes."

Magistrate: "Then why didn't you ever see him work?"

Overman: "They always stop work when they see an over-man coming and sit down and wait till he's gone—even take out their pipes, if it's a mine free from gas. They won't let anyone watch them."

An equally extreme standard was enforced for a part of the war period at a Clyde engineering works. The chairman of shop stewards was told one morning that there was a grievance at the smithy. He found one of the blacksmiths in a rage because the managing director in his ordinary morning's walk through the works had stopped for five minutes or so and watched this man's fire. After a shop meeting the chairman took up a deputation to the director and secured the promise that this should not happen again. At the next works meeting the chairman reported the incident to the body of workers, with the result that a similar demand was made throughout the works and practically acceded to, so that the director hardly dared to stop at all in his morning's walk.

I have seen similar instances cited. Many workmen feel that being watched is unbearable. What can we do about it? How can we get proper supervision without this watching which a worker resents? Supervision is necessary; supervision is resented,—how are we going to make the integration there? Some say, "Let the workers elect the supervisors." I do not believe in that.

There are three other points closely connected with the subject of this paper which I should like merely to point out. First, when and how do you point out mistakes, misconduct? One principle can surely guide us here: don't blame for the sake of blaming, make what you have to say accomplish something; say it in that form, at that time, under those circumstances, which will make it a real education to your subordinate. Secondly, since it is recognized that the one who gives the orders is not as a rule a very popular person, the management sometimes tries to offset this by allowing the person who has this onus upon him to give any pleasant news to the workers, to have the credit of any innovation which the workers very much desire. One manager told me that he always tried to do this. I suppose that this is good behaviouristic psychology, and yet I am not sure that it is a method I wholly like. It is quite different, however, in the case of a mistaken order having been given; then I think the one who made the mistake should certainly be the one to rectify it, not as a matter of strategy, but because it is better for him too. It is better for all of us not only to acknowledge our mistakes, but to do something about them. If a foreman discharges someone and it is decided to reinstate the man, it is obviously not only good tactics but a square deal to the foreman to allow him to do the reinstating.

There is, of course, a great deal more to this matter of giving orders than we have been able to touch on; far from exhausting the subject, I feel that I have only given hints. I have been told that the artillery men suffered more mentally in the war than others, and the reason assigned for this was that their work was directed from a distance. The combination of numbers by which they focused their fire was telephoned to them. The result was also at a distance. Their activity was not closely enough connected with the actual situation at either end.

One matter in regard to giving orders which seems to me of the utmost importance for business administration, I wish you would enlighten me about. When the numbers of employees are as large and as widely scattered as in the case of the Elevated and Telephone employees, how should the orders be conveyed? Someone said to me one day, "How do you suppose the Elevated gives its orders?" I didn't know what she meant and asked her, and she replied, "The uniform courtesy of the Elevated employees is such that I often wonder how the people at the top get their wishes across to so many widely scattered people."

Our time is more than up, but let me, in order to indicate the scope of this subject, mention some of the things we have not touched on, or not adequately: the relation of orders to training; the effect of the emotions (hope, fear, etc.) in the obeying of orders; how to keep control and yet give control and responsibility to subordinates. Moreover, perhaps I have not said explicitly that the participation of employees in the planning of orders should take place before the order is given, not afterwards. After the order has been given the subordinate must obey. I certainly believe in authority—of the right kind. And I am sure that I have not emphasized sufficiently the careful, painstaking study that is necessary if we are to anticipate how orders will be received. A man grumbles at an order; this makes trouble and the one over him says: "Why is that man kicking?" and he begins to study the situation. But perhaps by that time it is too late; the trouble has perhaps got too much headway. To anticipate the kicks, to learn the most successful methods of doing this, is an important part of the work of the order-giver.

I began this talk by saying that I was going to consider order-giving merely as an illustration of a method, the method of taking a conscious and responsible attitude toward our experience. I feel strongly on this point, on the nècessity of taking a responsible attitude toward our experience. We students of social and industrial research are often lamentably vague. We sometimes do not even know what we know and what we do not know. We can avoid this vagueness only (1) by becoming conscious of what we believe in, (2) of what we do not believe in, and (3) by recognizing the large debatable ground in between those two fields and trying our experiments there. Don't let us try experiments where they are not needed, in regard to matters about which we have already made up our minds. For instance, there are certain things which people continue to urge about employee representation which are almost universally accepted. There is no need of saying these particular things any longer, there is no need of studying them; let us give our efforts to the things we don't know—there are plenty of them.

Another point: we should always know whether we are considering principles or methods. A confusion here is disastrous, as we often see in discussion. I have heard a discussion on whether shop-committee meetings should be held in company time, which seemed to me quite beside the mark because the distinction was not being made between the principles underlying the matter and the possible methods of carrying out the principles. Some were talking about one, and some about the other. Moreover, let us not confuse our methods one with the other; let us try out one until we have come to some conclusion about it. As a coach used to tell the Harvard boat crew, "It's better to have a method and stick to it, even if it's not the best possible method."

This is all involved in what I spoke of as taking a conscious and responsible attitude toward experience. It is also taking a scientific attitude. The growing appreciation of the advantage of such an attitude is evidenced by the subject chosen for this course of conferences: *the scientific foundations of business administration.*

III

BUSINESS AS AN INTEGRATIVE UNITY[1]

A MAN said to me once, a man working on a salary as the head of a department in a factory, "I'm no wage-earner, working so many hours a day; if I wake up at midnight and have an idea that might benefit the factory, it belongs to the factory." His implication was that the wage-earner would not feel this. Can business reach its maximum of efficiency and service unless it is so organized that the wage-earner does feel this?

But the subject we are considering, that of integrative unity, goes far beyond the question of the worker's place in industry. It seems to me that the first test of business administration, of industrial organization, should be whether you have a business with all its parts so co-ordinated, so moving together in their closely knit and adjusting activities, so linking, interlocking, interrelating, that they make a working *unit*—that is, not a congeries of separate pieces, but what I have called a functional whole or integrative unity. I have taken these phrases from Kempf, the psychobiologist. They seem to me to represent one of the most profound of philosophical and psychological principles, and one which helps us very materially in working out practical methods of business organization. For this principle applies to the relation of men, the relation of services, the relation of departments, the last of which I have found one of the weakest points in the businesses which I have studied. How are we to get an integrative unity? How are we to know when we have it? What tests are there which will show us when we are approaching it?

I once asked a girl who worked in a factory where profit-sharing had been introduced, what difference it had made

[1] See note, p. 30; this paper was presented in January, 1925.

71

in her attitude, and she replied: "We have a garden in the factory grounds and of course I never used to pick any of the flowers, they didn't belong to me; but since I've felt myself a partner, I go in and pick the pansies." Remembering the Peter Piper of my nursery days, I said: "If all the partners picked the pansies, where would the pansies be for the partners to pick?"

What then does an integrative unity mean if it does not mean picking the pansies or taking a free ride on the railroad because I am a stockholder? Does employee representation give us the kind of unity we are seeking? This has seldom been even the aim of employee representation. To many the introduction of Works Councils, of Shop Committees, has meant merely changing the field of collective bargaining. Mr. W. L. Stoddard says, in his book on *The Shop Committee*, "Collective bargaining is the fundamental theory on which the shop committee rests." And he says it approvingly. We see the same thing stated again and again. I do not think we are going greatly to strengthen business and industrial organization by this conception. It seems to me that the aim of employee representation should be not merely to transfer the antagonism of "sides" to a different field, but to see how far sides—that is, controversial sides—can be done away with. Collective bargaining seems only a temporary expedient, for it has no real vitality as it does not create. It fixes the limits of wages, hours and conditions; it might be conceived perhaps as fixing certain limits to policies, but it does not create. It is on an entirely different principle that the policies of our great businesses are brought into being and operation. Collective bargaining will go on, I hope, until we have found something better, but I believe that something better will be found, is being found.[2]

[2] The term "bargaining" has come to be used pretty generally for all agreements between management and labour, yet some of these argreements are arrived at by a much more fruitful process than that of bargaining. I am not, when looking beyond "collective bargaining," thinking of these agreements, but of that bargaining which rests wholly on the balance of power and ends with compromise. (M. P. F.)

Conferring versus Fighting

Capital and labour must fight or unite. No gentlemanly name for fighting will change the essential nature of the relation between capital and labour in those plants where "sides" are sharply defined. Yet we must remember how strenuously the unions have opposed any blurring of the lines dividing management and workmen. Measures which aimed at greater unity of employers and employees have been denounced by the unions as class collaboration. W. Z. Foster and the extreme radicals attacked the Baltimore and Ohio Railway plan as class collaboration. Often I have heard that said of perfectly sincere efforts to bring the management and the workmen into closer working relations. It is openly voiced by some of the intellectuals of the English Labour Party. Those who prefer to see industrial relations as a fight do not wish to make a unit of the plant. There are unionists who, reading what I have to say, might think me unfriendly to labour. I think I am showing the only way that labour can permanently prosper.

We want to do away with the fight attitude, to get rid of sides. Yet there is a sense in which sides are necessary to the richness of that unity which we are here considering, essential even to its existence in any real sense. In any conference between managers and workers the representatives of the workers should represent the workers' point of view, but, as has been pointed out by one of our most thoughtful manufacturers, the workers' point of view of what is best for the plant as a whole. There is a vast difference here. And this principle holds good not only for conferences between management and workmen, but in any committee or conference in the business. In a meeting of the superintendents of departments, each should consider, not merely what is good for his department, but the good of the business as viewed from his department. Please notice the last phrase; I do not say that he should consider what is good for the whole business and end my sentence there, as is so often done. I say what is good

73

for the whole *as seen from his department.* We do want sides in this sense.

The question of pay for attendance at Works Councils is interesting in connection with this point, the viewing of the whole from an integral part of the whole. In some plants time spent in the Works Councils is paid for, in others not. In the latter case the assumption apparently is that the workmen are in those meetings looking after their own interests; if it were considered that they were working for the whole plant, then it would seem as if those meetings should be held in company time.

We have then a test for sides whenever they appear. Are they fighting sides or integrative sides? Are they sides which expect antagonism, arouse the impulse of self-protection against exploitation, or are they parts of a functional unity? If we wish to foster the latter and abolish the former, those set within the fight-pattern, let us see how it can be done.

It is, happily, generally recognized to-day that the first step in any controversy, in any discussion, and not only between managers and workmen, but on boards of directors, between fellow managers or wherever, should be to examine the situation irrespective of sides, to get at the facts. We spoke of this when we were considering the question of integration. In one factory I have visited, I found the workers much interested in time-studies, cost-of-living charts, etc., and it seemed to me very significant that it should be in this factory, where the facts relative to cost of production were being studied by the workers themselves, that I heard compromise denounced, surely an indication that the fight attitude was weakening among them. One man said to me: "When I worked in a shoe shop, the men were talking all the time of compromise, but here we are shown what we really earn." Others spoke of their objection to the Works Councils making requests on the compromise basis. "Let them ask," I heard said, "for what they really think right and then the managers will think them reasonable." This is interesting, I think, when we know so many college professors who are still preaching compromise, so many diplomats who are still

74

working for compromise as the apex of their endeavours.

Moreover, when we are looking at the actual situation we are more likely to follow the process necessary to integration, the breaking up of a whole situation into its component parts and considering these separately. My own experience is that nothing gets rid of sides so quickly as this process. When minimum wage boards vote on a cost-of-living budget as a whole, employees and employers are lined up on different sides; when they take up the items one by one I have invariably seen both employers and employees on each side in the vote. This is because each one is then looking at the facts, at what food, for instance, does actually cost in the year 1924; he is not thinking what his "side" would like to pay the girl.

Again, in a factory where I believe there is an honest endeavour to get at the facts irrespective of sides, one of the employees said to me of the conference committees: "The line-up is not always of managers on one side and workmen on the other; each question is considered on its merits, and managers as often change their opinions as workmen." Employers can take sides and fight over what wages they would like to give, the unions over what wages they would like to receive, but neither can fight over the question whether girls are actually paying $6.00 or $8.00 a week for board—this is an ascertainable fact.

I think it a good plan moreover, whenever possible, not only that a study of the situation should be made irrespective of sides, but that it should be co-operatively undertaken, as in the case of a board I was on where we could not agree even on the facts so long as each side was getting them separately and pitting one set of facts against the other. When a sub-committee of both employers and employees was appointed to gather these facts co-operatively, that was a big step toward final agreement.[3]

In the factory just spoken of, where the line-up in conference, it was said, is not always of managers on one side and workmen on the other, I heard few complaints of the

[3] *Cf. Creative Experience*, Chapter I, "Experience and the Expert."

management. But I found, on the other hand, that the representatives of the workmen were very wary about going back to their constituents and praising the managers because then their fellow employees might think they were trying to curry favour; as I heard one girl say, "Oh, he just wants to be foreman." But this fear of speaking well of the management, which at first glance might seem unfortunate, works out well, for finding it poor policy to praise, and having little fault to find, there is a tendency to describe to their fellow workers quite impersonally what has taken place. There is a tendency for the situation to be depersonalized and to be presented as depending on the facts of the case. This seems to me admirable.

When we have got thus far, we find that we have gone a long way toward looking at conference as a matter of conferring, not as a matter of fighting. It is indeed encouraging for the future of business administration that we see so many indications of a growing appreciation of this. A workman in a large plant said to me: "You don't go into a conference committee with a gun under your coat, and that does away with suspicion, for when a man has a gun under his coat, he always thinks the other fellow has two under his." One of the girls said: "When I first went to a conference committee, I thought I was going there to give my criticism to the management, but I came to understand that co-operation means also taking criticism from the management, and I am more willing now to take it." One man said: "I feel in a conference committee that I'm an agent for both sides." I think that a great achievement for that firm, as great as their success in production. I believe it contributes to their success in production, for this sense of double responsibility I could see increased this man's feeling of self-respect, of the dignity of his work, and everything which does that tends to increase the production efficiency of the plant.

I hope it will be understood that I do not intend all this to apply merely to managers and workmen. I think on every board, in every committee, the same effort should be made, namely, to substitute conferring for fighting, to recognize

76

that there are two kinds of difference, the difference which disrupts and the difference which may, if properly handled, more firmly unite, and to realize that if unity is the aim of conference, it is not because unity in the sense of peace is our primary object—you can get peace at any moment if your sledge hammer is big enough—but because we are seeking an integrative unity as the foundation of business development.

The Meaning of Collective Responsibility—Reconciling Centralization and Decentralization

An appreciation of the difference between controversial sides and integrative sides is necessary for the discussion of that "collective responsibility for production," which we hear so often advocated to-day. There are two quite different conceptions of collective responsibility depending upon whether one has accepted the notion of integrative unities. The Mines Act of 1911 gave the English miners power to appoint an inspector of their own to make a complete examination of the machinery once a month. This was called joint responsibility, but it was not the joint responsibility which is one of the tests of integrative unity. Some one writing approvingly of this Act said that it implied "a definite, statutory right of the workers to take an active and independent part in the prevention of accident." It is the "independent" part that I do not believe in. This Act was not taken advantage of widely because of the fear that adverse reports would mean loss of jobs, but even if it had been, it is probable that the reports of manager's inspector and workers' inspector would have differed; it is co-operative investigation and co-operative responsibility that we need. In the wood-working industries, however, another method was followed; a joint study was made of the dangers arising from the use of wood-working machinery. This seems to me to rest on sounder principles.

Responsibility for technique as well as for safety has been claimed and gained in many instances in England. The miners at a Yorkshire pit appointed a controller to supervise the distribution of mines underground and paid half his salary. Again, in the Nottingham lace factories, where deductions are made from the pay for spoiled work, quality is judged by a committee of the weavers. These are perhaps all good things as steps, as recognition of labour, but I do not think they should be cited as instances of joint responsibility. I think we shall be in danger of sides in the objectionable sense until all such activities are truly *joint* activities. The joint responsibility of management and labour is an interpenetrating responsibility, and is utterly different from responsibility divided off into sections, management having some and labour some. Mr. Tawney has advocated strenuously the maintenance of professional standards by crafts. This is excellent advice, yet we should remember that management too has something to do with the maintenance of professional standards among workmen. Indeed the responsibility of unions is perhaps something of an anachronism to-day, since the place of the crafts in modern industry is so very different from what it was in the early days of trade unionism.

We have in America an excellent example of a very real appreciation of joint responsibility for technique in the large unanimity of opinion that job analysis should be a matter for experts, managers and workers together.

I have been speaking of the demand of English workers for an "independent" responsibility. The fallacy involved in the word independent seems to me to run through much of the literature of the English Labour Party. Many of the Labour Party are suspicious of "joint control" because it might not allow room for what they call "independent" control. One writer says that the test of all forms of joint control "must be whether in the particular instance . . . the workers' side is independently active." Surely this is the wrong expression. The worker should be active in the fullest degree possible, but not "independently" active. The question, says this author, is: "Are the workers to play an active part in shaping policy?" Yes, but not an independent part.

This author speaks of "the test of actual independence of function," and again of "the test whether or not the workers' side does actually exert an independent force." Independent power? Are we always going to want independent power? Or shall we sometimes see that we actually get more independent power through joint power? Much could be said on this point.

On the employers' side there is often a corresponding mistake. Employers sometimes speak of *dividing* responsibility when they are merely *shirking* responsibility. Many people will avoid a decision in order to avoid being held responsible for the consequences. I know a case of a husband and wife where the husband is autocratic and likes to make the decisions, but when he thinks a particular decision may go wrong he leaves it to his wife! When, therefore, I hear that the workers are going to be given more responsibility, I do not rejoice over that fact at once; I wait to look into the matter and see what it means. A responsibility spread out thin may save your face when things go wrong, but will not correct the wrong. Responsibility will never take the place of technique; let us make no mistake about that.

It is evident, I hope, therefore, that I am not advocating the mere diffusion of responsibility. A large part of business success depends upon how far we can, after allotting responsibility to committees or division superintendents or foremen (we all know how dangerous it is to short-circuit the foreman), how far we can then make these various responsibilities interpenetrate.

I am often misunderstood on this point of collective responsibility. People sometimes think when I emphasize collective responsibility, that I do not believe in decentralization. I know no one who believes more strongly in decentralization than I do, but I believe that collective responsibility and decentralized responsibility must go hand in hand; more than that, I think they are parts of the same thing. Books on business administration often discuss concentrated authority versus distributed authority, but I do not think this discussible. I recently read in an article on business administration that we must find a happy mean between centralization and decentralization. I do not think that, for I believe we should have both. When the National Joint Council of Electrical Contractors and Electrical Workers was formed, it was found that joint local councils and joint district councils were necessary through which the national body could function and work out a national policy. That centralization and decentralization are not opposed is, I believe, the central lesson for business administration to learn. To understand this principle and to devise methods for its operation is what we must all work at daily if industry and the government of nations are not to fail. I do not minimize the difficulties we shall meet. This is one of our gravest problems: how to foster local initiative and at the same time get the advantages of centralization. The problem is grave, but we must face it; we want no compromise in this matter.

Let us note here a very marked difference between being responsible for a functional whole, what we are here considering, and being responsible for our function in the whole, which has been given far more consideration in the past. We have been so delighted with what has sometimes been called the functional theory, that is, the division of work so that each can do what he is best fitted for, that we have tended to forget that our responsibility does not end with doing conscientiously and well our particular piece of the whole, but that we are also responsible for the whole.[4] A business should be so organized that all will feel this responsibility. We see it in the case of the home. The wife has her duties and the husband his, but in addition to these, or rather by means of these, each has to do his and her part to make the home bear its significance in the life of the community, serve its maximum degree of service to the community. We do try to make our children feel this; I wish we could extend it to the rest of our household, to our servants.

[4] *Cf. The New State,* Chapter XXX, for a criticism of Vocational Representation. The underlying theory of the relation of functional parts to the whole is there developed in regard to the state in the same way as here applied to business organization.

What greater dignifying of labour could there be than that which comes from a sense of joint responsibility in community service?

This is the problem in business administration: how can a business be so organized that workers, managers, owners, feel a collective responsibility? The advantages of creating a sense of individual responsibility have long been noted as one of the cardinal principles of business administration, and many have leaned toward employee representation because they thought it was developing this. Some say in the language of the old maxim: Responsibility sobers. Or as one young manager said to me of his workmen, "They don't have so many darn fool ideas now." The idea of a collective responsibility, however, has been neither fully accepted nor the methods of obtaining it worked out.

I think myself that collective responsibility should begin with group responsibility, that a form of departmental organization which includes the workers is the most effective method for unifying a business.[5] In one business, where there is a strong feeling on the part of the managers that the worker should be given responsibility to his full capacity, group responsibility is encouraged wherever possible. For instance, the chauffeurs asked for shorter hours. They were given a fifty-four hour week with overtime, and the chairman and secretary of the chauffeur group, acting for the group, assumed the responsibility for each man giving an honest week's work. We see the next step in collective responsibility, *inter*departmental relations, in a store where, for instance, the elevator force has meetings at which are considered how the elevator force can help the store superintendent, how it can help the charge office, the advertising office, the information bureau, the mail order department, etc. Such steps are, of course, mere beginnings in the solving of what seems to me the crux of business administration, the relation of departments, of functions, however you wish

[5] *Cf. The New State*, p. 245: ". . . the State must be the actual integration of living local groups, thereby finding ways of dealing directly with its individual members."

to put it. Any study of business as an integrative unity should, I think, make this problem its chief concern.

An understanding of this principle of integrative unity which we are considering will keep us not only from a false individualism, but also from a false altruism. For instance, if we dislike many of the old ways of hiring and firing which often left too much to the mere whim of the foreman, we sometimes say that we dislike these methods because they are not fair to the workman, but the truth is that we do not change these methods in order to benefit the workman only, but because the change will benefit the business as a whole. Or take the necessity of regularizing employment so that seasonal or so-called "cyclical" fluctuations will be reduced. This need should not be taken up solely as a grievance of labour, for there is loss in overhead as well as loss to the employees. Again, the arbitrator should arbitrate for the institution. This should go without saying, but a union girl asked, "Is he pro-labour?" You can be *for* labour without being *against* capital; you can be for the institution.

When you have made your employees feel that they are in some sense partners in the business, they do not improve the quality of their work, save waste in time and material, because of the Golden Rule, but because their interests are the same as yours. Over and over again in the past we have heard it said to workmen, "If this were your material, you wouldn't waste it," and over and over again that admonition fails. We find, however, that when there is some feeling in a plant, more or less developed, that that business is a working unit, we find then that the workman is more careful of material, that he saves time in lost motions, in talking over annoyances, that he helps the new hand by explaining things to him, that he helps the fellow working at his side by calling attention to the end of a roll on the machine, etc. This is the Golden Rule taken behaviouristically. It is, by the way, the Golden Rule taken idealistically, too, for a functional whole is a much higher conception than our old notion of the Golden Rule.

Before we leave the subject of joint responsibility, I should like to consider the matter of how far it should go. We might base our discussion of this on a case which came up in Wisconsin some years ago. After the workmen's compensation law was passed in Wisconsin, a case in dispute came before the Industrial Commission for decision. A teamster got drunk in his employer's time, fell off his wagon and was killed. His widow petitioned for the amount of indemnity to be paid by the employer and won. The Supreme Court sustained the decision and later the Legislature sustained their opinion by making the law more explicit. Professor Commons tells us that back of the overt reasoning in this case there was the feeling of group responsibility. "On the former legal theory of individual responsibility," he says, "these decisions could not be justified. Only on a theory of partnership or solidarity of interest can they find justification. Employer and employee are engaged in a common enterprise. They jointly assume the risks and share the burdens and the benefits of the enterprise. More than that they share each other's frailties." I cannot see the matter wholly in this light, but a principle recently and soberly embodied in the law of one of our states is worth consideration.

I want to add one word more in regard to this conception of joint responsibility, joint control, and that is to point out that what we are considering is not at all the same as the conception of reciprocity so often advocated. I disagree with Professor Commons that "loyalty is an expectation of reciprocity." Our obligations, our responsibilities, our loyalty, should be, as we said of obedience in the previous lecture, to a functional unity of which we are a part. Robert Valentine said: "Employers should stop talking about the loyalty of their employees until they are ready to make an equal noise talking about their loyalty to employees." This was well worth saying, but if Mr. Valentine were here to-day he would say, I think, that this is a rather crude way of looking at the matter compared with our present conception of loyalty as part of the process of creating business unities.

Joint loyalty, then, joint responsibility, are very different conceptions when considered as an interweaving of obligations and when considered as a reciprocity of obligations. I wish you would make a note of this fallacy wherever you find it, in your reading or in your observation of business administration. For instance, Mr. Leiserson asks: "Does the company desire to do justice as the company sees it, or is the employer ready to administer justice to his employees as they understand justice?" But why should Mr. Leiserson think the latter any better than the former? It seems to me that it is just as true in regard to the standards for the conduct of business as it is for control, responsibility, loyalty, that standards, too, must be jointly developed. And the immediate moral of that is that the organization of the plant should be such as to make this possible.

The Redistribution of Function

The first test of any part of business organization and administration should be, I think: how far does this make for integrative unity? Take the question often discussed, and sometimes made a practical issue, whether foremen should belong to unions. The arguments in this discussion are not based on the theory of integrative unity, but on the theory of sides, controversial sides. Indeed perhaps no one subject could throw more light on this subject than the foreman's position, and if there had been time I had intended to give a section to that. If, however, we have not time for this or many other interesting questions, there is one point I wish to speak of, and that is that managing itself is an interpenetrating matter, that the distinction between those who manage and those who are managed is somewhat fading. We are on the way, it seems to me, to a different analysis of services from that which we now have. This is the most valuable suggestion, I think, in a very valuable paper read by Mr. Dennison to the Taylor Society. Mr. Tawney has also shown us that no sharp division can be drawn between management and labour, and that the line between them fluctuates widely from industry to industry with the nature of the work carried on. "There are certain occupations in

84

which an absolute separation between the planning and the performance of the work is, for technical reasons, impracticable. A group of miners who are cutting and filling coal are 'working' hard enough. But very little coal will be cut . . . unless they display some of the qualities of scientific knowledge, prevision and initiative which are usually associated with the word 'management.' What is true of miners is true, in different degrees, of men on a building job, or in the transport trades. They must exercise considerable discretion in their work because, unless they do, the work does not get done, and no amount of supervision can compensate for the absence of discretion." That is a sentence worth remembering—no amount of supervision can compensate for the absence of discretion.

We can all see daily the truth of the statement that not all the managing is done by the management, that workers are sometimes managing. I can see this clearly in my household; if my cook plans my meals as well as cooks them, she does some of the managing of my household. It is claimed that the plan of the Baltimore and Ohio, of bi-weekly conferences between managers and employees in the workshops, has produced the following results: reduction in labour turnover; routes of carrying material shortened and made easier; fuller and more regular operation made possible; the average delays per week behind schedule reduced; monthly materials per employee reduced; and the work of repairs greatly facilitated as well as the quality improved—the problem of getting a steady flow of adequate material was solved and certain difficulties in the tool-room which wasted time were straightened out. This is all part of the service of managing. But even when the workmen's managerial capacity is not tested so far as this, there is usually room for some. Whenever labour uses its judgment in planning, that perhaps is managing. If the worker is given a task and allowed to decide *how* he will do it, that perhaps is managing. It would not be possible to carry on a business if the workers did not do some managing.

There are two ways, however, of looking at this matter of

managing ability among the workmen. One executive says: "We wanted to get any managing ability there was, from counter, stock-room, truck delivery or wherever, into the management. We wanted it for ourselves as well as to help the people advance." This is certainly sound business sense, but then in addition to this, it seems to me that there is another attitude to be taken. It should be recognized that almost everyone has some managing ability, even if it be very little, and opportunity should be given each man to exercise what he has on his actual job. If all on the managerial force have—as, of course, they have—initiative, creative imagination, organizing and executive ability, there are many workmen who are not entirely lacking in these qualities. We want to make use of what they have.

If the job of every workman were analysed so that each could understand what opportunities he had for managing, that might have both a direct and an indirect influence on production. Indirect because this might greatly increase the workman's self-respect and pride in his work, which is so necessary for the best results. A workman who had sat on a good many conference committees said to me, with dignity and pride: "When I am on that committee I am the equal of anyone; of course when I go back to my work I am just a workman, but while I am on that committee I am the equal of the President himself." I told that to the President and he said: "He must be made to feel that all the time." Yes, but the difficulty is how. I wish you would consider that. Perhaps one way would be so to analyse each man's work that he would realize that he had some managing to do as well as the President.[6]

To be sure, the awards for suggestions given in so many plants now are a recognition that the workman has managing

[6] *Cf. Creative Experience*, p. 20: "Our aim in the so-called democratic organization of industry should be, not to give the workmen a vote on things they know nothing about, but so to organize the plant that the workmen's experience can be added to that of the expert; we must see just where their experience will be a plus matter, and we must plan to have the workmen learn more and more of the industry as a whole. To think that a man can come from his particular machine and vote intelligently on the running of the business is exactly the mistake we have made in politics."

ability. This recognition is, however, not yet sufficiently widespread. The post-office workers of England have repeatedly claimed that they have made suggestions for the improvement of the service which have been turned down. In a group of Derbyshire miners one man rose and said, "There isn't a man in this room who hasn't time and again made suggestions and been told that he was paid to work and not to think."

Whenever the trade unions show managing capacity, I think they do more for their cause than by any other of their activities. When the Amalgamated worked out a plan of employee insurance, when a few years ago the Photo-Engravers Union of New York drew up a new price-list, submitted it to their employers and won its acceptance, they went far beyond the function of unions as defence organizations.

In England we have several examples of plans from the workers actually making possible the continuation of production, as in the case of the British Westinghouse employees when the managers were thinking of closing down the foundry on account of the high cost of production. The fact that workers themselves have in many instances treated the disputed points between employers and employees as problems rather than matters of rights is a hopeful sign that the workers' demand for share in control is not a mere gesture for "power," that they feel in themselves managing capacity.

If the worker's job ought to be analysed to see what part of it is managing, so the managers' jobs should be analysed to see if to any part of those the workers could contribute anything. It may be found that even in those activities which have been considered exclusively the functions of the managers, as correlating the selling and production departments, the buying of material and equipment, the control of the flow of material through the plant so that there will be no congestion—even to these the worker can make some contribution.

The direct dependence of the worker on management is obvious. The piece-workers' earnings depend on the quality of material supplied by the purchasing agent, on the efficiency of the machinery and the flow of material. Unemployment depends partly on whether fewer orders have been taken than could be filled. If the sales department is over-zealous, profits may be wiped out by overtime. The hewer in the coal mines in England is paid for the amount of coal that gets to the surface, and that depends largely on the supply of tubs and the arrangements for haulage. In the charges before the Coal Commission, the following complaints were often heard: too little coal-cutting machinery; too little mechanical haulage; shortage of trains, tubs, rails, horses, and of timber for pit-props; bad distribution of rolling stock. It seems only fair that the workmen should not be held responsible for what the managers have a large share in through defective planning in the technique of the industry. It is obvious now, I think, that joint action is necessary in the development of industrial technique.

I should like to say, in summary of this section, that as we have always known that no sharp line could be drawn between planning and executing—one set of men does not do all the planning and another set all the executing; the higher executives are those who have the ability to contribute to the planning and are paid more for that reason—as we have always known this, so now we see that no absolutely sharp line can be drawn between management and labour, that the division between those who manage and those who are managed has been in part artificial.

There is one point, however, that needs further consideration. Should planning that is done incidentally as it were be called managing? Is not responsibility always a part of managing? Should anyone, strictly speaking, be said to manage unless he both plans and takes some responsibility for that planning? I should say that when men are allowed to use their own judgment in regard to the manner of executing orders, *and accept the responsibility involved in that,* they are managing.

We shall all agree on one point, however: there should be no haziness in regard to employee functioning in a managerial capacity; the limits of such functioning should be frankly and sharply defined. For instance, the Works Council is sometimes a judicial body; sometimes a legislative body; sometimes an advisory body; it is never an executive body. This should be openly recognized. To be honest and clear-cut in delimiting function is, I believe, essential to the success of the redistribution of function.

This matter of redistribution of function will not only, I think, have a direct influence in increased production and better conditions for workmen, but will indirectly affect policy. We cannot now foresee how far changes in internal organization will change business policy, but as the market-ing co-operatives have in some instances changed the agricultural policy of the farmers, so it may happen that the reorganization of business on the inside may change business policy. It may be indeed that the whole machinery of com-petitive capitalistic business will be in some degree altered.

Various Factors and Relationships Underlying Functional Unity

I have had time to give only hints of what I mean by functional unity in business. Let me emphasize a few points even if I can do so by scarcely more than headings. First, the interdependence of all the activities involved is clearly evident. There really is not such a thing, strictly speaking, as a departmental problem; there is hardly a problem, more-over, which can be considered purely one of production or distribution. The parts of modern business are so intricately interwoven that the worker, in order to have an intelligent opinion in regard to even his own problems, has not only to know something of processes, of equipment, has not only to consider the effect of the introduction of new machinery and the training of the worker; he should also understand the connection between the production and the commercial side, should know something of the effectiveness of the sales organization—misguided sales or purchasing policies may ruin a business. There are many now who think the worker should study unit costs, but he cannot understand low unit costs, can he, without knowing something of the terms of securing credit which help to determine unit costs? More-over, I think some knowledge of the general business and trade policy—adjustment of supply and demand, prospec-tive contracts, even the opening of new markets—would make the opinion of the worker on production processes more valuable.

While the necessity of team-work between the departments is recognized by everyone, the methods for obtaining it are not yet sufficiently worked out, and the matter is sometimes a little blurred by the fact that different departments are working at different things at any one moment. The manu-facture of cigars is almost a continuous process because cigars have to be fresh, but the buying of the tobacco has to be concentrated in short periods in spring and summer. The signing of contracts for delivery takes place at a different time from the manufacture of the product. This, however, does not change our problem; it merely makes it a more intricate one.

Besides all these relations which I have named, there is the newer one of production manager and personnel director, an important and often very delicate matter. As one Works Manager said, "Why is this young man of thirty-two sup-posed to know more of human nature than I at fifty-eight?" We are sometimes told how necessary it is that these two should "get on" together, but *you* all know that unless the personnel director does a good deal more than "get on" with Works Manager or Manufacturing Committee, he will not be of the greatest usefulness to his firm. In fact one of the things I feel most strongly about business administration as it exists to-day is that until we find some better way of uniting technical and so-called psychological problems than we have at present, we are far from efficient business administration.

Another necessary unifying we have not considered is the relation of the main firm to its branches—branch banks, branch stores, or a number of plants operating under one management. Many problems would meet us here, but we can use the same principles in trying to solve them.

In concluding my necessarily meagre treatment of what I have called integrative unity, I should say that the efficiency of many plants is lowered by an imperfectly worked out system of co-ordination of parts. In some instances what co-ordination there is depends chiefly on the ability of certain heads to get on together; their willingness to consult each other depends too often on mere chance qualities or conditions—perhaps whether certain men commute by the same train! An adequate system of co-ordination has not yet, so far as I know, been worked out for business administration.

It is impossible, however, to work most effectively at co-ordination until you have made up your mind where you stand philosophically in regard to the relation of parts to the whole. We have spoken of the relation of departments —sales and production, advertising and financial—to each other, but the most profound truth that philosophy has ever given us concerns not only the relation of parts, but the relation of parts to the whole, not to a stationary whole, but to a whole a-making. What does this mean in business? It means that the sales department, for instance, should have some principle by which to test the relation of a sales policy to general policy. Books on management sometimes tell us that the production manager should subordinate departmental policy to business policy. I do not agree with this. In the *Bulletin of the Taylor Society* for February, 1924, it is stated that "any department head should recognize organization policies as more vital than his own." I wonder why more "vital"? Or I have seen it stated that department heads should realize that general policy is more "important" than departmental policy. He should not, because it is not, any more than the United States is more important than New York, and I am no states-righter either. Co-ordinate manufacture and sales? Certainly, also work out the relation between manufacturing and general policy and between sales and general policy, always remembering that general policy is, or should be, no air plant, but that all the time manufacturing and sales policies are contributing to general policy. The production manager should not subordinate departmental policy to business policy; he should contribute it, and he should see that it is a contributable policy. That is the chief test of the production manager, whether his policy is a contributable policy.

I should like to say parenthetically that in order to consider this subject in one paper, we are leaving out many questions. Perhaps to secure independence of outside capital is necessary to functional unity, but such questions would carry us too far afield.

The Administrator as Integrator of the Interests of all Parties Concerned

So far we have been looking only at the unifying of a single plant in its many relations. We have left out of consideration the question of unifying a whole industry, although obviously that is very important. Many shortline railroads cannot pay if considered separately. In a number of industries, profits as a whole could make reasonable return on that industry as a whole. If the industry were considered as a whole, the so-called marginal plants might be kept going. Again, wages cannot be set by one plant; the tendency is toward equalization in the same trade over considerable areas. This applies also to hours of work. Moreover, it is the whole industry which should take into consideration the demand for its product; one plant cannot, to the greatest advantage, organize its production in relation to the demand. This is part of the problem of unemployment. The selling agencies throughout an industry should have some connection if production is to be regularized.

I need not speak at any length of how much competing firms have in common and the many instances we have of the increasing recognition of that, as in the case of the two rival Ohio firms which arranged for transfer from one plant to another for promotional purposes. (I am aware that the radicals would say that was probably a move against the consumer, but I do not want to go into that now.) The Joint Council of Electrical Contractors and Electrical Workers made an arrangement in New York in 1919 or 1920 for the exchange of skilled workers, and set up an employment bureau. It was thought at the time that statistics on cost of living, etc., could be pooled, wages and working conditions standardized, and the flow of labour to some extent controlled. The stated object of the National Industrial Council movement of England was increasing uniformity in labour standards *by industries*.

And beyond all this, beyond the matter of the unifying of single plants, beyond even the unifying of all the plants in the same industry, there is still another way of looking at business unity which should be one of the chief concerns of the business administrator. He sees the three classes: (1) workers, including industrial and managerial workers, (2) consumers, and (3) investors. The chief job of business is to find a method for integrating the interests of these three classes. I have said nothing of the consumer, because there has not been time, but when we find employers and employees uniting against the consumer to secure higher prices, tariff regulations or other preferential advantages, when we are told that the cotton industry in England will always, in case of anticipated government interference, respond to the call of "Lancashire against London," then we see how important is this branch of our subject.

Just as the *relation* of jobs is a part of job analysis, just as the *relation* of departments is a part of scientific management, so a study of all these relations just mentioned should be a part of the study of business administration. I wish it were not so often assumed that the subject of personnel relations in industry applies only to employers and employees. The manager has to get credit from the bankers, make dividends for the stockholders, and he has to deal with his competitors. To be more exact, the manager has relations with (1) bankers, (2) stockholders, (3) co-managers and directors, (4) wage-earners, (5) competitors, (6) the people from whom he buys, (7) customers.

The business man has probably the opportunity to-day of making one of the largest contributions to society that has ever been made, a demonstration of the possibility of collective creativeness. Many writers tell us that we are living in a barren age and deplore this as a sign of our degeneration. These writers look to the periods of creative energy in the past and find there their Leonardos and their Dantes; they then look around to-day and, seeing no Leonardos nor Dantes, deplore the unproductiveness of our modern civilization. Such people make the mistake of connecting creativeness always and inevitably with individuals. They do not see that we are now at the beginning of a period of creative energy, but that instead of being the individual creativeness of the past which gave us our artists and our poets, we may now enter on a period of collective creativeness if we have the imagination to see its potentialities, its reach, its ultimate significance, above all if we are willing patiently to work out the method.

In the field of politics we see little to encourage us; but in the League of Nations, in the co-operatives, above all in business administration, we see an appreciation emerging, not in words but in deeds, of what collective creativeness might mean to the world. Much of our theoretical writing accepts without analysis time-honoured phrases and notions, treats as fundamental ideas the crude, primitive attempts to get at democracy by rule of thumb. The world has long been fumbling for democracy, but has not yet grasped its essential and basic idea. Business and industrial organization is, I believe, on the verge of making large contributions to something far more important than democracy, democracy in its more superficial meaning—to the development of integrative unity. Business cannot serve its maximum degree of usefulness to the community, cannot perform the service which it has, tacitly, *bound* itself to perform, unless it seeks an enlarged understanding of the practical methods of unifying business organization.

IV

POWER[1]

I ASKED a number of workmen in two factories, both of which had some form of employee representation, "If a question came up where you had to decide between loyalty to your union and loyalty to the works, which would you choose?" The answer was always, "The union." Then I asked for their reasons, and here is the summary: (1) "I have taken an oath to the union; (2) the union is a permanent relation, the factory is not; (3) the unions have power back of them, the works council has not." Oath, permanency, power, but the greatest of these, I felt, was power.

Power, or control, is a word which we find on almost every page of English labour literature, and frequently enough in our own. One of the leaders of the Sheffield Shop Stewards movement said: "We organize for power," the baldest and most succinct statement I have seen.

One of the most urgent problems of business to-day is the relation of bargaining to value, and bargaining rests on power. He seems to get the best of the bargaining who has the greatest power. But is bargaining the only determinant of value, whether of goods, labour, or what not? What of scientific management? Does not every business man find one of his most pressing problems to be: how to integrate bargaining and scientific methods? As far as I have seen, scientific methods do not, cannot perhaps, set exact values; at present they merely set the limits of the bargaining process. Within those limits bargaining still goes on.

In discussing this question of power, we shall first give some general consideration to the subject and then to labour's demand for power.

[1] See note, p. 30; this paper was presented in January, 1925.
Cf. Creative Experience, Chapter X, "Power: the Condition of its Validity," and *The New State*, Chapter XXIX, "Political Pluralism and Sovereignty."

The "Urge" to Power

No word is used more carelessly by us all than the word "power." I know no conception which needs to-day more careful analysis. We have not even decided whether power is a "good" word or a "bad" word. Is the wish for power the desire of grasping and unscrupulous men, is it the "instinctive" urge of our lower natures; or is power a noble, the noblest, aim? Or is it neither of these? What is power? Is it influence, is it leadership, is it force? Why do we all like power? Because we wish to use it to satisfy our desires, or do we just like the feeling in itself? In the case of the men you meet every day in business, either your business associates or your workmen, do you find them trying to satisfy an "urge" to power; or do you find them merely trying to get what they want and seeking power in order to secure their ends? We are often told that there are many men who, after they have accumulated enough wealth to satisfy every want, keep on accumulating from mere love of power. Do you think this is so or do you think that there are still unsatisfied desires which motivate their activity?

Among the psychologists there is much difference of opinion on this subject. Some tell us that the urge to power is instinctive, is inherent in all human beings; others deny this and say that power is desired merely as means to an end. Dr. Floyd H. Allport, in his *Social Psychology*,[2] tends toward the former point of view. Dealing with social control, he tells us that there is a universal tendency to produce reactions in others, a tendency which probably originated in the habit developed in infancy and early childhood of controlling parents and nurses in order to secure satisfaction of the bodily needs. As we grow up and become more self-sufficient, the old habit persists in an inclination to control merely for the sake of controlling; not now, you see, means to end. I do not know whether this is so or not, for I do not think we have sufficient proof yet to establish its validity, but it is certainly interesting. Dr. Allport points out that the

[2] Houghton-Mifflin Company, Boston, 1924.

drive for the control of others (he has committed himself to a good deal by using the word "drive") often does not go to the extent of trying to determine their reactions, but simply to make them react. We could all give instances of this. My guide in the Adirondacks, if we came on a deer out of the hunting season, as we paddled up some lonely creek, would startle me, after an instant's silence, with a sudden yell. He could not shoot, but he could shout and make the deer run, make it *do* something.

We often see between two people the wish, not necessarily to get submissive reactions, but to get any reactions at all. A man will deliberately rustle his newspaper so that his wife will react in some way. She may not look up and smile either; she may frown, or she may irritably ask him to stop making a noise, but he gets some satisfaction even from that. (Perhaps I ought in fairness to add that the only time I have seen this done, it was the wife who rattled the newspaper.)

There are jurists also who talk of a "natural urge" to power, who tell us that the wish to keep a balance of power is such an urge. They say, for instance, that when you feel gratitude, it is the "urge" to regain an equilibrium which has been destroyed by the favour you have had conferred upon you. We can call it by a fine name, elevate it to a virtue, but what it really means is, we are told, that if I am under obligation to you for some favour conferred, I feel an unpleasant sense of your power, and so I return the favour in some way in order to restore the equilibrium between us which has been disturbed. This seemed to me a very strange idea the first time I came across it, but that very day I asked a man, staying in Boston to give a month's lectures at the Harvard Business School, what he thought of the idea, and instead of saying, as I expected, that it was absurd, he replied: "Of course it's so; here I am spending a month with [a well-known man in Boston] and I shall feel that I am in his power until I can think of some way of paying it back."

Some ethical teachers tell us that the whole subject resolves itself into the question: What do you want power for? This is not a wholly bad question for those interested in business administration. Take the alarm over absentee ownership voiced by a number of people. A good thing, too, that it should be; yet when we hear of the effort of some management to free itself from the domination of absentee-owned capital, we immediately think, What is their motive?

Bertrand Russell has had a good deal to say lately about the *motive* for power. He is very pessimistic over the development of science, for he says that the benefits go to the power-holders, and that the purposes of the power-holders are in the main evil.

But whether power is "good" or "bad," whether it is sought as means to end or as end in itself, most people are much of the time trying to get power. In conversation people try to impress others with their ideas, their feelings or their personal experiences. Some writers call this the egoistic impulse, but that seems too general; on further analysis we should probably find that it comes from the desire for ascendancy. For instance, the psychologists tell us that we like telling a good story because it makes us the centre of interest. Perhaps, in addition to this, it is because for that moment we are controlling others, for an instant we have others completely under our sway. And we must remember that this desire for ascendancy which we see in some form in almost every conversation, is by no means always, nor perhaps usually, because we wish to use at the moment the power gained; we like to bank our power, and keep a good balance on hand to use in large lumps as occasions arise when such use would be of distinct benefit to us.

I think the best way of understanding power would be to make some study of it in our daily lives—in our homes, in our business, or wherever we are—to observe when it appears and why and what the results are. I am always hoping in a group of this kind to find some one or two who will be sufficiently interested to do this with me, watch to see what gives one person influence over another: social position, professional standing, the special knowledge of the expert, wide experience, mere wealth, age, sex, certain personal characteristics, even physical strength. If any of you will do this I want to suggest that in such study you take provisionally the following definitions of power, control, authority, and see what you think of them. Power might be defined as simply the ability to make things happen, to be a causal agent, to initiate change.[3] Perhaps the "urge to power" is merely the satisfaction of being alive. Of course there are many different kinds and degrees of satisfaction. The boy throwing stones at a bird gives us an example of a very elementary kind; his "urge" is to make the bird do something—fly away. As a fuller kind of satisfaction we might note that of the violinist. It has always seemed to me that the violinist must get one of the greatest satisfactions of being alive; all of him is enlisted, he surely feels power. Probably the leader of an orchestra feels more. And this comes nearer the kind of power the head of a business feels.

Control might be defined as power exercised as means toward a specific end; authority, as vested control. And we should remember in this study that power and strength are not always synonymous; it is sometimes through our weakness that we get control of a situation. In the London Conference last summer Germany's greatest power was her economic impotence. That is, her bargaining power was the result of the economic condition to which she had been reduced by the demands made upon her by the Allies. We all know that the invalid in a household has, and sometimes exercises quite ruthlessly, power over the well and strong members of the family.

We should notice, too, in this observation of power which I am urging, all the different uses of the word. I saw the other day "the power of Wall Street" spoken of as an ominous thing. Is the power of Wall Street a good thing, a bad thing, or neither? A man said to me once: "I like deer shooting because it gives me a sense of power." Robert Wolf's method of beating one's own record, which he has used so

[3] This is not my own final definition of power, which I shall give at another time, but it is good I think so far as it goes, and therefore can be used legitimately without involving ourselves at present in a definition which might have fuller connotation, but which might not be so simple to handle and apply in our daily jobs. (M. P. F.)

successfully, is in part an appeal to the sense of power. As I have just mentioned Wall Street, we might perhaps to some advantage compare the power of Wall Street with the power aimed at by Mr. Wolf for his workers. I have found this observation of the way the word power is used an interesting study. I am making a list of all the different definitions I come across, by novelists or artists or wherever, and I find this all helping me in my observation of power in everyday life. I think it would help also in business administration, make us more alert and more discriminating; make us wiser in our decision when an employee asks for more "power," when he claims that something belongs to his province which we had taken for granted was in ours. We may decide for him or against him, I am not saying that this foretells what our decision will be, but if we have given some attention to this subject, we shall feel surer that our decision is just; we shall also be able to save time when examining his claims by this preliminary consideration of the subject, by knowing a little where we stand in general before we have to take up a particular situation.

A very interesting thing to observe, which I must not omit to mention, is the connection between rivalry and power. I wish you would watch yourselves and competing firms and see if you can draw any line between rivalry and "urge to power." The psychologists see a difference here. One tells us that in contests of strength of handgrip between two boys in laboratory experiments, it was found that the rivalry attitude gave way almost immediately to an attitude on the part of the stronger to *conquer* his opponent. This is significant for business competition.

We have innumerable opportunities for the study of power; we might to great advantage, I think, study the farmers' present striving for power. Are they seeking merely higher and more uniform prices; or do they wish to gain power over, or equal to, other groups?

I think one certain gain would come from a study of power: we should learn to distinguish between different kinds of power. For instance, there is the man who beats his rivals by getting, by hook or crook, special privileges in regard to freight rates. That gives him power. But the man who beats his rivals through better business administration, by producing better goods at equal price to the consumer, or the same goods at less price, has power too. We have here obviously two different kinds of power.

Power-with versus Power-over

We have been considering what we must watch if we wish to study the question of power. Let us see if we can get a little nearer the core of this question. So far as my observation has gone, it seems to me that whereas power usually means power-over, the power of some person or group over some other person or group, it is possible to develop the conception of power-with, a jointly developed power, a co-active, not a coercive power.[4] In store or factory I do not think the management should have power *over* the workmen, or the workmen over the management. It is right for the employers to resist any effort of the unions to get power-over. In discussing *Business as an Integrative Unity* we considered the difference between the "independent" power which the English labour unions are seeking (I use their expression) and joint power. Every demand for power should be analysed to see if the object is "independent" power or joint power. That should be one of the tests of any plan of employee representation— is it developing joint power?

If anyone thinks that the distinction between power-over and power-with is a fanciful or personal distinction, I am pleased to be able to say that these two prepositions are used to mark a distinction in law; you have rights over a slave, you have rights with a servant.

Of course at present, as I have said, most of us are trying to get power-over. Much of what is called "applied psychology" has this for its aim. The salesmanship classes teach this

[4] *Cf. Creative Experience*, p. xii: "Our task is not to learn where to place power; it is how to develop power. . . . Genuine power can only be grown, it will slip from every arbitrary hand that grasps it; for genuine power is not coercive control, but coactive control. Coercive power is the curse of the universe; coactive power, the enrichment and advancement of every human soul."

(although I tried to show in discussing "The Giving of Orders" that a sounder psychology could do better than this); the men being told how to conduct business interviews are being taught this. The so-called psychology of advertising is not concerned with giving information but with gaining power. Many of the trade unionists in the labour education movement wish education for power, that is, increased power in the fight with capital. The head of a Central Labour Union said to me: "I'm for the Trade Union College; we lose out because we send a $1,500 man to meet a $10,000 man; the trade unionists have got to educate themselves." I must in justice, however, add that I know unionists who are trying to develop power in the unions in the sense of increased ability to join with management in a co-operating efficiency, a co-operating responsibility, and this is a happy sign.[5]

And I certainly need not go to either capital or labour to find examples of power-over. Reformers, propagandists, many of our "best" people are willing to coerce others in order to attain an end which *they* think good. I have seen it stated, in what was supposed to be a progressive article, that workmen should be led, not driven. Well, leading is often power-over. The demagogue, the ward boss, the labour leader, the crowd orator, all lead, all try to "persuade"—a very innocent sounding word until you examine it. A workman, however, said to me: "In this factory they don't just try to persuade us, they try to convince us"—a very discriminating statement on the part of this man and a tribute to the management of that factory.

This is something we have to watch for in our study of power, in a conference between two or three business men, a consultation of doctors or wherever, namely, how far persuasion is taking the form of power-over. Some very keen observation and subtle discrimination are needed here, for you will see many ways by which this is sought: reason,

[5] *Cf. Creative Experience*, p. 184: "Some trade unionists are beginning to see the finer function of combination, combination in order to develop power in themselves rather than power over others."

suggestion, emotion, ascendancy of personality, etc. And since industry to-day is tending toward the conference method, toward committee government, this is an important study. One of the tests of conference or committee should be: are we developing genuine power or is someone trying unduly to influence the others? A workman in a plant where there is employee representation said to me: "I don't want to be led and I don't want to be patronized, and I watch all the time to see if I am." Notice particularly the first phrase, "I don't want to be led."

But we are now getting near a subject which I decided not to include in these talks because it has been treated so fully and so adequately by others—by Le Bon, by Martin, by Allport—and that is what crowd psychology tells us of power; it is obvious that the getting of power might be considered largely as a matter of creating conditions favourable to sug-gestibility. Much of the crowd literature assumes that ninety per cent. of our life is lived under the laws of suggestion and imitation, which means power-over. Granted as large a per cent. as you please, I still think we may recognize that there is such a thing as power-with.

The insidiousness of power-over is very well illustrated by Gandhi. Surely his method of non-co-operation was a use of power, the only power he and his followers had: the non-payment of taxes, the boycotting of English merchandise, refusal of honours and titles, of civil and military posts, refusal to attend schools, etc. Gandhi made declaration of "war to the end." Well, war is war. I cannot see that Gandhi's *method* is so different from that of any strike. In his *Letter to all the English of India* of October 27th, 1920, he said: "I wish to conquer you by my sufferings." Was not this a rationalization in effect? It was literally true, but while to Gandhi this had a high, spiritual sound, what was it really but a wish to gain power, to gain power through suffering? We find nowhere in Gandhi's life, letters or speeches any wish to discover a meeting ground for his party and the English. He says he believes in "the power of the humble," thus using the very word power. Was it their humility which gave Gandhi's party the measure of success which they had, or was it their unanimity, their earnestness and sincerity, their passion of conviction?

We see here how closely power is connected with the fight image when Gandhi calls his struggle a "war of the spirit." In order to make conflict constructive, I think we should try to abolish the war image as rapidly as possible. When the tobacco co-operatives of Greensboro, N. C., were invited to their second annual picnic at the Guilford Battle Ground, they were urged to come to "the spot where our fathers fell in deadly combat with the enemies of political freedom," and hear "the living heroes of to-day in mortal combat with the subtle, intriguing enemy of farm economic freedom." This is not the spirit of Gandhi, but the same fighting appeal is made in both cases.

This is a rather long introduction to our subject. And these preliminary considerations have been of the most general character. My aim has been, not exhaustive analysis, but to arouse in you a wish to be more analytical toward your own experience in regard to the matter of one person having what is commonly called power over another person, or one group over another group, one nation over another nation.

But even with all that I have left out we have time now to consider only two points, and those very briefly: how to reduce power-over, and labour's demand for power. One way of reducing power-over is through integration, which we considered in our first evening together. The integrating of desires precludes the necessity of gaining power in order to satisfy desire. Do you remember the instance I gave of the conflict in the Dairymen's League in regard to precedence at the creamery platform, a conflict which became so serious that it almost broke up the League? If either side had won in the fight, there would have been power-over, but by finding a solution by which the desires of both sides were satisfied, by integrating the desires of the two sides, power-over was prevented.

I hope it will be seen that what I have called legitimate power is produced by that circular behaviour described in our first talk. This is, I think, almost the heart of the whole matter and deserves more attention than this mere passing notice. Circular behaviour is the basis of integration. If your business is so organized that you can influence a co-manager while he is influencing you, so organized that a workman has an opportunity of influencing you as you have of influencing him; if there is an interactive influence going on all the time between you, power-with may be built up. Throughout history we see that control brings disastrous consequences whenever it outruns integration. Is not that the trouble in India? Russia has to use arbitrary authority because she has not yet learned to integrate. And was it not perhaps the greatest weakness in Woodrow Wilson that he thought control could outrun integration?

We can get still nearer the core of our problem in this matter of reducing power-over by recalling what we spoke of in our second paper, when we were considering the question of giving orders, as the law of the situation. If both sides obey the law of the situation, no *person* has power over another. The present-day respect for facts, for scientific methods, is the first step in this method of seeking the law of the situation, and already we see that it has influenced the whole tone of industrial controversy. Take the case of bargaining between employers and employees. As wages are coming more and more to be fixed by cost-of-living charts, by time-studies, by open books on cost of production, bargaining is more and more eliminated or, I should say, subordinated. It might be put thus: bargaining becomes limited by the boundaries set by scientific methods of business administration; it is only possible within the area thus marked out.

It is the same in international controversy. The pitting of power against power goes on, yet the reports of the expert are to-day taken into account to such an extent as appreciably to limit the bargaining process. Every commission, industrial or international, has its staff of economists, statisticians, accountants, engineers, experts of all kinds. The Dawes Plan has been spoken of as a triumph of the bankers.

Is it not rather a triumph of facts against empty assumptions? The Dawes Plan first of all disposes of certain fictions. Nowhere do we see more clearly than in the case of reparations the value of facts against assumptions; as time went on it came more and more clearly to be seen that it was not a question of "sympathy" for France or for Germany, but of the facts of the situation. Facts, by reducing the area of irreconcilable controversy, reduce power-over.

As clearly as we see that the consideration of facts reduces power-over, do we see that the withholding of facts is often used as a means to gain power-over. The chief weapon of the speculators is to keep facts from the public. Open prices have been fought for years because so many business men have been afraid they would mean a loss of power. The co-operatives have arraigned big business for its secretive methods, yet I know at least one marketing co-operative which refuses to publish warehouse receipts, or to give information as to solvency, to publish prices until the end of the year, to give overhead cost or number of members, because they fear that such information will give power into the hands of the middlemen.

Do we not see now that while there are many ways of gaining an external, an arbitrary power—through brute strength, through manipulation, through diplomacy— genuine power is always that which inheres in the situation? Our first search should always be to discover the law of the situation. For instance, the middlemen are preventing the farmer from having the power which belongs to his situation; it is hoped that the marketing co-operatives will give him that power. Yet, as I have indicated above, we have not got rid of power-over in the co-operatives. I do not think we shall ever get rid of power-over; I do think we should try to reduce it.

To sum up our consideration of power-over. Power-over can be reduced: (1) through integration, (2) through recognizing that all should submit to what I have called the law of the situation, and (3) through making our business more and more of a functional unity. In a functional unity each has his function—and that should correspond as exactly as possible with his capacity—and then he should have the authority and the responsibility which go with that function.

Labour's Demand for Power

Perhaps it will throw some light on the subject of power if we consider labour's demand for power. While the employer's attitude on this question of workers' share in management has radically changed of late years; while the employer no longer says, or not often, "These men have the damned impudence to want to run my business," still he has not sufficiently analysed the workers' démand for power. Let us ask ourselves some questions in regard to the workers' wish for what they call share in control.

1. Is this the instinctive urge to power?
2. Is it, on the other hand, a means—to higher wages, shorter hours, better working conditions?
3. Is it the "instinct" of workmanship, and therefore a means to an end? That is, does the workman, suffering sometimes under inefficient management, wish enough share in management to enable him to do his work as he thinks best? The glass-bottle makers in England will not work under a man who is not trained as a glass-bottle hand. It seems obvious that we should encourage all the "power" which tends to increase pride in craft skill.
4. Is it because so many "instincts" are thwarted by modern machine industry; do all these instincts cry out together for "power"?
5. Is there more in the old claim than has yet been recognized, that the worker wants to be treated as a man, not as a "hand"?
6. How far is it an expression of an inferiority complex?
7. Is it to improve status?
8. How far is it a reaction against officialism or the abuses of officialism?
9. Does the worker want to accumulate power to use in the struggle between capital and labour?
10. Is the worker trying to get power without responsibility, those two which can never be divorced? I have seen it stated: "Labour wants wages, hours and security without financial

responsibility but with power enough to command respect."
How naïve. Many of us would like power without responsibility!
Is that possible, or is it the old story of eating and having your
cake?

11. Is it that the most fundamental thing in man is his "urge"
to self-expression and self-determination, combined with his ever
seeking the larger, the more complete? Are these twin impulses
at the heart of his being perhaps the chief reason for the workers'
demand for power?

You can probably think of other reasons, I have put these
eleven down quickly. Further with respect to this point, let
us consider especially those two expressions which we hear
daily, the delegation of power and the balance of power.

In the literature on employee representation, we read
much of the delegation of power. Myers[6] tells us that the
power of the Works Committee is "delegated," that the
board of directors or the stockholders have the ultimate
authority. The Nunn, Bush and Weldon Shoe Co. say that
they have "delegated" to their employees the power of fixing
wages and hours of work and the right to discharge. I read
again, "Authority must be distributed from its source, and
filters down through delegation to all parts of business
organization." Power must be distributed from its source?
Very well, but what is the source? A workman in a factory
I was visiting said to me, "Who do you think is the boss
here?" It seemed, he said, difficult to discover him. "Is it the
Manager of the Works," he asked, "or is it the President?
But these are responsible to the Directors. Is it then the
Directors? But they are responsible to the people. Is it then
the people?" I tried to find out what he meant by the people,
but he was rather vague about that. This interested me,
however, because I had not thought I should find the old
question of sovereignty, which I had struggled with in
political and legal science, cropping up in modern industrial
organization in such direct manner. The only legitimate boss,
sovereignty, is, I believe, the interweaving experience of all

6 *Op. cit.* See p. 64.

those who are performing some functional part of the activity under consideration.[7]

I do not think that power can be delegated because I believe that genuine power is capacity. To confer power on the workers may be an empty gesture. The main problem of the workers is by no means how much control they can wrest from capital or management, often as we hear that stated; that would be a merely nominal authority and would slip quickly from their grasp. Their problem is how much power they can themselves grow. The matter of workers' control which is so often thought of as a matter of how much the managers will be willing to give up, is really as much a matter for the workers, how much they will be able to assume; where the managers come in is that they should give the workers a chance to grow capacity or power for themselves.

There are many ways in which power develops naturally if there is no hindrance Let me give this as an illustration. We often think of the development of large-scale industry as limiting the individual's opportunity for managing. In some ways this is not true. Take, for instance, what is called "the instinct for workmanship." Formerly, in the time of individual production, this "instinct" was expressed in the individual's own work. Now that individual production has given way to group production, this "instinct" cannot be expressed unless the individual workman has something to say about group organization and the technique of group production. This seems to me a natural development of genuine power.

It is true indeed that the workmen cannot have anything to say about the technique of group production, about group organization, without the co-operation or even the initiative

[7] *Cf. The New State*, p. 271: "Real authority inheres in a genuine whole. The individual is sovereign over himself as far as he unifies the heterogeneous elements of his nature. Two people are sovereign over themselves as far as they are capable of creating one out of two. A group is sovereign over itself as far as it is capable of creating one out of several or many. A state is sovereign only as it has the power of creating one in which all are. Sovereignty is the power engendered by a complete interdependence become conscious of itself."

of management; but there is something here which is not covered by the word "delegation."

Interest, Responsibility, Power—an Indissoluble Partnership

One thing should be borne in mind beyond anything else in the consideration of this subject, and that is that you should never give authority faster than you can develop methods for the worker taking responsibility for that authority. We may find also that we should not give workers authority without some corresponding stake in the business. In a certain store which has a form of profit-sharing, the employees voted one December not to open the store on the day after Christmas, after taking into account the number of people likely to come out on that day against the expenses of operation. But in the case of another holiday when the same question came up, thinking that this time there would be no appreciable effect on the numbers of people shopping, they voted to open. They had the "power" in both cases, and if that "power" had been divorced from a stake in the business they would probably have voted in both cases to close the store. Interest, responsibility, power—perhaps here is an indissoluble partnership. Of course in a case like this the responsibility may have been enough without the sake in the business.

We have an unfortunate precedent in the use of such phrases as the delegation of power, etc. Many writers on government say that the power of the State should be *divided* among various groups; many tell us that power should be *transferred* from one group to another; many that it should be *conferred* on the smaller nations. Hence it has been natural for many economists who write of something they call "industrial democracy" to tell us that the power now held by owners and managers should be *shared* by the workmen. These expressions, while containing indeed a partial truth, nevertheless at the same time *hide* an important truth, namely, that power is self-developing capacity. This fact is hidden by that expression which has become a pet phrase of the guild socialists, "encroaching control." Divided or conferred authority is non-psychological authority; "encroaching control" is not a genuine control. Power is not a pre-existing thing which can be handed out to someone, or wrenched from someone. We have seen again and again the failure of "power" conferred. You could give me dozens of cases. The division of power is not the thing to be considered, but that method of organization which will generate power. The moral right to an authority which has not been psychologically developed, which is not an expression of capacity, is an empty ethics. This applies to management as well as to workers. We have always to study in a plant how far the authority of the management is real, how far it comes from fulfilling function, from knowledge and ability, and how far it is a nominal or an arbitrary authority.

The difficulty of the political scientists quoted in the above paragraph is that they are confusing power and authority. To confer authority where capacity has not been developed is fatal to both government and business. Those political scientists who use the words power, control and authority as synonymous, are confusing our thinking.

If you want the best philosophical as well as the best psychological principle by which to test the legitimacy of "power" (by which you probably mean authority), you will ask whether it is integral to the process or outside the process, that is, whether, as we have said, it grows out of the actual circumstances, whether it is inherent in the situation. You cannot confer power, because power is the blossoming of experience. I think a non-understanding of this is the limitation of an article on "Authority" by Ludwig Stein which came out in the September *Atlantic* and was a good deal talked about by business men. Professor Stein says: "That the Bolsheviki had to substitute for the dictatorship from above one from below is a classical example for the sociology of authority." And again, later on: "The fact that old authorities are overthrown only to permit new ones to be created in their stead irresistibly forces the conclusion that authority represents a social-psychological necessity." It does not force me to that conclusion, but to the conclusion that we shall always be seeking an external, and arbitrary authority until we learn to direct our efforts toward seeking— the law of the situation.

There is something in regard to an authority which is not the recognized law of the situation which we should not fail to note in passing, and that is, that an arbitrary authority may rouse very disagreeable reactions. These not only make things difficult for you, but actually reduce your power. Charles Francis Adams used to say: "Increase powers and you decrease power." And only the other day I heard it said that commissions with mandatory powers have less power than those with advisory powers because they put people's backs up. All this is worth consideration.

And we must not omit to mention that most common of fallacies, that when we join with others, we deliberately give up a part of our "power," as it is called, in order to get certain privileges which will issue from the union. When a grower signs a co-operative contract, he is supposed to give up a certain amount of "power." Does he? His marketing capacity is certainly increased by his joining with others. The delusion of the "independent" farmer is now exposed to all. Take again the notion of the sacrifice of sovereignty, that each nation must sacrifice a part of its sovereignty for the sake of the benefits which will come from a League of Nations. This is the rationalization of the sentimentalist. No nation intends to sacrifice anything; when a nation sees that it is to its interest to become a part of the League of Nations it will do so. Sovereignties must be joined, not sacrificed. We find this fallacy expressed in regard to business administration by those writers who tell us that the manufacturer ought to surrender a part of his power in order to gain a spirit of contentment in the factory.

As a summing up of this question of conferring or sharing power, I should say that if we have any power, any genuine power, let us hold on to it, let us not give it away. We could not anyway if we wanted to. We can confer authority; but power or capacity, no man can give or take. The manager cannot share *his* power with division superintendent or foreman or workmen, but he can give them opportunities for developing *their* power. Functions may have to be redistributed; something the manager does now had better perhaps be left to a division superintendent, to a foreman, even to a workman; but that is a different matter; let us not confuse the two things. Indeed, one of the aims of that very redistribution of function should be how it can serve to evolve more power—more power to turn the wheels. More power, not division of power, should always be our aim; more power for the best possible furtherance of that activity, whatever it may be, to which we are giving our life.

So much for the delegation of power; and now let us consider balance of power. It almost seems as if our conclusions in the preceding paper in regard to joint power did away automatically with the conception of balance of power; yet no conception is more widely held. A labour leader said a few years ago: "We must give up each trying to wrest power from the other side"; so far a very good idea, but he added, "and find an absolute balance of power." He had no notion of a unit of power. I do not think the balance of power will get labour much further than a domination of power.

Myers[8] evidently believes in the balance of power between workers and executives, as do many others. So does Professor Commons, who, in speaking of the desired equilibrium between capital and labour, says: "If one is suppressed the other becomes dictator." Certainly, but it seems to me that there is a way out of the difficulty other than the one indicated by Professor Commons.

Many people make co-ordination and balance synonymous, which seems to me a mistake. The guild socialists do this. Their co-ordinating congress, they tell us, is an arbitrator or court of appeal to keep the balance of power between co-ordinate autonomies. This is surely poor philosophy and the religion of the fearful; they are so afraid of power that they say: "Let us all have equal power." I think the aim of co-ordination should be the building up of a functional total. I think we may learn that a jointly developing power

[8] *Op. cit.* See p. 64.

means the possibility of creating new values, a wholly different process from the sterile one of balancing. Not to rearrange existing values, but to bring more into existence is the high mission of enlightened human intercourse.

Collective Bargaining as the Determinant of Value

I began this paper by asking: "What is the determinant of value?"—surely the most important consideration for business administration whether we are speaking of value of services or what not. Most labour men tell us that value is, or should be, determined by collective bargaining. Many business men say that value should be determined by scientific methods which will do away with collective bargaining. But trade unionists do not want to do away with, or even to narrow the field of, collective bargaining; they want to bargain over everything. They have bargained over wages and hours; now many of them say that they should have the opportunity of bargaining over changes in the technique of industry, since these involve changes in the working conditions. If you tell them that industrial technique is a purely scientific matter, then they reply: "It is never the question alone of the advantage of a new method; but of who is going to get the advantage? If the worker is to get his share that must be bargained for."

This is true as far as it goes. Bargaining is at present necessary, and the result of bargaining rests on the relative strength of the two sides. If we are studying any particular industrial controversy, one of the first steps is to seek the sources of power of the moment. We ask, "What are the general conditions which give to capital or labour the greater economic power of the moment?" Unemployment gives power to the employer; also lack of education among the workmen; also the fact that the employees are not in a position to wait. On the other hand, the power of the workers is reinforced by the strength of the unions back of them, and their strength has increased with the number of unions and the numbers in them.

It is true, therefore, as things are now, that everything

should be done to reduce the inequalities in the bargaining power of labour and capital, but I think at the same time we should see beyond that, that our ultimate aim should be different. I do not think this the final secret of solving the problems of business administration. Professor Commons says: "Unless the labourer can speak as a representative of associated labourers, he cannot speak with equal power." While I believe in encouraging employee associations, while I think it a grave weakness of some systems of employee representation that there is not adequate connection between Works Councils and the whole body of workers, still my reason for my very strong advocacy of employee association is not chiefly to bring about equal power, but because this helps us to approach functional unity. I should want to make a "side," not for a fair fight, not for fighting at all, but in order that it should enrich the whole. If I were a manufacturer I should want to consolidate my workers, not in order to give them greater strength in a fight, but in order that they should, by conscious unity, be a stronger part of my plant and thus strengthen my whole organization. I think we should never forget, what we spoke of at greater length in the preceding paper, that there are two kinds of "sides." There is all the difference in the world between controversial sides and integrative or contributing sides. I am interested only in the latter. I differ therefore from those people who say that the greatest fairness to the worker is to give him equal power in the bargaining process. My whole business philosophy is different from this. I think we owe both the worker and ourselves more than that.

I trust that the difference between this "equal power," so much talked of, and the power-with we have been considering, is evident. Equal power means the stage set for a fair fight, power-with is a jointly developing power, the aim, a unifying which, while allowing for infinite differing, does away with fighting. When the Sheffield Shop Stewards said, "We organize for power," did they mean power-over, equal power, or power-with? The history of the Shop Stewards' movement in England is sufficient answer to this question.

Yet I do not want to be misunderstood on the matter of collective bargaining. It is of course necessary at present; without it both wages and working conditions would fall below even minimum standards.[9] And, of course, if we do have bargaining we should give the two sides equal advantage as far as possible. I am trying to say merely that I think it is wise to decide, before we begin on any reorganization of our business, whether we believe in collective bargaining as an *ultimate* aim, or whether we accept it for the moment and surround it with the fairest conditions we are able to, at the same time trying to make our reorganization plan look toward a functional unity, which if it does not abolish collective bargaining (it may not) still will give to it a different meaning from that which it has at present. The best point about collective bargaining is that it rests on conference and agreement (there are methods of adjustment, as arbitration, which do not), but I believe in conference, not as an episode of war, but as one of the necessary activities in the process I have called a functional unifying. Would not the unqualified acceptance of collective bargaining as now generally understood commit us to the view that industry must remain at the mercy of shifts in "power" from employer to workman, from workman to employer? And is there any hope for a steady and wholesome progress with that condition of things?

But I am aware that we have begun on what ought to be another talk, and must therefore end rather abruptly. Should collective bargaining, we asked, be the determinant of value? Not for ever, I think; certainly not in the narrower meaning of that term. It seems to me that value is an interweaving, and that the clever business administrator must know both the strands and the pattern they make.

[9] Moreover, I should not include in an objectionable kind of collective bargaining all of the present "agreements" between capital and labour, some of which are arrived at by a different process than that of bargaining alone. (M. P. F.)

V

HOW MUST BUSINESS MANAGEMENT DEVELOP IN ORDER TO POSSESS THE ESSENTIALS OF A PROFESSION?[1]

THE word "profession" connotes for most people a foundation of *science* and a motive of *service*. That is, a profession is said to rest on the basis of a proved body of knowledge, and such knowledge is supposed to be used in the service of others rather than merely for one's own purposes. Let us ask ourselves two questions: (1) How far does business management rest on scientific foundations? (2) What are the next steps to be taken in order that business management shall become more scientific?

Present Signs of a Scientific Basis for Business Management

We have many indications that scientific method is being more and more applied to business management.

First, of course, is the development of so-called "scientific management," which, after its early stages, began to concern itself with the technique of management as well as with the technique of operating.

Secondly, there is the increasing tendency toward specialized, or what is being called "functionalized," management. Functionalized management has, indeed, not yet been carried far. In some cases the only sign we see of it, beyond the recognition that different departments require different

[1] This paper was presented on October 29th, 1925, and, with the three succeeding papers, reprinted from *Business Management as a Profession*, Henry C. Metcalf, *Editor*, A. W. Shaw Company (now McGraw Hill Book Publishing Company), 1927. Miss Follett gave one additonal paper in this series of conferences, entitled "What Type of Central Administrative Leadership is Essential to Business Management as Defined in this Course?" This paper appears in the Shaw volume, but is omitted in this collection as the same line of thought is developed in two of the later papers, Nos. XII and XIII.

kinds of knowledge, different kinds of ability, is the employ-ing of experts for special problems. In other cases a further step is taken and a planning department is created; but the powers given to planning departments vary greatly from plant to plant—some take up only occasional problems as they are asked, some are only advisory bodies. Yet in most plants the functionalization of management is a process which in one way or another has gained a good deal of ground recently. That is, the fact is very generally accepted that different types of problems require different bodies of knowledge.

In the third place, arbitrary authority is diminishing, surely an indication that more value is being put on scientific method. The tendency to-day is to vest authority in the person who has most knowledge of the matter in question and most skill in applying that knowledge. Hiring, for instance, is now based on certain principles and special knowledge. The job of hiring is given to those who have that knowledge. It is not assumed by someone by virtue of a certain position.

Perhaps nowhere do we see more clearly the advance of business management toward becoming a profession than in our conception of the requirements of the administrative head. It would be interesting to take some firm and note how one duty after another has in recent years passed from the president to various experts, down to that most recent addition to many businesses, the economic adviser. One president, of whom I enquired what he thought exactly his job to be, said to me: "I can't define my job in terms of specific duties because I can't tell what special duty which I have to-day may be given at any moment to someone better able than I to handle it." One of the interesting things about that remark (there are several) is that he recognized that someone might handle some of his duties better than he could; and yet he is an exceedingly able man. He saw that some particular task might develop a special technique and that men might be trained as experts in that technique.

The stereotype of the successful business man is indeed

changing. The image of the masterful man carrying all before him by the sheer force of his personality has largely disappeared. One good result of this is that we now consider that executive leadership can in part (remember, I say only "in part") be learned. Oliver Sheldon[2] calls executive leadership "an intangible capacity." I do not wholly agree. Someone else says it is "beyond human calculation." There are many things, we hope, which have not yet been calculated which are not beyond calculation. I think that one of the hopes for business management lies in the fact that executive leadership is capable of analysis and that men can be trained to occupy such positions. I do not, of course, mean every man; but not every man can become a doctor or an architect. I mean that for business management, exactly as for other professions, training is gaining in importance over mere personality. I know a man who told me ten or fifteen years ago that he relied on his personality in business dealings. He has not made a success of his business. It was once thought that the executive's work rested largely on "hunch," and his subordinates' on obeying—no science in either case. The administrative head who relies first on the magic short cut of "hunch," and secondly on his adroitness or masterfulness in getting others to accept his "hunch," is, I believe, about to be superseded by a man of a different type.

Can you not remember the picture we used to have of the man in the swivel chair? A trembling subordinate enters, states his problem; snap goes the decision from the chair. This man disappears, only for another to enter. And so it goes. The massive brain in the swivel chair all day communicates to his followers his special knowledge. An excellent plan if—there seem to be too many if's in the way! And so we resort to the humbler method of scientific research, the method of all the professions.

But with this agreed to, there is another misconception in regard to the administrative head. Many writers speak as if he were only the glue to hold together all these departments and functions of our big modern plants. As the need

2 See notes, p. 123.

of co-ordination is daily and hourly felt in these vast, complex organizations, it is said that the president must do the co-ordinating. True; but I think that co-ordination is very different from matching up the pieces of a picture puzzle, to change our metaphor. Later, I am going to say just what I think it is; but let me say now that those of us who think of the administrative head as more than a mere co-ordinator and those of us who think that administrative decisions should rest on more than "hunch" (although "hunch," too, is important) are thinking of scientific foundations for business management.

A significant indication of the different type of management required to-day is the fact that managers are somewhat less inclined to justify their behaviour by a claim of abstract "rights." An employer used to say, "I have a right to treat my men so and so." Or, "My behaviour in this matter is perfectly reasonable." To-day there are many who are more inclined to say: "If I treat my men so and so, how will they behave? *Why* will they behave in that way?" It takes far more science to understand human beings—and their "rights"—than to proclaim loudly our own rights and reasonableness.

We have a very interesting indication of the new demand made upon management in the fact that the idea, which is everywhere gaining ground, that we may have greater conscious control of our lives is seen in the business world most significantly. For example, those fatalistic rhythms, business cycles, are now considered susceptible to study, not as mysteries wholly beyond the comprehension of man. Again, take unemployment. Consider the steel industry. There you have an imperishable commodity. Moreover, you can calculate pretty well the demand. And you have rather permanently located firms and mills. There seems no reason, therefore, why the steel industry should not eventually be stabilized. Every time we take a problem out of the unsolvable class and put it into the solvable, and work at it as such, we are helping to put business management on a scientific basis. Mr. John Maynard Keynes, in a recent address,[3] spoke of the three great epochs of history described by Dr. John R. Commons, and stated his belief that we are on the threshold of the third of those epochs. The first of these was the era of scarcity, which came to an end in about the fifteenth century. Next came the era of abundance, the dominating idea of which was the doctrine of *laissez-faire*. Finally, there has come the era of stabilization upon which we are now entering and in which the doctrine of *laissez-faire* must be abandoned in favour of deliberate, conscious control of economic forces for the sake of the general social good.

Many people to-day think of business not as a game of chance, not as a speculative enterprise depending on rising and falling markets, but as largely controllable. The mysteriousness of business is in fact disappearing as knowledge in regard to business methods steadily increases.

This is seen in the increased sense of responsibility for failure. You know the old excuses if a business failed or was not getting on well: the hard terms of bankers, the unscrupulousness of competitors, the abominable behaviour of trade unions. I think that to-day there is less inclination to take refuge in such excuses; that there is a tendency to seek the difficulty in the running of the business. There is greater frankness in facing difficulties and a keener zest in overcoming them. You know, perhaps, the story of little Mary, who was naughty and was told by her mother to go into the next room and ask God to forgive her. When she came back her mother said, "Did you do what I told you to?" And received the reply, "Yes, I did; and God said, 'Mercy me, little Mary, I know heaps worse'n you.' " Many an employer takes this attitude, but their numbers are diminishing.

Moreover, many of the points disputed with trade unions, many points which both sides have thought to be legitimate fighting issues, are now considered problems which we should try to solve. To increase wages without increasing price is sometimes a solvable problem. Wherever thinking takes the

---

[3] "Am I a Liberal?", subsequently published in *Essays in Persuasion* (by J. M. Keynes), Macmillan & Co., 1931.

place of fighting, we have a striking indication that management is coming to rest on scientific foundations. In international relations—but I have only to mention that term for you to see the analogy, for you to see the barbarous stage we are yet in, in international relations. Business men have the chance to lead the world in substituting thinking for fighting. And business men are thinking. One of the things I have been most struck with in the last four or five years has been the vitality of the thinking of business men. I once said to a professor of philosophy, "Do you realize that you philosophers have got to look to your laurels, that business men are doing some very valuable thinking and may get ahead of you?" And he acknowledged this fully and generously, which I thought was a significant concession.

Finally, management, not bankers nor stockholders, is now seen to be the fundamental element in industry. It is good management that draws credit, that draws workers, that draws customers. Moreover, whatever changes come, whether industry is owned by individual capitalists or by the state or by the workers, it will always have to be managed. Management is a permanent function of business.

There are many circumstances, let us note in concluding the first part of this paper, which are impelling us toward a truly scientific management: (1) efficient management has to take the place of that exploitation of our natural resources whose day is now nearly over; (2) keener competition; (3) scarcity of labour; (4) a broader conception of the ethics of human relations; (5) the growing idea of business as a public service which carries with it a sense of responsibility for its efficient conduct.

What are the Next Steps Toward Making Business Management More Scientific?

Recognizing that business management is every day coming more and more to rest on scientific foundations, what has it yet to do? First, the scientific standard must be applied to the whole of business management; it is now often applied to only one part. Business management includes:

(1) on the technical side, as it is usually called, a knowledge of production and distribution, and (2) on the personnel side, a knowledge of how to deal fairly and fruitfully with one's fellows. While the first has been recognized as a matter capable of being taught, the latter has been often thought to be a gift which some men possess and some do not. That is, one part of business management rested on science; the other part, it was thought, never could.

Oliver Sheldon says: "Broadly, management is concerned with two primary elements—things and men. The former element is susceptible to scientific treatment, the latter is not."[4] And again: "Where human beings are concerned, scientific principles may be so much waste paper."[5] If we believe that, we should not be here in a Bureau of Personnel Administration Conference. Let us take that statement— that human relations are not susceptible of scientific treatment—and ask what scientific treatment is. Science has been defined as "knowledge gained by systematic observation, experiment, and reasoning; knowledge co-ordinated, arranged and systematized." Can we not accumulate in regard to human relations knowledge gained by systematic observation, experiment, and reasoning? Can we not co-ordinate, arrange, and systematize that knowledge? I think we can.

Sheldon says further: "There may be a science of costing, of transportation, of operation, but there can be no science of co-operation."[6] The reason we are here studying human relations in industry is that we believe there can be a science of co-operation. By this I mean that co-operation is not, and this I insist on, merely a matter of good intentions, of kindly feeling. It must be based on these, but you cannot have successful co-operation until you have worked out the methods of co-operation—by experiment after experiment, by a comparing of experiments, by a pooling of results.

[4] Oliver Sheldon, *Bulletin of Taylor Society*, Vol. 8, No. 6, December, 1913, p. 211.
[5] Oliver Sheldon, *The Philosophy of Management* (London, Sir Isaac Pitman & Sons, Ltd., 1923), p. 36.
[6] *Ibid.*, p. 35.

It is my plea above everything else that we learn *how* to co-operate. Of course, one may have a special aptitude for dealing with men as others may have for dealing with machines, but there is as much to learn in the one case as in the other.

In all our study of personnel work, however, we should remember that we can never wholly separate the human and the mechanical problem. This would seem too obvious to mention if we did not so often see that separation made. Go back to that sentence of Sheldon's: "There may be a science of costing, of transportation, of operation, but there can be no science of co-operation." But take Sheldon's own illustration, that of transportation. The engineering part of transportation is not the larger part. Please note that I do not say it is a small part. It is a large part, and it is the dramatic part, and it is the part we have done well, and yet the chief part of transportation is the personal things. Everyone knows that the main difficulty about transportation is that there have not always been sensible working arrangements between the men concerned.

But you all see every day that the study of human relations in business and the study of the technique of operating are bound up together. You know that the way the worker is treated affects output. You know that the routing of materials and the maintenance of machines is a matter partly of human relations. You know, I hope, that there is danger in "putting in" personnel work if it is superadded instead of being woven through the plant. You remember the man who wanted to know something about Chinese metaphysics and so looked up China in the encyclopædia and then metaphysics, and put them together. We shall not have much better success if we try merely to add personnel work. Even although there is, as I certainly believe there should be, a special personnel department run by a trained expert, yet it seems to me that every executive should make some study of personnel work a part of that broad foundation which is to-day increasingly felt to be necessary for the business man.

If, then, one of the first things to be done to make business management more scientific is to apply scientific methods to those problems of management which involve human relations, another requirement is that we should make an analysis of managers' jobs somewhat corresponding to the analysis of workers' jobs in the Taylor system. We need. to get away from tradition, prejudice, stereotypes, guesswork, and find the factual basis for managerial jobs. We know, for instance, what has been accomplished in elimination of waste by scientific methods of research and experiment applied to operating, to probable demand for commodities, and so on. I believe that this has to be carried further, and that managerial waste, administrative waste, should be given the same research and experiment. How this can be done, I shall take up later.

The next step business management should take is to organize the body of knowledge on which it should rest. We have defined science as an organized body of exact knowledge. That is, scientific method consists of two parts: (1) research, and (2) the organization of the knowledge obtained by research. The importance of research, of continued research, receives every year fuller and fuller appreciation from business men; but methods of organizing the results of such research have not kept pace with this appreciation. While business management is collecting more and more exact knowledge, while it is observing more keenly, experimenting more widely, it has not yet gone far in organizing this knowledge. We have drawn a good many conclusions, have thought out certain principles, but have not always seen the relation between these conclusions or these principles.

I shall mention here only one way of organizing in industrial plants our accumulating knowledge in regard to executive technique. There should be, I think, in every plant, an official, one of whose duties should be to classify and interpret managerial experience with the aid of the carefully kept records which should be required of every executive. From such classification and interpretation of experience—this experience which in essentials repeats itself so often from time to time, from department to department, from plant to plant—it would be possible to draw useful conclusions. The importance of this procedure becomes more obvious when we remember that having experience and profiting by experience are two different matters. Experience may leave us with mistaken notions, with prejudice or suspicion.

A serious drawback to a fuller understanding and utilization of executive experience is that we have at present (1) no systematic follow-up of decisions, of new methods, of experiments in managing; and (2) no carefully worked out system of recording. Poorly kept records, or the absence of any systematic recording, are partly responsible for what seems in some plants like a stagnant management, and in all plants for certain leaks in management. For instance, the fact that we have no follow-up for executive decisions with a comparing of results—a procedure necessary before business management can be considered fully on a scientific basis—is partly a deficiency in recording. The fact that an executive, if he wishes to introduce a certain method (not in operating, but in management itself), cannot find in any records whether that method, or anything like it, has been tried before, and what the results have been, is a serious deficiency in recording. If an executive is facing a certain problem, he should be able to find out: (1) whether other executives have had to meet similar problems, (2) how they met them, (3) what the results were. It seems to me very unfortunate that it is possible for one man to say to another, as I heard someone say at the suggestion of a new method, "I believe our department tried that a few years ago, but I've forgotten what we thought of it."

I have heard it said that the Harvard football team was put on its feet when Percy Haughton introduced the system of recording football experience. After that, if someone thought he had a brilliant idea that such and such a play could be tried on Yale, the first thing done was to examine the records; and it might be found that that play had been tried two years before and failed. It might even be discovered why it had failed. This system of recording—I believe it already existed at Yale—was Mr. Haughton's great contribution to Harvard football. Because of it, the team could not, at any rate, go on making the *same* mistakes.

The recording of executive experience, which will probably need a technique somewhat different from that used for the rest of business recording, should have, I think, our immediate attention. The system of both recording and reporting should be such that records and reports can be quickly mastered, and thus be practically useful to all, instead of buried underneath their own verbiage, length, and lack of systematization. And there should be required of every executive training in the technique of keeping records and making reports.

But we need more than records. We need a new journal, or a new department in some present journal; we need sifted bibliographies of reports, ways of getting information from other parts of the country, from other countries; above all, we need executive conferences with carefully worked out methods for comparing experience which has been scientifically recorded, analysed, and organized. When many different plants are willing to share with one another the results of their experience, then we shall have business policies based on wider data than those of the present.

The Graduate School of Business Administration and the Bureau of Business Research of Harvard University are now collecting cases of business policy, thus opening the way for classifying and cross-indexing. Harvard has, of course, been able to get hold of a very small number of cases, but this seems to be a valuable and significant undertaking.

I have been interested also in what a certain recent committee, with representatives from various firms, deliberately stated as its object: "the comparison of experience." I should like to know how frank and full their exchange of experience was; but any attempt of this kind is interesting, indicating, as it does, the attitude on the art of those participating that they expect to gain more by working together than they will lose (the old idea) by allowing other firms to gain any intimate knowledge of their affairs.

Moreover, not only should we analyse and compare our experience, but we should deliberately experiment. We should make experiments, observe experiments, compare and discuss these with each other, and see what consensus we can come to in our conclusions. For this we should be wholly frank with one another. If we have the scientific attitude toward our work, we shall be willing to tell our failures. I heard of a man who made an ice machine which did not work, and the following conversation took place between him and a friend he met:

Friend: "I was sorry to hear your experiment was a failure!"

Man: "Who told you it was a failure?"

Friend: "Why, I heard your ice machine wouldn't work."

Man: "Oh, that was true enough, but it was a great success as an experiment. You can learn as much from your failures as from your successes."

From such experimenting and from the comparison of experience, I think certain standards would emerge. But we should remember that, as no Taylorite thinks there is anything final in "standardization," so we should not aim at a static standardization of managerial method, executive technique. We should make use of all available present experience, knowing that experience and our learning from it should be equally continuous matters.

If science gives us research and experimentation as its two chief methods, it at the same time shows us that nothing is too small to claim our attention. There is nothing unimportant in business procedure. For instance, I have mentioned record keeping. I know a firm where they tell me that they are not getting nearly so much advantage as they should from their records because they have not yet worked out a system of cross-indexing. Yet to some, cross-indexing may not seem to be of great importance. I know a man who says frequently about this detail or that, "Oh, that doesn't matter." Everything matters to the scientist.

The following incident seems to me to have some significance. I told a man that I was working at the technique of the business interview, at which he seemed rather amused and said, "I guess most business men know how to conduct interviews." It was evident that he thought he did—but he is a man who has never risen above a small position. Later, I said the same thing to a clever man in a good position, a New York man, by the way. I said it a little hesitatingly, for I thought he too might consider it beneath his notice, but he was much interested and asked whether he might see my paper when finished.

I have spoken of the classification of experience, the organizing of knowledge, as one of the necessary preliminaries to putting business management on a scientific basis. This organized body of knowledge tends at first to remain in the hands of a few. Measures should be taken to make it accessible to the whole managerial force. There should be opportunities for the training of executives through talks, suggested readings (including journals on management), through wisely led discussion groups and conferences, through managers' associations, foremen's associations, and the like. The organized knowledge of managerial methods which many of the higher officials possess should spread to the lower executives.

In some cases, the higher official does not even think of this as part of his responsibility. He will say to a subordinate, "Here is what I want done; I don't care how you do it, that's up to you." Indeed, many an official has prided himself on this way of dealing with subordinates. But this is changing. It is part of the Taylor system that standards and methods for each worker's job are made accessible to the worker; also knowledge of the quality of work expected, which is shown him by specifications or drawings. Some such system should be developed for management. To develop it might be made part of that analysis of managerial jobs which I spoke of above. Indeed, more and more of the higher executives are seeing now that managers' jobs as well as workers' jobs are capable of carrying with them accepted standards and methods.

Of course, it is recognized that many of these standards and methods need the sanction of custom rather than of authority, that they should be indicated rather than prescribed, also that much more elasticity should be allowed than in the detailed instructions of the Taylor system—but this is all part of that large subject, the method of training executives.

Possibly in time, as business organization develops, we shall have an official for executives corresponding to the functional foreman who is sometimes known as the "methods instructor," an official whose duty it will be to see that certain managerial methods are understood and followed, as it is the duty of the functional foreman to see that certain operating methods are understood and followed. But I should not advocate this unless the executives were allowed fullest opportunity for contributing to such prescribed methods. The development of managerial technique has been thought by some to involve the risk of crushing originality, the danger of taking away initiative. I think that, rightly managed, it should give executives increased opportunity for the fruitful exercise of initiative and originality, for it is they themselves who must develop this technique even if helped by experts. The choice here presented is not that between originality and a mechanical system, but between a haphazard, hit-or-miss way of performing executive duties and a scientifically determined procedure.

Yet when business management has gained something of an accepted technique, there still remains, as part of the training of executives, the acquiring of skill in its application. Managerial skill cannot be painted on the outside of executives; it has to go deeper than that. Like manual workers, managerial workers have to acquire certain habits and attitudes. And, just as in the case of manual workers, for the acquisition of these habits and attitudes three conditions must be given: (1) detailed information in regard to a new method; (2) the stimulus to adopt this method; and (3) the opportunity to practice it so that it may become a habit.

A business man tells me that I should emphasize the last

point particularly. He says that his firm has been weak just here; that they have done more preaching than they have given opportunity for practice. He says: "We've given them a lecture on piano playing and then put them on the concert stage. This winter we are going to try to invent ways of giving real practice to foremen so that a set of habits can be formed."

No subject is more important than the training of executives, but as it is a subject which would require a whole paper for even the most superficial consideration, we cannot speak further of it here. Let me just say, however, as a hint of what I shall elaborate later, that if you wish to train yourself for higher executive positions, the first thing for you to decide is what you are training for. Ability to dominate or manipulate others? That ought to be easy enough, since most of the magazines advertise sure ways of developing something they call "personality." But I am convinced that the first essential of business success is the capacity for organized thinking.

In conclusion: What does all this imply in regard to the profession of business management? It means that men must prepare themselves as seriously for this profession as for any other. They must realize that they, as all professional men, are assuming grave responsibilities, that they are to take a creative part in one of the large functions of society, a part which, I believe, only trained and disciplined men can in the future hope to take with success.

VI

HOW MUST BUSINESS MANAGEMENT DEVELOP IN ORDER TO BECOME A PROFESSION[1]

I said in the preceding lecture that for most people the word "profession" connotes a foundation of science and a motive of service. It would be well, therefore, for us to examine the idea of service. I do not wholly like the present use of that word. In the first place, it has been so over-used that we are tired of it—"Service is our motto," "Service with a smile," and so on. Moreover, this word is often used sentimentally, or at least vaguely, to express good intentions, or even, like charity, to cover a multitude of sins. "Public service" is not always genuine service; public service corporations are not wholly self-sacrificing associations. "Social service" often means the work necessary to make up for certain defects in society, as pure-milk stations. It is well to have healthy babies; but we are looking forward to the time when the making of healthy babies will not devolve on extra-social agencies, on agencies which would be unnecessary if society were what we hope it will some day become. You see, I do not call pure-milk stations social agencies, as do most people, but extra-social; and the distinction I am making here seems to me to have some value. Business is, and should be considered, truly a social agency.

The Meaning of Service—Function

Underneath all the various current uses of the word "service," there is the idea of service as expressing man's altruism, labour performed for another, doing good to others. I think there is a more profound meaning to service than this. Let us look at the matter historically. Is there any

[1] See note, p. 117; this paper was presented on November 5th, 1925.

foundation in the development of our early communities for the notion of business based on altruistic service? A group of people settling in a new region first plant and sow. But other things have to be done. One buys groceries and sells to his neighbours. He does this expecting someone else in the community to build his store and house and keep them in repair, and someone else to make his shoes, and someone else to look after him when he is ill, and so on. This is an exchange, or interchange, of services. When we say "reciprocal service" it seems to me that we are nearer the facts and also that we are expressing that give-and-take of life which is its noblest as it is its most profound aspect. That person is intellectually or morally defective who is not taking part in the give-and-take of life.

With this understanding of the word "service," I think it a good word. Its connotation of self-sacrifice, of the recognition of other aims than private gain, makes it a high motive for individual lives and a social asset. If a man thinks of his business as a service, he will certainly not increase private profits at the expense of public good. Moreover, "business as service" tends to do away with one conception which was very unfortunate. There was a notion formerly that a man made money for himself, a purely selfish occupation, in the daytime, and rendered his service to the community by sitting on the school board or some civic committee at night. Or he might spend his early and middle life in business, in getting money, and then do his service later by spending his money in ways useful to the community—if he did not die before that stage arrived! The much more wholesome idea, which we have now, is that our work itself is to be our greatest service to the community.

There is, however, a word which gives us a truer idea of the place of business in society than even the expression "reciprocal service." I refer, of course, to the word you have been thinking of as you have been reading this paper, the word "function." A business man should think of his work as one of the necessary functions of society, aware that other people are also performing necessary functions, and that all together these make a sound, healthy, useful community. "Function" is the best word because it implies not only that you are responsible for serving your community, but that you are partly responsible for there being any community to serve.

For some time there has been emerging a sense of industry as a function. And this among employees as well as among employers. Someone who attended the La Follette Convention told me that the reason the locomotive engineers had so much influence there was that they had a sense of railroads as functional instruments and brought in a programme which resulted, not in oratory, but in discussion. A good many unionists are beginning to see that labour's stake in industry is not its stake in collective bargaining, but its stake in maintaining a useful enterprise. This is an understanding of function. And this gives actual, not evangelical, value to the idea of service.

I said that the chief reason we often hesitate to use the word "service" is that it has been abused. But so was the word "efficiency," which preceded it, and so certainly is this word "function" which is succeeding it. We need all these words—efficiency, service, function—but we need to use all three discriminatingly.

Assuming, then, that a profession (1) is exercised as one of the necessary functions of society, not purely for private gain, (2) that it is the application of a proved and systematic body of knowledge; recognizing, that is, that it rests on the double foundation of science and service, reciprocal service— what are some of the other implications involved in regarding an occupation as a profession?

One is certainly love of the work. A doctor or a lawyer, a teacher, a chemist, or an engineer usually cares greatly for his work, chooses it usually for that reason, voluntarily goes through the training necessary for it, often a long and strenuous training. But many a boy drifts into a business without having felt any particular urge to do that particular thing.

And love of work usually includes satisfaction in work well

done. Craftsman and artist and professional man have aimed at this satisfaction, and more and more this is becoming true of business men. There is an expression which I like very much, "honest" work. We speak of a certain carpenter or plumber as giving us honest work. It would be profitable, I think, for each one of us to scrutinize his own work rigorously to see if it is as "honest" as, say, the surgeon's standard. In a recent book, the author speaks of the business man's zeal for service, and says that long after the clerks have departed from the office of a big corporation you can see lights burning in the rooms of the executives. Much fun has been made of this sentence, but I think a good deal of overtime work is done, if not for service, at any rate with the craftsman's love of doing a job well. And it seems to me that this is too fine an aim to be made second even to that of service, which sometimes narrows us down to too meagre an ethics. The *whole* grandeur of life is not there. It is indeed a noble word, but so also is self-expression, the love of work, the craftsman's and artist's joy in work well done. It seems to me, in short, that some people have their imagination aroused by the idea of service, others by high standards of accomplishment; that usually these go together; and that no occupation can make a more worthy appeal to the imagination, either from the point of view of the service it can perform or from the tremendous interest of the job itself, than that of business management.

Professional Standards Developed and Effected through Group Organization

Men have been greatly helped in developing standards and in adhering to standards by combining into some form of association. Each profession has its association. While I object to the idea that individual professional men have necessarily a higher code than individual business men, I do think that the professions are ahead of business in the fact that their codes are group codes. The errors of the personal equation are thus often corrected. Moreover, members know that they cannot have the respect of their group unless they follow its standards. But business, too, has begun to develop group codes. We can see how various trade associations, begun chiefly for such objects as central credit records or to secure legislation favouring their particular industry, have already improved trade practices and raised trade standards. And managers have now their associations, too. This is a step toward management's becoming a profession.

A professional association is an association with one object above all others. The members do not come together merely for the pleasure of meeting others of the same occupation; nor do they meet primarily to increase their pecuniary gain; although this may be one of the objects. They have joined in order better to perform their function. They meet:

To establish standards.
To maintain standards.
To improve standards.
To keep members up to standards.
To educate the public to appreciate standards.
To protect the public from those individuals who have not attained standards or wilfully do not follow them.
To protect individual members of the profession from each other.

These objects of a professional association may be summed up by saying that a profession provides a corporate responsibility. As most of the objects speak for themselves, I shall refer further to only three: corporate responsibility for maintenance of standards, for the education of the public, and for the development of professional standards.

In regard to the first, maintenance of standards, business can certainly learn a lesson from the professions, where the ideal is loyalty to the work rather than to the company. An architect feels primarily that he belongs to a certain profession, only secondarily that he is working for a particular firm. He may change his firm; but he remains permanently bound to the standards of his profession. I recognize that there is very serious trouble when the standards of one's firm and one's profession clash—*there* is indeed a difficult integration for you. What I am emphasizing here is that in the profession it is recognized that one's professional honour demands that one shall make this integration. If business management were a profession and had its own recognized code, differences between executives and company heads could perhaps be more easily adjusted. I know a man who recently left a Southern firm because, he told me, he could not reconcile his principles with the way that firm conducted business. When he put the matter to the firm, his principles were treated as a purely individual matter. If he had been a doctor, or if business management were a profession, he could have prevented the matter becoming personal by referring to the accepted standards or methods of the profession.

When, therefore, I say that members of a profession feel a greater loyalty to their profession than to the company, I do not mean that their loyalty is to one group of persons rather than to another; but that their loyalty is to a body of principles, of ideals; that is, to a special body of knowledge of proved facts and the standards arising therefrom. What, then, are we loyal to? To the soul of our work. To that which is both in our work and which transcends our work. This seems to me the highest romance as it is the deepest religion, namely, that by being loyal to our work we are loyal to that which transcends our work. The great romance of business is not, as sometimes supposed, the element of chance. That spells adventure only for him with the gambler's temperament. The high adventure of business is its opportunity for bringing into manifestation every hour of the day the deeper thing within every man, transcending every man, which you may call your ideal, or God, or what you will, but which is absent from no man.

In regard to the second point mentioned above, responsibility for the education of the public, it is considered one of the duties of a profession to train the public by sticking to professional standards instead of merely giving the public what it wants. An architect, to be sure, may put cupolas and gimcracks on a house he is building, a portrait painter may get rich by painting portraits flattering his sitters, but when architect or portrait painter does these things he is outside professional standards, outside the accepted tradition of a group of people. If business management is to become a profession, business management, too, will have to think of educating the public, not merely of giving it what it asks for. The head of a string of restaurants, one who thinks of business as a public service and is trying to give wholesome food as a public health measure, was trying to reduce the bacterial count in ice cream. A customer asked one day, "Why doesn't the ice cream taste as it used to?" "We are trying," said the waitress, "to reduce the bacterial count." "Oh, give us our old bugs. We liked 'em," said the customer.

Oliver Sheldon says, "Management acknowledges as master the public will of the community alone." I do not agree with that. The public will of a particular community may have to be educated to appreciate certain standards. That is exactly what is going to make business management a profession: to realize that it is responsible to something higher than the public will of a community, that its service to the public does not lie wholly in obeying the public.

And this brings us to our third point. One of the aims of the professional man is not only to practise his profession, to apply his science, but to extend the knowledge upon which that profession is based. A profession means, not only a tradition, but a developing tradition. There would be no progress if men merely lived up to the standards of their profession. The judge makes a decision which not only disposes of the case in hand, but becomes a precedent. A lawyer often handles a case in such fashion that certain principles are established or strengthened. The doctor not only cures a particular person, but has something to tell his profession about that particular disease. Business lags behind the professions in this respect. You know how often you hear the expression "get by"—"I guess we can get by on that." Men tide over certain situations without doing that which means a progressive policy for their business, or that which helps to establish a standard for business management.

There is one thing which I think all executives should

remember every hour of the day. You are not helping to develop your profession only when you are discussing its demands in the managers' association. The way in which you give every order, the way in which you make every decision, the way in which you meet every committee, in almost every act you perform during the day, you may be contributing to the science of management. Business management cannot become a profession unless business men realize fully their part in making it such. All professions have been developed by the work of their own members. If there were people somewhere in the world creating executive technique, and you were applying it, your job would be big; but it is just twice as big as that, for there is no one else in the world but yourselves to create the science, the art, the profession of business management. This is pioneer work and difficult, but it has always been pioneer work to which men have responded with courage and vigour.

We have been speaking of professional standards as formed and developed through group association. Is there not something in the manner in which those ideals are followed which we have hitherto connected more closely with the professions than with business? There is a word which means a great deal to me; I wonder if it does to you. That is "style." Whatever a man does, whether he is a statesman or artisan, whether he is poet or tennis player, we like his activity to have the distinction of something we call style. Style, however, is a difficult thing to define. I have seen it defined variously as adapting form to material, as calculation of means to end, as restraint, as that which is opposed to all that is sloppy and bungling, the performance of an act without waste. Others speak of style as broad design, noble proportion. A manager's job performed with style would have all these characteristics.

I have looked for style in literature and art, games and statesmanship. It is interesting to watch polo from this point of view. In all the games of polo I have seen, the best players have usually had style: no waste of muscle, calculation of means to end, yes, and proportion and design, too. Again, watch a good actor when his acting has the distinction of style. There is restraint, calculation of means to end, no waste of energy. A physiologist watching a scene of agony on the stage will, if the acting is of the first order, tell you that he sees no waste of muscular force. In poor acting, however, there is such waste. Such acting lacks, among other things, style.

Professor Whitehead gives attainment and restraint as the two chief elements of style and says:

"Style is the fashioning of power, the restraint of power. The administrator with a sense of style hates waste, the engineer with a sense of style economizes his material, the artisan with a sense of style prefers good work. Style is the ultimate morality of mind."

And further:

"With style, the end is attained without side issues, without raising undesirable inflammations. With style, you attain your end and nothing but your end. With style, the effect of your activity is incalculable, and foresight is the last gift of gods to men. With style, your power is increased, for your mind is not disturbed with irrelevances, and you are more likely to attain your object. Now style is the exclusive privilege of the expert. Whoever heard of the style of an amateur poet, of an amateur painter? Style is always the product of specialist study, the contribution of specialism to culture."

That is an interesting phrase, "the contribution of specialism to culture." Then you need not, according to this definition, give your daytime hours to a low thing called business, and in the evening pursue culture. Through your business itself, if you manage it with style, you are making a contribution to the culture of the world. It makes business management interesting, doesn't it? I take it that you are taking this course throughout the winter to learn how to give to your work of management the distinction of style.

I have left to the last what seems to me the chief function, the real service, of business: to give an opportunity for individual development through the better organization of human relationships. Several times lately I have seen business defined as production, the production of useful articles. But every activity of man should add to the intangible values of life as well as to the tangible, should aim at other products than merely those which can be seen and handled. What does "useful" mean, anyway? We could live without many of the articles manufactured. But the greatest usefulness of these articles consists in the fact that their manufacture makes possible those manifold, interweaving activities of men by which spiritual values are created. There is no over-production here.

Suppose the doctors should tell us that it would be more healthy to go barefoot, and we should all take their advice. What would become of all the shoe factories? Of course, the manufacturers would find out how much of their equipment could be used in making something else, and they would turn to the manufacture of that other article. In that case, must they consider their previous work of no value? Must an old man who has been a shoe manufacturer think he has wasted his life in producing something actually injurious to the community? I think he would have to, if all he had produced was boots and shoes, the material product. But not if the men who worked in that factory, managerial or manual workers, had through their work become more developed human beings. And the tendency to-day in many plants is, most happily, to make that development one of the objects of the industry. It is the development of the individual involving the progress of society, that some of our finer presidents are aiming at, not pecuniary gain only; not service in the sense of supplying all our present crude wants, but the raising of men to finer wants. If the aim of the lawyer is justice, if the aim of the doctor is health, if the aim of the architect is beauty, business, I am sure, may have as noble an aim. There are business men to-day who perceive that the *process* of production is as important for the welfare of society as the *product* of production. This is what makes personnel work in industry the most interesting work in the world.

If business offers so large an opportunity for the creation of spiritual values, and I think it offers a larger opportunity than any single profession in the possibilities of those intimate human interweavings through which all development of man must come; if many business men are taking advantage of that opportunity, should we any longer allow the assumption which I have seen stated three times since last summer, that the professions are for service and business for pecuniary gain? I have seen the expression "the greed of the business man." I have seen it stated that the business man's test of an undertaking is, "Will it increase income?" while the professional man's test is, "Will it increase the sum of human welfare?" But I do not think this distinction valid. I object to dividing us off into sheep and goats and putting all the goats on the side of business. Professional men as well as business men used to think less of pecuniary gain. But that is *their* responsibility. Ours, it seems to me, is to redeem the word "business." We are told that business should have a professional conscience. Why not a business conscience? Why not business pride as well as professional pride?

It is unfair to think that all business men have only as high a code as is compatible with keeping profits at a certain level. I have known business men who were willing to make sacrifices to maintain certain standards. Napoleon called England a "nation of shopkeepers." That was an epitome of his own character. Shopkeeping did not have the pomp and glory of *his* trade. It had none of the deceptive values on which his life was based.

We have progressed in a hundred years beyond Napoleon's notion of shopkeeping; yet in an interview reported in the *Boston Herald* the artist, Cecilia Beaux, said in effect, "The business man aims at success in the sense of wealth or prominence; the artist's idea of success is the satisfactory development of an idea." If I were a business man, I would not let business lie any longer under this stigma. It is true that the artist or the professional man undertakes to solve his problems, he does not try to "get by." He would rather be lamely and blunderingly trying to solve his problem than brilliantly escaping it. But why should not the business man have the same attitude? Cecilia Beaux said in this interview, "The artist grips his idea and will not let it go until it has blessed him, as the angel blessed Jacob."

I see no reason why business men should have lower ideals than artists or professional men. Let us, indeed, do everything possible to make business management a profession, but while we are doing it, I think we may feel that business men can make as large a contribution to professional ideals as the so-called learned professions. I think, indeed, that the business man has opportunities to lead the world in an enlarged conception of the expressions "professional honour," "professional integrity." That phrase which we hear so often, "business integrity," is already being extended to mean far more than a square deal in a trade.

I have tried to show in this and the previous lecture that business management has already acquired some of the essentials of a profession, that it is on the way to acquire others. By far the most significant sign that business management is becoming a profession is that the old idea of business as trading has begun to disappear. The successful business man of the past was thought to be the one who could get the best in a trade. This required neither great intelligence nor special training. A man used to think that if his boy was not clever enough for a profession he must be put into business. To-day we think that business management needs as high an order of intelligence, as thorough a training as any of the "learned" professions.

It seems to me very significant that we seldom hear to-day the expression so common twenty or even ten years ago—"captains of industry." While all captains of industry did not fly the black flag, still in the nineteenth century ruthlessness and success too often went together; buccaneering and business were too often synonymous. Even when this was not so, the captain of industry was at best a masterful man who could bend all wills to his own. This is beginning to change. Success is now seen to depend on something other than domination. It is significant that two ideas which so long existed together are disappearing together—namely, business as trading, and managing as manipulating.

As arbitrary authority in the management of business has decreased, as authority has come to be associated less with mere position and more with actual capacity, the whole executive force has more opportunities to exercise creative ability in contributions to organization. Please bear in mind that by the word "organization" I mean far more than constructing a system. As Mr. Dennison has told us, "We have to reorganize every day." By which he means, I think, that many of the daily executive duties contribute to a developing organization.

Organization is the word most often heard to-day in all discussions of business development. The greatest weakness in most industrial plants is seen to be organization. The organization engineer is the one most in demand. Do you not think that the recognition of organization as the chief need of business is rather interesting when we remember that conscious organization is the great spiritual task of man? We speak of the "composition" of a picture; it is the way the artist has organized his material. The harmony of a piece of music depends on the way the musician has organized his material. The statesman organizes social facts into legislation and administration. The greater the statesman, the greater power he shows in just this capacity. It might be fun to try to do it in one's own life, to say: "Here are the materials of my life. How would the artist arrange them in order to make the composition the most significant? How would he subordinate lesser values to higher values? How would he manage to give everything its fullest value? Or we might ask ourselves the craftsman's question, "How can I make of my life a whole whose beauty and use shall be one?" Organization is what separates mediocre endeavour from high endeavour. No one has a better opportunity than the business manager to take part in this the highest endeavour of the human race.

It occurs to me that you may think, because I have hardly mentioned the profit motive in business, that I have deliberately avoided it. I assure you I have not. We all want profit and as much as we can get. And this is as it should be when other things are not sacrificed to it.

When people talk of substituting the service motive for the profit motive, I always want to ask: Why this wish to simplify motive when there is nothing more complex? Take any one of our actions to-day and examine it. There probably have been several motives for it. It is true that if anyone asked you why you did so and so, you would probably pick out to present to the public the motive which you thought did you the most credit. But the fact of the actual complexity remains. We work for profit, for service, for our own development, for the love of creating something. At any one moment, indeed, most of us are not working directly or immediately for any of these things, but to put through the job in hand in the best possible manner, which might be thought of, perhaps, as the engineer's motive. But whatever these motives are labelled—ethical or service motive, engineer's motive, craftsman's motive, the creative urge of the artist, the pecuniary gain motive—whatever, I say, these various motives, I do not think we should give any up, but try to get more rather than fewer. To come back to the professions: can we not learn a lesson from them on this very point? The professions have not given up the money motive. I do not care how often you see it stated that they have. Professional men are eager enough for large incomes; but they have other motives as well, and they are often willing to sacrifice a good slice of income for the sake of these other things. We all want the richness of life in the terms of our deepest desire. We can purify and elevate our desires, we can add to them, but there is no individual or social progress in curtailment of desires.

VII

THE MEANING OF RESPONSIBILITY IN BUSINESS MANAGEMENT[1]

The Illusion of Final Responsibility

As our subject, "The Meaning of Responsibility in Business Management," would require more than one paper for adequate consideration, I have decided to centre this discussion on what is called "final" responsibility. Let us think of that in connection with certain other expressions which are akin to it, such as "ultimate authority," "supreme control." When Sidney Webb, in *The New Spirit in Industry*, writes of "ultimate authority," as do many others too, when Oliver Sheldon writes of "final determination" of policy and "supreme control" as two of the functions of administration as so many do, I think that expressions are being used which are a survival of former days.

These expressions do not seem to me accurately to describe business as conducted nowadays in many plants. Business practice has gone ahead of business theory. So much goes to contribute to administrative decisions before the part which the administrative head takes in them, which is indeed sometimes merely the official promulgation of a decision, that the conception of final responsibility is losing its force in the present organizations of business. This is as true of other executives as of the head. Here, too, final decisions have the form and the force which they have accumulated. I have seen an under-executive feel a little self-important over a decision he had made, when that decision had really come to him ready-made. An executive decision is a moment in a process. The growth of a decision, the accumulation of responsibility, not the final step, is what we need most to study.

[1] See note, p. 117; this paper was presented on April 29th, 1926.

146

The most fundamental idea in business to-day, that which has permeated our whole thinking on business organization, is that of function. Each man performs a function or part of a function. Research and scientific study determine function in scientifically managed plants. A man should have just as much, no more and no less, responsibility as goes with his function or his task. He should have just as much, no more and no less, authority as goes with his responsibility.[2] Function, responsibility, and authority should be the three inseparables in business organization. People talk about the limit of authority when it would be better to speak of the definition of task.

If, then, authority and responsibility are derived from function, they have little to do with the hierarchy of position. And in scientifically managed shops this is more and more recognized. The dispatch clerk has more authority in dispatching work than the president. When we find foremen jealous of their "authority," jealous, for instance, of the part the employment manager has in "hiring and firing," they have to be led to see that authority is not the important thing which has been given to the employment manager, but the function of hiring and firing. Or we might say that one of the foreman's jobs has been given to someone else, just as one of the president's jobs is often nowadays given to some specialist engaged to do that particular thing. One of the differences between the old-time foreman and the present is that the former was thinking in terms of his authority; he thought he could not keep up his dignity before his men unless he had this thing which he called "authority." Many foremen of to-day are learning to think in terms of responsibility for definite tasks or for a defined group of tasks.

Or, to take another illustration, I read in some plans of employee representation that authority has been granted to

---

[2] Cf. The New State, p. 232: "Moreover, at present representative government rests on the fallacy that when you delegate the job you delegate the responsibility. . . . What we need is a kind of government which will delegate the job, but not the responsibility. The case is somewhat like that of the head of a business undertaking, who makes the men under him responsible for his own work and still the final responsibility rests with him. This is not divided responsibility but shared responsibility—a very different thing."

employee representatives to discharge and discipline. Those who devise plans of employee representation should not be thinking of authority to discharge and discipline, but where the function of discharge and discipline should be placed— with management, with workers, or with both. This may seem a matter of mere language to you, but I do not think it is; I think it will affect your attitude on this subject very materially in which of these terms you are thinking.

This conception of authority as bound up with function does away with that bugbear of many political scientists, "central interference." As business is being organized to-day there is less and less chance of central interference, for we find authority and responsibility with the head of a department, with an expert, with the driver of a truck as he decides on order of deliveries. I know a man in an industrial plant who is superintendent of a division which includes a number of departments. He tells me that in many cases he says to the head of a department, "With your permission, I do so and so." This is a decided reversal of the usual method, is it not? In the old hierarchy of position, the head of the department would be "under" the superintendent of the division; the "lower" would take orders from the "higher." But my friend recognizes that authority should go with knowledge and experience; that that is where obedience is due, no matter whether it is up the line or down the line. Where knowledge and experience are located, there, he says, you have the key man to the situation. If this has begun to be recognized in business practice, we have here the forerunner of some pretty drastic changes in organization.

This conception of authority and responsibility should do away also with the idea almost universally held that the president *delegates* authority and responsibility. One of our ablest writers says: "The chief executive should define clearly each staff executive's responsibility and its relation to general purposes and plans, and should grant each staff executive adequate corresponding authority." But is that exactly what happens in business? Is not this, as a matter of fact, decided by the plan of organization? When a plant reorganizes and introduces staff management along with line management, the duties, authority, and responsibility of the staff executives are inherent in the plan of organization. Whatever formality is necessary on the part of the president *is* more or less of a formality.

This phrase, "delegating authority," assumes that the owner or chief executive has the "right" to all the authority, but that it is useful to delegate some of it. I do not think that the president or general manager should have any more authority than goes with *his* function. Therefore I do not see how you can delegate authority except when you are ill or take a vacation. And then you have not exactly delegated authority. Someone is doing your work and he has the authority which goes with that particular piece of work. Authority belongs to the job and stays with the job.

I have just denied the "right" of the chief executive to all the authority. The idea of function changes very materially our conception of "rights," a term which is, happily, rapidly disappearing. Our activities are not determined by any abstract notion of rights. The head of a branch bank may decide on small loans, while large loans have to go up to the executive committee. This is not because the executive committee has the "right" to pass on large loans, but because it is recognized that the combined judgment of the executive committee and the head of the branch bank is probably better than that of either alone.

The Interweaving of Authority and Responsibility

We are now ready to take a second step in the consideration of this subject. Authority and responsibility go with function, but as the essence of organization is the interweaving of functions, authority and responsibility we now see as a matter of interweaving. An order, a command, is a step in a process, a moment in the movement of interweaving experience. We should guard against thinking this step a larger part of the whole process than it really is. There is all that leads to the order, all that comes afterwards—methods of administration, the watching and recording of results, what flows out of it to make further orders. If we race all that leads to a command, what persons are connected with it and in what way, we find that more than one man's experience has gone to the making of that moment. Unless it is a matter of purely arbitrary authority. Arbitrary authority, or the "power over," which we considered in the paper on "Power," is authority not related to all the experience concerned, but to that of one man alone, or of one group of men.

The particular person, then, identified with the moment of command—foreman, upper executive or expert—is not the most important matter for our consideration, although, of course, a very important part of the process. All that I want to emphasize is that there is a process. A political scientist writes, "Authority co-ordinates the experiences of men." But I think this is a wrong view of authority. The form of organization should be such as to allow or induce the continuous co-ordination of the experiences of men. A practical business man, the member of a firm of manufacturers in one of our Western States, said to me, while speaking of the necessity of business management's becoming a profession: "And the essence of any profession is finding the law. That is what makes business management a science. The business manager has to find the law of every managerial activity in question." This means that this man recognizes authority as inherent in the situation, not as attached to an official position. He would not agree with the political scientist that authority co-ordinates the experiences of men, because he sees that legitimate authority flows from co-ordination, not co-ordination from authority.

It would seem to go without saying that you cannot hold people responsible for anything unconnected with their experience. Yet this was what the Allies tried to do when they sought power over Germany through the Treaty of Versailles. The Treaty of Versailles failed because, not being related to the experience of the Germans, the Allies found it impossible to hold Germany responsible for the results. I am not responsible for anything which has not its roots in my experience or my potential experience, that is, the experience I am in a position to acquire by reason of my function.

It is because responsibility is the outcome of an inter-weaving experience that we often find it so difficult to "fix" responsibility, as it is called. Is it the head of a manufacturing department who is responsible for the quality of a food product, or is it the consulting chemist? If a certain method you are using in your business proves a failure, who is responsible? The expert who suggested it? Or the head of the department who accepted it? Or those who engaged expert and head of department? Or the man who carried it out and knew it wouldn't work but obeyed orders? Again, if the quality of a piece of work is poor, it may be the fault of the last worker on it, or it may have been handed to him in poor condition from a previous operation, or the workers may have been given poor material, or all of these causes may have led to the final result. We might multiply these instances indefinitely; every one agrees, for instance, that managers and operators are both responsible for waste. This pluralistic responsibility, this interlocking responsibility, makes it difficult to "fix" responsibility, yet business success depends partly on doing just this. We have a problem here to think out. We have to discover how far each one con-cerned has contributed to the failure or partial failure, not in order to blame, but in order to learn all we can from this experience.

Another corollary from this conception of authority and responsibility as a moment in interweaving experience is that you have no authority as a mere left-over. You cannot take the authority which you won yesterday and apply it to-day. That is, you could not if we were able to embody the conception we are now considering in a plan of organiza-tion. In the ideal organization authority is always fresh, always being distilled anew. The importance of this in business management has not yet been estimated.

Of course, you will understand that in all this I am speak-ing of business organization in the more progressive plants, but there are as yet far more plants organized under the old doctrines.

It seems to me that there should be one very important consequence of this conception of authority and responsibility which we are considering, as it permeates more and more the theory and practice of business organization, and that is that it should greatly dignify the position of under-executive and operator, for this conception makes each one's work tremendously important. If you see that your activity is, in its measure, contributing to authority, in the sense that it is part of the guiding will which runs the plant, it will add interest and dignity to the most commonplace life, will illumine the most routine duties.

Evidences of the Diffusion of Responsibility

Having cleared the ground to some extent by these general considerations, let us ask ourselves what there is in the present organization of business which tends to diffuse rather than to concentrate responsibility. First, management is becoming more and more specialized. The policies and methods of a department rest on that department's special body of know-ledge, and there is a tendency for the responsibility to be borne by those with that special body of knowledge rather than by a man at the top because of his official position.

I saw the statement recently that the administrative head should hold frequent consultation with the heads of all departments and from the facts thus gained make his "final" decisions, construct his policies. But it is a matter of everyday knowledge to business men that their heads of departments pass up to them much more than mere facts. They give interpretations of facts, conclusions therefrom, judgments, too, so that they contribute very largely to final determination, supreme control, ultimate responsibility, even to what has been called "administrative leadership." In fact, as to both the information and the conclusions handed up from the executives, it is often not possible for the head to take or leave them. These conclusions and judgments are already, to a certain extent, woven into the pattern, and in such a way that it would be difficult to get them wholly out. Hence, while the board of directors may be theoretically the governing body, practically, as our large businesses are now organized, before their decisions are made there has already taken place much of that process of which these decisions are but the last step.

Another indication of the view of responsibility which I am considering is that the planning department provided in so many plants is passing from a tool of management to a part of management, a part of a functionalized management. But here again I should like to point out that business practice is going ahead of business theory, for in articles in business magazines we often see the planning department referred to as a tool of management. To be sure, the planning department is still so much of a novelty that there are many different ideas in regard to its place in the plant. It may be asked for purely statistical information. In the case of a decision pending for the sales department, for instance, it may be asked for a record of past sales, with analysis in regard to volume, localities, and so on. Usually, however, it is asked for more than this—for the probable future developments of certain localities, what the future demand will probably be, the probable effect of the raising of price. By the time this has all been passed over to the head, his decision is already largely predetermined.

Whatever our exact idea of a planning department, I think we shall agree that functional management means that authority and responsibility go with function and not with a certain position at the top of the chart. There is hardly a staff official, is there, who provides merely the material on which some line official bases his decision? Take the industrial relations manager. He is usually given a staff position. His work is largely research and planning, but in the presentation of results there is advice, either given openly as advice or suggestion, or else veiled under his general conclusions. Therefore, even if this official does not issue orders, does not exercise authority in the usual sense, he has as real an influence as the line official who issues orders and who influences his subordinates by direct contact with them.

Another notion which is doing away with our idea of "finals" as of supreme importance is that conception of the relation of department policy to general policy which we discussed in last winter's conferences. When we realize that sales policy and production policy are contributing to general policy as well as general policy "dictating" (the word we often see) departmental policy, we have got out of the region of finals and absolutes. When you tell me that sales planning is but a division of business planning, when you tell me that sales research is only part of a broader function which might be designated commercial research, wherever, that is, you show me functional parts, then I say to you that you are going beyond our old notion of ultimate authority, that you are enlarging its meaning, extending its scope. It is interesting, is it not—it is to me the most interesting fact about business—that functional management, as we are coming to see its deeper implications, is changing our whole philosophy of business organization?[3]

Still another evidence of the diffusion of responsibility is the tendency in present business practice to solve problems where they arise, to make reconciliations at the point where conflict occurs, instead of the matter being carried "up" to someone. This means that department heads are being given more and more responsibility within their own units. Of course, all methods of decentralization tend to weaken the significance of "final" responsibility, and the tendency to-day is to decentralize.[4]

Cumulative Responsibilities as Opposed to Ultimate Authority—Co-ordination

Instead, then, of final determination, supreme control, ultimate authority, we might perhaps think of cumulative

[3] I wish it to be noted that I have left out all consideration of general policy as formed by president, general mnager, executive committee or board of directors. (M. P. F.)

[4] This tendency to decentralization exists side by side with that centralization required by functional management. The two are not inconsistent, as will be shown later. (M. P. F.)

control, cumulative responsibility. I am indebted to Mr. Henry S. Dennison for this phrase, which seems to me to have implicated in it one of the most fundamental truths of organization, whether we are thinking of industrial or political organization. That one person or board becomes the symbol of this cumulative responsibility should not blind us to the truth of the matter. To be sure, it is the chief executive, or one of the upper executives, to whom we look to tide over unexpected difficulties, or when instant decisions are necessary. In the big snowstorm last February, several hundred telephone girls had to be sent to hotels for the night. Their rooms, suppers, and breakfasts made a cost of about $1,500. This had to be taken to the general manager for decision. But when it is not a question of meeting emergencies or filling up gaps or strengthening weaknesses in organization, ultimate authority is a good deal overrated. It is the diffusion of authority and responsibility which strikes you in the study of business to-day. What Filenes,[5] and many other firms, too, have done is to make their formal organization coincide with a decided tendency in business practice. They found that there was power, leadership, responsibility all along the line. They recognized the existing. They sought means to take advantage of it, to make this scattered power cumulative and hence more effective. There is nothing academic about the recent organization of business plants. There is nothing self-sacrificing, either. The upper executives have not given up anything. They have gathered into the management of their business every scrap of useful material they could find.

That business men are facing this undoubted fact of cumulative responsibility, of pluralistic authority, that modern business organization is based to some extent on these conceptions, is very interesting to me, for I have been for many years a student of political science, and it seems significant to me that now I have to go to business for the greatest light on authority, responsibility, sovereignty—these concepts which have been supposed to be peculiarly

[5] Boston (Massachusetts) Department Store.

the concepts of political science.[6] For instance, in the last book I read on government, a recent one, the writer speaks of "a single, ultimate centre of control," but I do not find that practical men are much interested in ultimates. I think that with political scientists this interest is a survival from their studies in sovereignty. The business man is more concerned with the sources than with the organs of authority. Mr. Laski makes much of the fact that "there should be in every social order some single centre of ultimate reference, some power that is able to resolve disputes by saying a last word that will be obeyed." This is, of course, true, but it should not be *over*-emphasized. Moreover, this view disregards one of the most important trends in the recent development of thinking on organization: "central control" used to mean the chief executive; now it is a technical expression of scientific management indicating the point where knowledge and experience on the method in question are brought to a focus.

I should like, however, over against these statements made by students of government, to give some words of a practical administrator. In Franklin Lane's report to President Wilson on leaving the Cabinet, in suggesting that the heads of departments should be the advisers, the constructors of policies, he said, "in a word, we need more opportunity for planning, engineering, statesmanship above, and more fixed authority and responsibility below." This is interesting as taking some of the circumstance that once attached to the word "authority" and making it a part of routine detail. Indeed, authority and responsibility seem to be becoming humbler virtues.

And as it is the idea of pluralistic authority, of cumulative responsibility, which is dominating progressive business organization to-day, so the crux of business organization is how to join these various responsibilities. Take the purchasing of materials. The responsibility for this should be shared by the purchasing agent and by the production department

[6] *Cf. The New State,* Chapter XXIX, for the corresponding political theory that sovereignty is evolved through the interdependence of the groups.

which gives its specifications to the purchasing agent. If the purchasing agent thinks that some of these specifications could be changed and cost thereby reduced without decreasing quality, he should discuss this with the production department. While I realize that much can be accomplished by friendly relations between individuals, I think that organization should have for one of its chief aims to provide for joint responsibility in those cases where combined knowledge is necessary for the best judgment.

This problem is being solved in a number of plants by a system of cross-functioning. In one factory I know they are trying to build up a structure of interlocked committees. This is perhaps the most important trend in business organization.

Let me take the New England Telephone Company as providing an example of this trend, although, of course, there are many other companies which would do equally well for illustration. Here we find the four departments— traffic, engineering, plant, and commercial—constantly conferring, one with another or all together. These conferences are often informal, but are expected of all officials. A superintendent told me: "Each department is supposed to get in touch with certain others. We are not told to, but if we don't it is considered poor judgment on our part." The district traffic manager asks the wire chief from the plant department to talk a matter over with him, or if it is a commercial matter he calls in the commercial manager of that district, or if it is a question of blue prints or costs he asks the engineering department if they will send a man over. They may settle it among themselves. If not, the traffic manager puts it up to the division superintendent of traffic and he may consult the division superintendents of plant and commercial departments. Here, you see, we have a combination of going both across and up the line.

When the Main exchange in Boston was cut into two last summer, the question came up whether to cut thirty-five a day or 500 in a blanket order overnight. This affected all four departments—traffic, engineering, commercial, and plant. They agreed, after discussion, on the blanket order. If they had disagreed, they would have taken it up to the general superintendent of each department—*up* the line, note. And then the four general superintendents would have consulted—here a *cross*-relation. If these had agreed, the matter would have ended there. If not, it would have had to go to the general manager—now *up* the line. This combination of across and up exists, as I have said, in many plants to-day, and I have found it an interesting thing to watch, interesting because significant, perhaps, of a change in the accepted principles of organization which will eventually change, not only business, but government as well. It is noteworthy, in connection with this point, that the Telephone Company does not have, and does not seem to need, any special co-ordinating department, because there is a "natural" continuous co-ordinating inherent in their form of organization.

I have told you that the chief weaknesses of those businesses which I have studied was lack of co-ordination. Yet there is much talk of co-ordination. Why, then, do we not get it? First, because its advantage, its necessity, is not yet seen with sufficient clearness. Secondly, the system of organization in a plant is often so hierarchical, so ascending and descending, that it is almost impossible to provide for cross-relations; the notion of horizontal authority has not yet taken the place of that of vertical authority. We cannot, however, succeed in modern business by always running up and down a ladder of authority. In the third place, cross functioning seems often to be conceived of as useful only when difficulties arise, or when it is obvious that joint consultation on some specific problems would be desirable. But as such consultation is necessary all the time, some machinery which will operate continuously should be provided.

Of course, one difficulty about a degree, or a manner, of working together which hides individual effort comes from the egotism, a perfectly natural and to some extent justifiable egotism, of the persons concerned. Each executive wants his special contribution to get to the ears of the boss.

The chief reason, however, why we are not more successful with this problem is, I think, because it is not sufficiently recognized that co-ordination is a process which should have its beginnings very far back in the organization of the plant. You cannot always bring together the *results* of departmental activities and expect to co-ordinate them. You have to have an organization which will permit an interweaving all along the line. Strand should weave with strand, and then we shall not have the clumsy task of trying to patch together finished webs. Mr. Dennison says that in his factory they have found that a small committee of workers and foremen, or sub-foremen, will come to some plan of co-operation sooner than a committee further along; that the nearer you get to specific cases, the better chance you have for agreement. He also tells us that when they set tasks and rates in his factory, they do the mechanical work of time study first and get what facts can be disclosed with relative accuracy, and then, if there is any doubt, they bring in "a small committee of the employees for consultation at the very early stages, so that they may have their opportunity in the very discovery of the facts that lie at the basis of further understanding."

That expression, "the very early stages," expresses the essence of my whole philosophy of organization, in business or in government. I believe in decentralization, but not in the kind advocated by many political pluralists. The Guild Socialists, for instance, plan for the uniting of their separate units at the top, in the Guild Congress. I do not believe there will ever be any genuine, any effective, uniting except that begun in "the very early stages." In government this will mean in the smallest units, whether these be geographical or vocational; in industry, in joint sub-committees.

To sum up: final responsibility is, I think, partly an illusion. You will not find the pot of gold at the foot of that rainbow. The best method of organization is not that which works out most meticulously or most logically the place for "finals" and "ultimates," but that which provides possibilities for a cumulative responsibility, which provides for gathering together all the responsibility which there actually is in the plant, which provides for making the various individual and group responsibilities more effective by the working out of a system of cross-relations. And as a business is organized to-day, with its many experts, its planning department, its industrial psychologist, its economic adviser, and its trained managers, the illusion of final responsibility is disappearing.

I do not wish to minimize the amount of autocracy there is in the business world; I deplore it as much as anyone. But I think that the way it is going to diminish is not by sub-stituting "democracy," whatever that means, but by some of the methods of organization which I am indicating to you, and which I am not theorizing about, for the beginnings of these methods can be seen at work, some in one place, some in another. The emphasis to-day is on specific respon-sibility and interweaving responsibilities. When, however, I take up later the question of administrative leadership and emphasize the importance of that, you may think that I am taking back some of the things I have been saying, and yet I hope I shall be able to prove to you then, not only the importance of able administrative leadership, but that in fact the administrative leader has more responsibility, not less, because of all the recent tendencies in business practice which we have discussed in this paper. In the following paper we shall consider what we have only hinted at this evening, the function of the worker in relation to the problems of authority and responsibility.

A Telephone Case

Something occurred not long ago to make me look into the organization of the telephone company which serves the city in which I live, and I seemed to find there a very interesting corroboration of some of the things I have just been saying. Let me first run over the incident and then consider the significance of what was disclosed.

One day I sat down at eleven o'clock to telephone to my bank. It took me until 11.45 to get it, and I immediately made notes of how this time was spent. I will give them in substance as I wrote them down.

Two minutes were spent in getting a wrong number, as someone else answered. Four minutes were then spent in ringing the bank, and four minutes is an unusually long time for a ring at the switchboard of a large bank to go unanswered. At the end of the four minutes I received the report, "No one answers." I then spent three minutes in getting Information and confirming the fact that I had the right number, as it occurred to me that the number might have been changed since I last called the bank. Again for four minutes I endeavoured to put through the call, and at the end of that time received the reply, "No one answers." This made eight minutes that the switchboard of a large bank was apparently dead at the busiest time of day. I had now consumed thirteen minutes. I therefore then called the chief operator to ask her to get the number for me. For five minutes there was silence—no number and no report. At the end of this time I again asked the chief operator to get the number. Again silence—no number and no report on the matter for a further space of four minutes. From 11.22 to 11.30 (eight minutes) I spent in trying to get the manager of the exchange in which I was making the call, but I could get no response from his office, although I asked ten or twelve times. At 11.30 I finally got the manager's office, and eight minutes were then spent by his clerk in trying to locate him. I learned later that the manager was responsible for four central offices and was probably going from one to another. At 11.42, I called the head office of the New England Telephone and Telegraph Company, asked for some official of the company higher than the manager whose office I had been trying to get, and was connected with a superintendent, who instantly got my bank for me, at 11.45.

I supposed the incident then closed, but in the afternoon a traffic representative in the office where I had had my trouble telephoned to me and asked what had happened, and we had a long talk. Later the company sent a service representative to see me, and we had a much longer conversation. After that I talked the matter over with the president of the company, who felt that my experience was an instance of exceptionally poor service, and who arranged that I might have an opportunity to see something of the management of the company in action. But I am not telling this story as illustrating poor telephone service. On the contrary, before I was through with the matter, I came to think that the organization of this telephone company illustrates some of the basic principles of sound organization.

In the first place, each official seemed to be thinking more in terms of his job than of his position. The first thing that struck my attention was the minor importance of hierarchy of rank. This was rather a good joke on me. Forgetting all my beautiful theories, all my preaching against one man having power over another, the mental habits of a lifetime asserted themselves without my being aware of it, and I started out, as I realized when the incident was over, on a hunt for someone in authority over others. I called the chief operator because I thought she was "over" the operator; I called the exchange manager because I thought he was "over" the chief operator. I asked for a superintendent because I thought he was "over" the exchange manager. But I found that the officials of the telephone company did not seem to be thinking in those terms. When I said to the superintendent with whom I was connected, "Are you over the exchange manager?" he said in rather bewildered tones, "No, I am not over him." When a superintendent called me up in the afternoon, the first thing I said to him was, "Are you over the superintendent I talked with this morning." He replied, "Oh, no. I'm not over him." You see, in spite of all my principles, I was so used to the old way of thinking that I couldn't adjust myself quickly; I kept straight on in this search for someone above others instead of asking: Whose particular job is this?

And later I found that this lack of emphasis on hierarchy of rank went all down the line. The chief operator did not have, or did not exercise, authority over the operators in exactly the old sense, neither did the supervisors nor the instructors. The girls were being trained, not ordered. Command and obedience did not seem to be exactly the thing going on. There was either no position which as such carried with it the right to "boss" or else no one took advantage of such a position. I was much interested in this because only the week before, in talking to a member of a well-known firm, I had asked him a certain question to which he replied, "We don't bother about co-ordination and all that. We tell people what to do and they have to do it."

In the second place, in the telephone company there was substituted for hierarchy of rank an amount of cross-functioning which, while it, of course, exists in all plants where there is functional management, seemed to me to work with special efficiency here. I have already described this in the first part of my talk.

A third suggestion of some of the things we have been considering I found in the general attitude toward responsibility. Each one seemed to be thinking not so much in terms of to whom he was responsible as for what he was responsible. You will remember, perhaps, the nurse I spoke of who told me: "The doctors are not over us; they can't tell us what to do. They have their work and we have ours." At first, I did not like this—it seemed like chaos indeed. I thought the old way much better, of the doctor's having full responsibility, of his giving all the orders and seeing to it that the nurse obeyed his orders. But on second thought it seemed to me that this might perhaps have a good side; perhaps the nurse might do better work if she felt the larger responsibility which the attitude of my nurse indicated. And this view was strengthened by what I saw in the telephone company, where there seemed less feeling of responsibility of one man to another than one expects to find in such an organization. The attitude common to most seemed to be that of interest in their jobs and a feeling of responsibility for them. Responsibility "for" seems to me a little higher conception than responsibility "to."

Moreover, my fourth point, everyone with whom I talked seemed to be thinking of his job not just as that of wire chief, manager, superintendent, or whatever it might be, but as the whole enterprise of telephone service. This must be a great asset to the company. It seemed to me a triumph for someone, I do not know whether for the president of the company or for that particular form of organization.

In the fifth place, blame was not made personal. When, for instance, there is a large number of answers taking over ten seconds, disclosed by a system of observation, this matter comes to the chief operator, who discusses it with the chief supervisors. What I noted was that it is not instantly assumed that some particular operators are to blame. It is recognized that this may have come from distribution of business on the boards, lack of teamwork between operators, or other causes. Still, the possibility of tracing it to particular persons was recognized, but then the matter was in the hands of the instructor for that division. Then it became a matter of further instruction. No one suggested blame, reprimands— the old weapon of authority. The official who was showing me around said, "We are not looking to blame an individual, but to improve service." This point of educating instead of blaming seems to me important. Nothing stultifies one more than being blamed. Moreover, if the question is, Who is to blame? perhaps each will want to place the blame on some- one else, or, on the other hand, one may try to shield his fellow worker. In either case the attempt is to hide the error, and if this is done, the error cannot be corrected. And it is true of executives also, as well as of operators, that mistakes should serve as the opportunity for further development of the individual, only in the case of the executive it will probably be a matter of self-training encouraged by an upper executive.

Another way in which an organization of this kind gives scope for the development of individuality is that in the cross- functioning a man is constantly meeting his equals in position —the head of a division, the head of another division, or a subhead, another subhead. And this, for one thing, gives a man a much greater sense of responsibility, for when you are constantly in contact with those above you, there is a tendency to think that the man over you will bear the brunt of the responsibility. To be sure, you bear it for those under you, but it is all too easy to pass it on up the line.

Another evidence that one of the aims of that telephone company is to develop the individuality of its executives was the amount of independence of thinking I seemed to find. I am speaking of independence of thinking in regard to daily management, not in regard to company policies. Moreover, a great deal of thinking seemed to go into decisions. Two executives made a great point of this to me. They said that things were not sprung on them; they were expected to bring to the conferences the best thinking of which they were capable.

In talking of the conferences between departments, I asked, "What takes the place of authority in all these conferences of parallel heads?" And the reply came instantly: "Sportsmanship. Our method of organization depends for its success on the good sportsmanship of the executives. I [traffic manager] say to the wire chief, 'I fell down on that.' "

One of the higher officials of the company said to me: "The kind of management we are aiming at is management with authority all down the line, as contrasted with management by edict from a central source. The latter kind of management—by edict from a central source—consists in carrying out that central edict whether or not it is wise, as the soldier who obeys orders literally is the satisfactory soldier. We are trying to teach our men what their jobs are with the idea that they shall use their brains, their discretion, having in mind certain fundamental principles. We teach people what their job is, and then insist that they shall exercise the authority and responsibility that goes with that job instead of relying on the fellow above them."

It occurs to me that I have not yet told you why it took me three-quarters of an hour to get my bank. One trunk line was out of order. The chief operator ought to have thought of that and tried another, which was what was done by the superintendent who finally got my number. I was interested to know whether that information ever reached that chief operator. I was told that it did. I also wanted to know whether the exchange manager ever knew that someone had spent eight minutes trying unsuccessfully to get his office. I discovered then that I ought not to have called the exchange manager, as he has nothing to do with the public, which I did not know. I was told, nevertheless, that this information did reach him. In fact, I was very much struck with the way the two superintendents of the company involved in this very slight and unimportant matter handled the case. Their object did not seem to be to appease me, a subscriber; they evidently wished to use the occurrence to improve service.

I am aware that I am running the risk of criticism from those who complain of our telephone service in speaking thus favourably of the organization of a telephone company. I am willing to run that risk, for it seems to me that anyone who has looked into the difficulties and complexities of telephone management, both on the mechanical and the personal side, will not make severe strictures on telephone service.

VIII

THE INFLUENCE OF EMPLOYEE REPRESENTATION IN A REMOULDING OF THE ACCEPTED TYPE OF BUSINESS MANAGER[1]

In order to discuss this subject, we have first to consider what we mean by "employee representation," for it has meant, and still means, very different things to different people.

Inadequate Concepts of "Employee Representation"

Many think of employee representation merely as a sop to labour—to quote a phrase I have seen, "a concession to turbulent labour." I object to this concession theory. I do do not see why workers, or any of us, should be given "concessions," "privileges." If employee representation is sound organization, sound management, let us have it. If it is not, we do not wish it, for labour will in the long run be most benefited by the best management.

Again, many think of employee representation as providing a procedure for collective bargaining. The bargaining which has taken place between employers and trade unions is now to take place between employers and employee representatives. But this is not an entirely different method of dealing with labour. If the basis and the purpose of employee representation are collective bargaining, then the qualities of management required are not so very different from those which have always been required—those which help you to get the best in a bargain. But, and as it seems to me happily, the conception of employee representation as the field for

---

[1] Although the technically so-called "Employee Representation Plan" has been outlawed in the United States, the principles and procedures thereof discussed by Miss Follett in this paper and permeating her philosophy of industrial relations are as sound and practicable to-day as ever; we are therefore including this paper as it was originally given. See note, p. 117; this paper was presented on May 6th, 1926.

collective bargaining is yielding a little, only a little as yet, to the conception of employee representation as an opportunity for joint determination.[2]

It is yielding to this conception even where the term "collective bargaining" is retained. The plan adopted by the Baltimore and Ohio Railroad, and since extended to other roads, is called "union-management co-operation," and in descriptions of this plan we find the word "co-operation" employed again and again. Yet at the same time it is called an extension of collective bargaining. That is the title of an article by B. M. Jewell, President of the railway employees department, published by the American Federation of Labour—"Recent Extension of Collective Bargaining." In that article Mr. Jewell states, "Co-operation is the essence of collective bargaining." We cannot think this literally true, for the process of co-operation is, strictly speaking, very different from the process of bargaining. Yet it is obvious how this use of words has come about.

Collective bargaining is taken as an expression which indicates an accepted method of contact between employers and employees, and then the aim is that this contact should be a co-operative one. But I deplore the language. While it is serving its purpose as a useful step because we get thereby the continuity we must believe in, and because it has its tactical use as the banner under which labour has improved its position so greatly, and also because it has a very real use in its implication that labour and management meet in a sense as equals—a hard-won victory which labour should not relinquish—still, the idea of bargaining is a survival of anything but a co-operative attitude and must in time, I think, be abandoned. Indeed, Otto S. Beyer, consulting engineer of the railway employees department, says that the joint conferences set up by the union-management co-operation plan are not for bargaining in the narrow sense of the

[2] *Cf. The New State*, p. 114: "Even collective bargaining is only a milestone on the way to the full application of the group principle. It recognizes . . . that some adjustment between the interests of capital and labour is possible, but it is still 'bargaining.' . . . We see now the false psychology underlying compromise and concession. . . . Nothing will ever truly settle differences but synthesis."

term; that for this there is other machinery. This slight discrepancy of statement on the part of the advocates of the Baltimore and Ohio plan shows us the transition stage in which we find ourselves to-day. Indeed, I have been rather amused at the fact that I have had to rewrite this paper three times in order to keep up with current events. Things have been happening faster than I could get their significance down on paper.

Another view of employee representation is the extremely restricted one that it exists primarily as a method of forestalling "trouble," as a sort of lubricating oil. It is indeed true that with employee representation you do get fewer kicks or, to put it more elegantly, you have a more smoothly running operating machine, and that is an excellent objective. Moreover, it does mark an advance in organization through its method of dealing with grievances, for it recognizes the right to make complaints. The worker who makes a complaint not only is not penalized, but machinery is provided by which his sense of justice is more likely to be satisfied. And this method has usually some educational value as well as that of settling the matter in dispute.

Yet employee representation as anticipating trouble, as adjusting grievances, is not what is changing management so greatly. Moreover, this view implies that employee representation makes management easier, whereas, as a matter of fact, it makes it harder. Take wage cuts, for example. Compare the method of making an arbitrary decision and posting notices of wage cuts with the method employed under employee representation, where wage cuts are not only discussed with employees, but where a joint investigation is often made of cost of living and of the condition of the industry. No; employee representation makes things harder for management except in the sense that whatever makes your plant more efficient and its running more harmonious does in the end make management easier. Autocracy is, of course, always for the moment the easiest way of governing—in your household or in your shop.

What are some of the other objectives given for employee

representation? One of the most common is, as expressed by one writer, "to provide a double-track channel of communication for exchange of information, opinions, and desires." This is indeed of great value. The managers have not known, and have had no way of knowing, enough of the desires, conditions, aspirations of the workers, and the workers have known very little, if anything, either of the purposes of the company or of its problems. To provide, therefore, some way for managers to get the workers' point of view and for workers to get the managers' point of view was certainly a necessary step. Yet this is not the greatest value of employee representation. And the double track is at least an unfortunate metaphor, for it does not imply that meeting and readjustment of the two points of view which is the important thing about employee representation. It is obvious, too, that this mere communication does not require an entirely different type of manager. He has, to be sure, to be more open-minded than the old-fashioned manager, more willing to listen to labour, and that does, I realize, mean for many employers a pretty big change. Still it is, and always has been, an essential of management that it should be able and willing to get all the information and light it could from all quarters. The fact about employee representation that is remoulding management is that it requires, not merely the giving and receiving of information, but a uniting of information, of opinion, of judgment—a wholly different matter.

Another view of employee representation which affects our question is that which sees it as a branch of what is called personnel relations. It is often called a solution of human problems, an experiment in human relations. I do not at all agree with this view. Employee representation should be considered as an aspect of organization engineering. It should not be thought of as something added on to any scheme of organization in order to facilitate relations with labour. It should be an integral part of a certain plan of organization, a plan of organization resting on certain fundamental principles.

Still another view of employee representation considers it primarily as a method of getting the consent of employees to certain decisions with the expectation that the workers will then be more likely to co-operate heartily in carrying them out. Those who hold this view consider that to his other gifts the manager must now add that of persuasion, that he has to be able to present company policies to Works Councils or joint committees in such a way that the workers will be persuaded to accept them. I agree partly with this, but not wholly. The most progressive view of employee representation to-day, as of democracy, is not consent of the governed, but participation. Some of us, indeed, think that consent is a thoroughly overrated matter. An able writer on industrial questions says that everyone will agree that the free man is the consenting man. I cannot agree to that. To say "Yes" implies that the alternative is to say "No," and there is not much freedom there. Men were supposed to be politically free because they had the vote. Even if employee representation plans gave much more power to employees than at present, even if the employee representatives voted on every· thing, "consented" to everything, that would not make them free. The vote is a deceptive business altogether. How often we used to see a tiny child driving with his father made happy by being allowed to hold the end of the reins. The vote makes many people happy in the same way; they think they are driving when they are not.

Moreover, consent is sometimes a matter in which managers deceive themselves. It is possible for consent to be so perfunctory that managers are willing to give the workers a vote on many more matters than they would really yield control of. I know an institution where this takes place. The director says to his staff: "We will have democracy here. You will vote on everything." But I have never known his subordinates vote against anything he proposed. Such unanimity seems to me suspicious.

Everyone talks to-day of co-operation, but there is no way of making consent spell co-operation. You have to have participation before you can get co-operation. What I said about pluralistic responsibility in the preceding lecture shows us the something more than consent. One of the very encouraging things about business practice to-day is that in some instances workers are being given a genuine participation in the control of industry.

Many thoughtful people, who have welcomed employee representation as a measure of what they have called industrial democracy, have considered that its greatest promise lies in the fact that it indicates on the part of management a recognition of the "rights" of labour. I do not find the greatest promise of employee representation in this, but in the fact that management has seen that an enterprise can be more successfully run by securing the co-operation of the workers. The "rights of labour," the "rights of capital"—these are barren expressions as usually employed. Yet I do not wish wholly to discard the expression "rights of labour," for in some degree it indicates a growing sense of justice towards labour. With many a business man, however autocratic he is by nature, however autocratically he conducts his business, there is an increased recognition of the different status in business which is coming to labour.

Another view of employee representation, and one which I think particularly unfortunate, or rather, not so much a view as a use to which it is sometimes put, is when it is employed to avoid managerial responsibility. When managers have a grave problem they should never avoid trying to solve it or shirk the onus of the possible consequences of their decision by handing it over to employee representatives. I once heard two heads of departments discussing something on which they could not agree. At last one of them said, in some heat and exasperation, "Oh, well, take it to your employee representatives." He was in that instance obviously avoiding responsibility instead of continuing the discussion, or the necessary study, long enough to discover what both could agree on as sound policy. But as I have said before, and want to say again and again, whatever managerial problems you have must be squarely met. If there is any weakness in organization or management, it can never be remedied by making the responsibility for it cover a larger area.

Thus far I have been giving some of the current conceptions of employee representation with which I do not wholly agree. I do not say that I think they are wrong views. Employee representation certainly does help oil the wheels, and it is a good thing that it should. There is something to be said for bargaining inside the shop rather than outside. As an exchange of information and opinions employee representation has great value. To get the consent of the governed is better than not to get the consent of the governed. I think the interests of the worker need protecting. Yet these are all, it seems to me, only partial views. I wish now to consider employee representation, not as bridging a gap here and there, not as a concession to labour or as a help to management, but as part of a sound scheme of organization.

Employee Representation as Part of a Sound Scheme of Organization in the Application of Functional Power

As we said in the preceding paper, one of the basic principles of organization was a pluralistic responsibility; that authority and responsibility should not depend on hierarchy of rank, but that they should go with function. This principle should be applied to labour as well as to executives. As we saw before, there were companies whose executives were not thinking so much of one executive being "over" another as that each man had a different task for which he was responsible, that men exercised authority, not in virtue of their place in an ascending scale, but in virtue of what they were doing, so now we see that this conception of functional authority can be applied, is being applied, to the workers, to the executives' relation to the workers. Some time that wife will seem very antiquated who said with pride, "John has seventy in his department that he's boss over."

One step towards this consummation will be taken when we begin to think of control in connection with concrete instances, in connection with the best way of handling actual cases, instead of talking so much about control in the abstract. Authority, power, control, sovereignty are big words, and much has been written about them by learned people in learned language. I was therefore much interested when a manufacturer said to me, pricking the bubble, I thought, of many a high-sounding phrase, "Management is really only sensible working arrangements." Someone else has told the story of a works committee meeting on a certain morning when there was no work ready for the piece-workers. If anyone had suggested that this was a question of management, the writer tells us, these particular employers would probably not have allowed the discussion which took place, but everyone was thinking of it merely as a question of how to make sure that the piece-workers should find the work ready for them when they came in the morning.

This story seems to me significant. This whole change in our thinking, from management as a dominant force to management as sensible working arrangements, gives us a new outlook on the worker. When labour asks for control, it should be asking only for what goes with its function. One of the tasks of organization is to find what that is.

Another task of organization is to join managerial capacity of worker with managerial capacity of executive.[3] Functional authority, pluralistic responsibility, requires conference as its method. And genuine conference requires on the part of management very different qualities from those demanded by bargaining, with its concealments, its use of economic power, its aim of compromise. Here in the joint committees executives and workers meet, or should meet to get from each other the special knowledge and experience each has; also to get to know each other's points of view, desires, aims. More than this, they should meet to pool their knowledge

[3] Cf. The New State, p. 119: "Workshop committees should be encouraged, not so much because they remove grievances, etc., as because in the joint workshop committee, managers and workers are learning to act together. Industrial democracy is a process, not a growth. The joint control of industry may be established by some fiat, but it will not be the genuine thing until the process of joint control is learned."

174

and experience, to unite their desires and aims. For this we need the kind of men who are able to make vital contacts, able both to give themselves and to learn from others. This means, first, more open methods than we have had in the past. The old managerial tactics of suppressing knowledge, of keeping most managerial matters within the executive circle, must disappear if we are to have successful employee representation.

Secondly, the conference method demands from managers the ability to explain. And I mean by this not merely or chiefly the ability to state a case, although that also is valuable, but even more than that, the power to analyse a situation. Of course, the man who does the analysing reaps as great an advantage as his hearers. The fact that managers have to explain to employee representatives a good deal about the running of the business makes them look at some of their problems a little differently. If they cannot make out a good case, they see that there are things to be changed or greater efforts to be made. At any rate, they see their problems more clearly when they have to meet employee representatives and place certain situations before them. In a study on employee representation, it is stated that it is coming to be the practice in many manufacturing companies for the chief executive of the plant to report regularly, usually at the monthly meeting attended by the employee representatives, on the conduct of the business—new orders, trend of manufacturing costs, and the like. We cannot doubt that this makes a new demand on the chief executive far beyond that of merely presenting his case.

In the third place, the conference method demands from managers the ability to make of differences a unifying, not a disruptive, factor, to make them constructive rather than destructive, to unite all the different points of view, not only in order to have a more contented personnel, but in order to get incorporated into the service of the company all that everyone has to contribute. There are only two things to do with energy, the inventiveness of your workers—let it gather force against you or for you. It seems more sensible to make use of it. And in the conference committees you have your chance.[4]

In order to utilize this opportunity, there must be new attitudes toward conference on the part of both workers and executives. Business agents have been sent from the unions to meet employers, and in these meetings there has been on both sides the fight attitude. The business agent is supposed to be a skilled negotiator. But the methods of those who come to negotiate are wholly different from those who come to confer. It is possible for the negotiator's attitude completely to stultify proceedings in a conference.

I sat once on a wage board, two of the labour members of which were agents from two trade unions. The board failed. And I am sure the reason was that these two members came to fight, and could not perceive quickly enough that that was not what was required in this case, that they were defeating their own aims. For we had not met for negotiation. We had been asked by the Massachusetts Board of Labour and Industries to see whether we could come to some agreement, after an investigation of cost of living and the condition of the industry. But these two members showed no interest either in cost of living or the condition of the industry. They had come to bargain. We could make no headway against this attitude, and these members lost for the girls of that industry the increased wages they should have had and which it would have been easy to secure for them by the conference method.

To change the traditional fight attitude into a co-operative attitude is no small task for the executives who meet the workers in conference. They have, of course, what is sometimes forgotten, to acquire it themselves first. It has been often said that one of the chief aims of employee representation is to secure a partnership spirit. But when this is said, the speaker is almost always thinking of a partnership spirit on the part of the workers. It is just as essential that the

---

[4] *Cf. Creative Experience*, p. 82: "Some people want to give the workmen a share in carrying out the purpose of the plant and do not see that that involves a share in creating the purpose of the plant."

executives should have this spirit else they would be like the man who wrote to a Christian Scientist: "There is disharmony between my wife and me. Will you please give my wife treatments?"

To sum up this point, I should say that as we have been told over and over again that trade-union development requires managers to learn the skilful use of bargaining, now we have to emphasize the fact that the employee representation movement requires managers to learn the skilful use of the conference method.

The fact that there is to-day a growing appreciation of this on the part of both employers and employees is a promising sign. One of the most interesting things that happened in America during the year 1925 was the attitude taken by the American Federation of Labour, under the leadership of Mr. Green, toward union-management co-operation. In 1925, at the American Federation of Labour Convention at Atlantic City, resolutions were adopted which in effect declared that "labour is ready to co-operate with ownership and management in eliminating waste in industry and generally in improving and regularizing industrial operations." When in December of that year Mr. Green spoke before the Taylor Society, he said:

"Labour is willing to make its contribution to assist management and to bring about the right solution of problems dealt with by management. . . . The mental attitude of labour toward industry and industrial processes is undergoing revision and readjustment. . . . Labour is understanding more and more that high wages and tolerable conditions of employment can be brought about through excellency in service, the promotion of efficiency, and the elimination of waste. . . . Chief among the ideals of labour is the development of cordial relations between the workers and management. The workers believe that through understanding and co-operation the best interests of all those associated with industry can be served."[5]

Mr. Green said more than this. I have taken sentences here and there in one of the most significant utterances of

[5] William Green, *Bulletin of the Taylor Society*, December, 1925, pp. 244-5.

the century in regard to industrial relations. Significant because we hear nothing here of the efficacy of fighting, but everything of the value of mobilizing all the associated productive powers of industry into a sustained, impelling force for the development of industry and the equitable distribution of its rewards. In so many words, Mr. Green speaks of a "contact between management and workers which is free from suspicion, antagonism, and hatred." Already a committee representing labour is being formed to co-operate with management in a study of waste in production.

Significance of the Parallel Development of Business Management as a Profession and Employee Representation

The vitality of the employee representation movement, the interest in industrial relations and personnel management, is to be accounted for in a number of ways. We have come to the end of our quick exploitation of our natural resources. We got rich quickly and easily without paying much attention to ways and means. Success to-day depends far more on organization and management than it has in the past, depends partly on management's getting all the help it can from the workers. On the workers' side there is the wish to share in the wealth American industry is producing. There is also the general movement throughout the world for self-determination. We might add to these causes for the progress of the employee representation movement the more and more complete separation between ownership and management, the fact that our sellers' market is becoming a buyers' market, and the fact that the United States is becoming increasingly a credit nation.

I think, therefore, we may say that, though the employee representation movement began partly as a concession, partly to make things go more smoothly, partly to counter trade unions, to-day it is considered by many men as an asset, as an essential part of sound organization. But it needs a certain type of manager to make it an asset. The fact that employee representation and the study and development of business management are two parallel movements seems to me very significant. At the same time that a share in management is being given to workers, we find that there is a rapidly increasing sense of the need for executives with a training which shall enable them to turn to account labour's possible contribution to management. And what I want to emphasize particularly is that the willingness to do this, the clearness of vision which makes a manager see the advantage of doing this, is not enough. He must be expert in the methods which will enable him to deal with case after case as they arise in labour-management co-operation. The primary thing he has to learn about his dealings with labour is not how to "treat" with labour, but how to use labour's ability, yes, even labour's aspirations, as someone has pointed out, as an asset to the enterprise.

Two facts stand out: (1) organized labour has become aware that it can offer substantial assistance to management; (2) management on its side has awakened to an appreciation of this, and wishes to understand how to use such assistance. Management sees also that it is not a question of consulting labour in emergencies, but that "the intelligence of labour can be mobilized in a systematic and sustained way to promote the success of an industry."

Employee representation is indicative of certain fundamental changes in the thinking of our times. It is in these changes—something going on in the thinking of people, not in certain events connected with industrial or international affairs—that I find our greatest hope in the muddle we have got into all over the world in these early years of the twentieth century.

A good illustration of this change in our thinking was seen in the recent controversy between Arthur Nash and the Amalgamated Clothing Workers of America. At the beginning of this controversy, the Amalgamated thought Nash simply a hypocrite going round talking of the Golden Rule and paying his men less than the going trade-union wage. Nash did not think any better of the Amalgamated. There seemed at first little chance of these two coming to any agreement satisfactory to both sides. But certain people who thought this controversy might be an opportunity for a genuine integration of interest arranged a number of conferences which brought together friends of Mr. Nash and friends of the Amalgamated for discussion of the issues involved. The men who arranged these conferences were present at them, men who were interested in, who were, one might say practising, the new type of thinking of which I am speaking. Their endeavour was to find and bring out the real values on both sides in order to prepare a way for the joining of these values. For instance, was it possible for the idealism which exists in Sidney Hillman, along with his shrewdness, to find any common ground with what sincerity, what genuine religious feeling, there was in Mr. Nash's protestations? And so on and so on. I am not going to give a history of those conferences—this is not the place for that—but merely to point out the result. When Nash and Sidney Hillman finally met, that meeting was successful because the new type of thinking which had been injected into the matter had meant an interpenetration of values. It was seen that the Nash business could be run so as to produce the values which he cared for and also the values which the Amalgamated cared for. That a genuine interpenetration of thinking took place was shown by the following incident. After his shop had been unionized, Mr. Nash, with the Vice-President of the company and some representatives from the Amalgamated, sat down to look over the pay roll. Discovering that all the wages were below the union scale, the Vice-President suggested that the pay be raised. Mr. Nash said: "No; these people have just been unionized; they must see the value of the union. We must let the union ask to have the pay raised." Here we have an employer who had been thought of as caring for publicity, for reputation, deliberately forgoing the credit of raising the pay.

I am speaking of this controversy because it is an illustration of a change in the method of thinking which seems to me one of the most important things that is happening in the world. Its connection with our present subject is that here

I find what I think the most essential qualification for management necessitated by employee representation, namely, the ability to do this kind of thinking—the willingness to search for the real values involved on both sides and the ability to bring about an interpenetration of these values.

A second change in our thinking is the full recognition that labour can make constructive contributions to management. We see this in many cases, but nowhere more conspicuously than in the success of the Baltimore and Ohio Railroad plan. At a meeting of the Taylor Society held in February, 1926, in conjunction with several other societies of railway men and mechanical and industrial engineers, the subject of the evening was "Union-Management Co-operation in the Railway Industry." The speeches reveal much, by implication, of the demands made on managers to-day by labour's co-operation in management. Under the Baltimore and Ohio plan it is distinctly understood that the joint conferences are not for the consideration of grievances. Complaints and the adjustment of disputes are handled by the machinery provided by the wage agreement which exists between the union and the management. It was stated by Otto S. Beyer that "the nature of the subjects discussed at the co-operative conferences, in keeping with the basic principles underlying them, are constructive in nature." Mr. Beyer's list of subjects, which I have not space for here, is very interesting.

The chief interest to me in the acceptance of the fact that labour can make constructive contributions to management is the principle at its very heart and core, that management is not a fixed quantity. When we used to talk of "sharing" management, it was because we tended to think then of management as a fixed quantity. We thought that if someone was given a little, that amount had to be taken from someone else. But the fact is that the successful business is one which is always increasing management throughout the whole enterprise in the sense of developing initiative, invention. Any manager who is looking with far-seeing eyes to the progress of his business wants not so much to locate authority as to increase capacity. The aim of employee representation, because it should be the aim of every form of organization, should be not to share power, but to increase power, to seek the methods by which power can be increased in all. The real reason that labour rebels is not the money reason given by the economists, is not, moreover, the psychologists' instincts of self-respect and the like, but that the fundamental law of the universe is the increase of life, the development of human powers, and either you keep yourself in obedience to that law or for you the universe breaks around you and is shattered.[6]

[6] *Cf. The New State*, p. 119: "The labour question is—Is the war between capital and labour to be terminated by fight and conquest or by learning how to function together? . . . I believe that the end of the wars of nations and of the war between labour and capital will come in exactly the same way: by making the nations into one Group. . . . Then we shall give up the notion of 'antagonisms,' which belong to a static world, and see only differences—that is, that which is capable of integration."

IX

THE PSYCHOLOGY OF CONTROL[1]

LAST summer in England I was interested in two letters on the coal strike sent to the London *Times* by two bishops. One said that we must not confuse economic and moral issues, that the coal strike was a purely economic issue and should be treated as such. A few weeks later another bishop wrote to *The Times*, not in answer to the first, but independently, and said that the coal strike would never be settled if it was not understood that the issues involved were not economic but moral issues.

Undepartmentalized Thinking—Emphasis on the Whole as a Unit of Study

I was interested in these letters because I am coming more and more to think that we cannot departmentalize our thinking in this way, that we cannot think of economic principles and ethical principles, but that underneath all our thinking there are certain fundamental principles to be applied to all our problems.

Let me give another illustration. A man, the owner of a store, marked a certain grade of women's stockings which he had been selling for $1 a pair down to 87 cents, because he thought the price had been too high. His son reported later that the reduction had spoiled the sale of that item, that customers felt that something must be the matter with it; they wanted a "dollar stocking" as they had always had. Now I do not know what the rest of that story was, but one

---

[1] This paper was presented in March, 1927, and, with the three succeeding papers, reprinted from *Psychological Foundations of Management*, Henry C. Metcalf, *Editor*, A. W. Shaw Company (now McGraw Hill Book Publishing Company), 1927.

can imagine the son, being modern, talking of the "psychology" of the customer, while one can imagine that the father, brought up in an age which did not talk psychology in season and out, and being an upright, conscientious business man, was thinking of something he called an "economic" price. Here again I should like to ask: Could not that problem have been solved by some principle which was not wholly psychological or wholly economic? Here again, would it not be possible to undepartmentalize our thinking? I think we should do this—undepartmentalize our thinking— in regard to every problem that comes to us. I am going to say before the end of my talk how I think this could have been done in the stocking controversy. I do not think we have psychological and ethical and economic problems. We have human problems with psychological, ethical, and economic aspects, and as many more as you like, legal often. I know a lady who asked her maid to lift a large pot of ferns from one place to another in the room. The maid replied that the lady was stronger than she was and she thought she should do the lifting. Here you see was a problem with an economic aspect and a psychological and an ethical. It could not have been satisfactorily solved by any one of these disciplines alone.

If we have to undepartmentalize our thinking and get down to principles that are fundamental for all the social sciences, fundamental indeed for all the life processes, surely we have to do that especially for the subject of this paper. The aim of organization engineering is control through effective unity. If, therefore, we wish to understand control, we should begin by trying to understand the nature of unities. And as our thinking on this subject has of recent years been greatly enriched by the thinking in other fields, I want to speak briefly of what we are learning of unities from biologists, psychologists, philosophers. Professor Henderson, a biological chemist, tells us that we have to study a whole as a whole, not only through an analysis of its constituents. He says: "The old physiologists described the circulation of the blood, the beating of the heart, or the properties of gastric juice, and could tell you separate facts, but could not connect these facts so as to make a satisfactory picture of the organism." Again he says: "Physiology is far from seeing the organism as a whole yet, but we can put together the carriage of oxygen, of carbonic acid, the alkalinity of the blood, and see how these three are parts of one process. We can study how this bit of integration is itself an adaptation." Professor Henderson is always looking on the functioning of a whole as the adapting and integrating of parts. (Is not that the chief job of the organization engineer?) And he goes so far as to say—after stating the fact that doctors used to study separate diseases but now tend to study man as a whole —that this may be the beginning of a new science, the science of human biology.

This emphasis on a whole as a unit of study we see in many places. Dr. Cannon's physiology is the physiology of the integrated organism rather than of analysed parts. J. B. S. Haldane points out that the metabolic activity within the organism is a "whole" activity, the different sides of which are indissolubly associated, instead of being, as was formerly thought, isolable physical or chemical processes. A very suggestive treatment of wholes has come from those who have been working at the integrative action of the nervous system. Sherrington has shown us convincingly that the simple reflex, which has been treated as an isolable and isolated mechanism, is an artificial abstraction, that the nervous system functions as a whole. Kempf, a psycho-biologist, deals with what he calls "whole personalities." He tells us of an integrative unity, of a functional whole. Many psychologists to-day are taking the idea of "organization," "integration," "total activities of the individual," as the pivotal point in their psychology. (Here again are words and phrases with which we are coming to be very familiar in business management.) The *Gestalt* school gives us what is called explicitly the doctrine of wholes, which denies that physical, psychical, or social situations are made up of elements in a plus-plus relation. The whole, they tell us, is determined, not only by its constituents, but by their relation to one another. This is not new doctrine, but, being put forward as the cardinal feature of a whole school of psychology, it is having a large influence.[2]

Moreover, those engaged in personality studies have been especially influenced by the *Gestalt* school, and they are having a direct influence on industry through personnel directors, employment managers, industrial psychologists. Their enlarged understanding of the nature of unities has affected hiring, promotion, and dismissal, for this view of wholes rather than of parts is what now guides us in our estimates of individuals. We used to describe people by naming a number of characteristics—he is selfish and he is so and so and so and so. But now we know that we do not get a very correct idea of a man thus described. We know that it is the way these characteristics are related that makes a man's personality. Aggressiveness in Roosevelt[3] may mean something quite different from aggressiveness in someone else. It is certain that biographies of the future will be very different from those of the past because of the larger understanding of this point.

Again, consider the way we now use intelligence tests. Here is one list: "reasoning ability, imagination, verbal memory, incidental learning, judgment, learning in specific fields of knowledge." It used to be thought sufficient to get percentages for each of these. Now we ask how they modify one another. If a man is over-confident (or over-cautious, either) that may affect his reasoning ability so that his judgments may not be so good as one might expect from the way his reasoning ability was rated.

All this is reflected in placement or promotion in industry. The men who hire have discovered that skill is often overestimated in determining industrial value. They ask (if they are up to their job) what that man's interest in his job is and how that affects his skill. They ask also his ability to work in a group or get along with his foreman, and how that

---

[2] *Cf. Creative Experience,* Chapter IV, "Experience in the Light of Recent Psychology: The *Gestalt* Concept."

[3] Theodore Roosevelt.

affects his skill. Of course, it is equally true the other way round, that his degree of skill may be affecting his other qualities. He may, for instance, take so much interest in doing his work well that any resentment he may have against foreman or fellow worker gets smoothed out.

The importance of noting the relative significance of the different factors concerned has been pointed out by Cyril Burt, in his *Study in Vocational Guidance*, and also by Dr. Yoakum when speaking at these Bureau of Personnel Administration Conferences.[4] And I think it is Dr. Yoakum who has also told us of another unity which it is necessary to consider. The personnel manager has to think of the efficiency ratings of the man, of the job analysis, of the promotion policies of the company, and of production and sales figures; and it is recognized to-day by some of the best personnel managers that the crux of their job is to understand the relations between these factors.

Let me give one more illustration from the field of industrial psychology. Fatigue studies used to consider the monotony of the task and its effect on the individual. Now a study is made of the different modes of expenditure of energy natural to that individual. In other words, we are always studying the total situation. All industrial psychologists feel that Dr. Mayo[5] has added a very valuable contribution to their work by his insistence on "the total situation." And we must remember that we should always mean by that not only trying to see every factor that influences the situation, but even more than that, the relation of these factors to one another.

This is the most important, far the most important, trend in the thinking of to-day. In a certain hospital there is a consultation clinic for the man of moderate means. For the sum of $10 he can be examined by specialist after specialist. But there is no one doctor who reads the opinions of all these specialists to see what they amount to all together. The

[4] *Psychological Foundations of Management*, Henry C. Metcalf, *Editor*, A. W. Shaw Company (McGraw Hill), 1927; Chapters II–VI, by C. S. Yoakum.

[5] *Ibid.*, Chapters XVI–XVII, by Elton Mayo.

reports of the neurologist, the radiologist, and the others are forwarded to the doctor who has sent the patient to the hospital, and he says, "What on earth does all this mean? What does it add up to?" But certain doctors are hoping to remedy this defect, and that is yet another indication of the growing appreciation of wholes.

We see this in almost every field of study. You will find it very explicitly stated in an article in *Science*, on "Emergent Evolution and the Social," written by Professor William Morton Wheeler, an eminent zoologist who has written on the social life of insects. I do not think he has sufficient grounds for his conclusions in that article, but the first part of the article is an interesting statement of the principle we are here considering.

Again, another illustration from .zoology, an article on wild mice in the *Journal of Mammalogy*, shows that the local distribution of wild mice is not controlled by any single factor of the physical environment—by climatic conditions, or food and water supply, or antagonism between species, or nesting material—but is due to the relation of the mice to the biotic community as a whole of which they are members. This relating of the "behaviour of animals to the environmental complex" marks an interesting correspondence in the thinking in different fields. It has exactly the same significance as Dr. Mayo's "total situation."

In the field of anthropology, Malinowski says cultures are wholes, and you cannot alter any feature without producing repercussions which alter the whole.

In philosophy, our greatest thinkers have given us more than indications of this view of unity. Among living philosophers, I think Professor Whitehead is contributing most to our understanding of this truth.

To turn to the field of the social sciences, we find in our study of government the same truth—namely, that unities are determined not only by their constituents but by the relation of these constituents to one another. We see, for instance, how the realignments of nations change each nation. As the biologist tells us that every organism has a form or structure which is determined by the way the elements are placed in that structure, so we find on the social level, too, that rearrangement is always more than rearrangement; it changes the character of the things arranged.[6] The regrouping of European nations has its effect on each nation.

In the study of government we find many examples which throw light on unities—genuine unities, pseudo-unities, attempted unities. We have not time for the many, but one may point to the League of Nations. One might point to the crop of autocrats which southern Europe seems to be reaping. I believe the cause of that lies in the fact that these nations find that unity is necessary and that they have not yet found out how to get it in a better way, or rather how to get nearer a genuine unity.

Some political scientists make the mistake of considering co-ordination and balance synonymous. Most of the political pluralists do this.[7] The guild socialists tell us that their co-ordinating congress is an arbitrator, or court of appeal, to keep the balance between co-ordinate autonomies. According to the doctrine I am expressing, "co-ordinate autonomies" is an impossible expression. You cannot have co-ordinate autonomies because co-ordination is the building up of a functional total.

One of the most interesting indications in the field of government of the appreciation of the principle we are considering is the present effort in England to functionalize the departments of government and to provide for cross-relations between the departments which shall bring about a closer and more effective unity, not an arbitrary or artificial unity based on the dictum of constitution or law, but a functional unity.

[6] Cf. *Creative Experience*, p. 171: "Yet while I think that all talk of the sacrifice of interests is ruinously sentimental, there is something else which is an essential part of any unifying process, and that is a revaluation of interests. For individuals and nations alike, this is the course of progress. We wish to join the League of Nations when a revaluation of our interests shows us that it is to our advantage to do so."

[7] Cf. *The New State*, Chapters XXVIII–XXXII, for a full discussion of Political Pluralism.

To take another illustration from the field of government, many people think that democracy means all taking part. If it means only that, I do not believe in democracy. It is the fruitful relating, the interacting of parts, a co-functioning, that we want. We must provide the organization necessary for such interactions and also recognize and control those which we now have. To deny that they exist is a basic error. Professor Dewey says that it is the role of the public in government (I am using his words) to intervene not continuously but at certain junctures. He explains the phrase "not continuously" by saying that the public has its own life to lead, it is preoccupied with its own work and amusements. I do not think that there is any possible way in which Professor Dewey can support this statement. We have our own work? As a Vermont farmer, I go out and shear my sheep, but at Washington they are putting a tariff on wool— I hope. My amusements? I go to the movies and at the same time the government is censoring them—I fear. But I must not go into such questions as this. I have taken a moment for this only because I want to show that the basis for understanding the problems of political science is the same as the basis for understanding business administration—it is the understanding of the nature of integrative unities.

In economics, too, we find this same development in thinking. Ten or fifteen years ago we heard a great deal from certain economists about instincts; one instinct was to be satisfied thus and so, another by some other means. To-day I do not know any economist who is thinking in this way. They see that instincts interact, that the result depends on the way in which they interact.

We hear also from both economists and psychologists of a "want-system," by which they mean that we cannot satisfy one want or desire after another, that my different desires act on each other, and that the total want-system is different from the addition of separate wants. Their use of the word "system" is significant. They are using it in the technical sense in which biologists use the word, in the sense of organized activity. We are all coming to see that our lives are controlled not so much by certain "drives" or wants as by their relation to one another.

I think the general recognition of want-systems would do away with a great deal of unnecessary discussion. Arthur Pugh, one of the ablest of the trade-union leaders in England —some people think the ablest—said to me this summer, "It isn't more pay the workers are usually after; it is improvement in status." I do not suppose he could have meant that literally, so I suppose he meant to emphasize a want-system in which status has an important place. We know that the worker wants a good many things—security in his job, work that interests him, congenial companions, recognition of his special ability, decent work conditions. Now, these wants have some relation to each other; they form, in the words we are using, a structure, a pattern, a whole, a unity.

In another field, psychiatrists look for a complex, not a single cause. There has been a marked advance in psychiatry in this respect.

Again, the probation officer, too, recognizes wholes, or the environmental complex, to use the expression of the zoologist. He sees not only that a number of things are influencing the boy's life, but he tries to understand the way in which they are influencing one another.

Take an instance of a social worker. She is dealing with a girl of a difficult temperament who has a nagging stepmother, a job for which she is not fitted, and evening recreations of not the most wholesome character. The most successful social worker is not the one who deals with these one by one merely, but who sees their relation to one another. A more suitable job may change all the others and therefore the total.

I am emphasizing this matter of relation because, while it is customary now to speak of "the total situation," that phrase means to many people merely that we must be sure to get all the factors into our problem. For instance, some of the industrial psychologists who are using this phrase tell us that when a workman is grossly rude to his foreman we must not jump too quickly to the conclusion that he has an

habitually bad temper or an exasperating foreman; the cause
may have been a quarrel with his wife at breakfast. That
is, these psychologists are warning us that we must be sure
to get all the factors in. What I am emphasizing is not merely
the totalness of the situation, but the nature of the totalness.

I am taking some time to speak of the nature of unities
because if unity is the key-word for biology, psychology,
philosophy, the same thing, what we call co-ordination, is
certainly the crux of almost every problem the organization engineer or the business manager has to deal with. In
talking with organization engineers in both England and
America, I am always told that co-ordination is their most
important, as it is their most difficult problem. And they
are coming to understand co-ordination as the making of an
"integrative unity" (Kempf's expression). They know that
the parts of a business should so move together in their
reciprocally adjusting activities (almost Professor Henderson's phrase) that they make a working *unit*, not a congeries
of separate pieces. They are coming to see also that you do
not have co-ordination by two units existing harmoniously
side by side, that these units have to make a unity before
you can say that you have co-ordination. And they are also
coming to know, as the biologist and psychologist and
philosopher know, that we advance by progressively evolving unities.

The possible examples from business management of the
working of this fundamental principle are innumerable. In
considering any business problem, you always find that what
you have to consider in a situation is not all the factors one
by one, but also their relation to one another. This means,
among other things, that when a factor is added to or sub-
tracted from a situation, you have not that situation minus
or plus that factor, for all the rest will be changed. You
see it in a board of directors. One man leaves and all the
rest become a little different. The influence of that board
of directors as a total is not the same as it was minus that
man's influence, because his withdrawal, by changing
slightly every other man, has made the total different. Every

business man knows that the president of a company in relation to one board of directors may be very different from that same president in relation to another board.

An organization consultant, called in to find why a certain department in a business was not keeping pace with the rest of the business, told me he found the solution of the problem was not to change any one thing or any two or three things in that department, although that was what the board of directors had expected him to do. But what he suggested to the board was certain changes in the relation between the factors or sections of which the department was composed.

Take a situation made by credit conditions, customers' demand, output facilities, and workers' attitude. They all together make a certain situation, but they constitute that situation through their relation to one another. If you change one, usually some, if not all, of the others are changed.

I was very much interested in something the head of a large business said to me just the other day, since I began writing this paper. I will quote it, and while I am quoting please think of what the *Gestalt* school is telling us of a unity, that is not a plus-plus relation of parts. He said:

"If my heads of departments tell me that Department D and Department E are co-ordinated, and then I find that Department D and Department E are exactly the same as they were before, then I know that what I have been told is not true; they are not co-ordinated. If they have been co-ordinated, then the parts will be changed, that is, the practice of Department D will differ in some respects from what it was before co-ordination."

This statement contains a very profound truth, but it was a practical business man who made this statement, not a philosopher.

One might think that this is a statement affirming that the whole determines the parts as well as that the parts determine the whole, but that would not be strictly accurate. The same activity determines both parts and whole.

My illustrations serve, I hope, to show that the same fundamental principle holds good in various fields of study, namely, that the reciprocal activity of the parts changes the parts while it is creating the unity. That is the first point of this paper.

The Nature of Reciprocal Activity in Creating Unities

My second point concerns the nature of the interacting. If we could discover that, I think we should have arrived at something very fundamental. Suppose you have two factors, or I should prefer to say two activities, A and B, reciprocally influencing each other. The key to our problem lies in what we mean by reciprocally influencing. Do we mean all the ways in which A influences B, and all the ways in which B influences A? Reciprocal influencing means more than this. It means that A influences B, and that B, made different by A's influence, influences A, which means that A's own activity enters into the stimulus which is causing his activity. This is something like what on the physiological level has been called circular response, the full significance of which was well shown by Bok, the Dutch physiologist. In every situation our own activity is part of the cause of our activity. We respond to stimuli which we have helped to make. Capitalism is not responding to trade unionism but to the relation between itself and trade unionism.[8] As soon as we take any actual instance like that, we see how inadequate it would seem not to take this fact into consideration. It is the fact which is of the greatest importance for all consideration of conflict. I am never fighting you, but always you plus me, or, more accurately, the relation between you and me. France is not responding to Germany alone, because so much of Germany's activity has been brought about by the actions of France. The behaviour of France is not a function of the behaviour of Germany,

---

[8] Cf. *Creative Experience*, p. 67: "Let us take an illustration which involves all the points so far given:

The workman responds to
1. Employer: wages, share in profits or management, conditions of factory, etc.
2. General conditions: cost of living, etc.
3. His own desires, aspirations, standards of living, etc.
4. The relation between his responding and the above."

but of the interweaving between France and Germany. We need an understanding of this law for any situation where human beings are concerned. I think it is the key to history, law, economics, and to business administration.

Let us note this, too—When we say that the behaviour of France is a function of the interweaving between France and Germany, we are speaking of a unity which is not the result of an interweaving, but *is* the interweaving. Unity is always a process, not a product. I suppose that is really the pivotal point of this paper. Unless we are thinking wholly in terms of process, the statements I am making will be meaningless. With this in mind we see that when we say that the behaviour of France is a function of the interweaving between France and Germany, we are saying much more than that the parts are altering each other; we are saying also that the whole a-making is altering the parts.

Please notice that we have now carried our argument a step further. I have been saying that the whole is determined not only by its constituents, but by their relation to one another. I now say that the whole is determined also by the relation of whole and parts. Nowhere do we see this principle more clearly at work than in business administration. Production policy, sales policy, financial policy, personnel policy, influence one another, but the general business policy which is being created by the interweaving of these policies is all the time, even while it is in the making, influencing production, sales financial, and personnel policies. Or put it the other way round—the various departmental policies are being influenced by general policy *while* they are making general policy. This sounds like a paradox, but it is the truest thing I know. Business unifying must be understood as a process, not as a product. We have to become process-conscious. I believe that is the first essential to the understanding of business organization. We sometimes hear the question discussed whether general policy should dictate departmental policies or departmental policies contribute to general policy. There is a deeper truth than either of these, and that is this something which I am trying to express to you—namely, that it is the same activity which is making the whole and parts simultaneously. We never "put parts together" even when we think we do. We watch parts behaving together, and the way they behave together *is* the whole. I say "parts," and people often speak of "factors" or "elements" in a total, but when we use any of these words we must remember that we are talking of activities.

I wish I had time to show how this fundamental principle works on the personal level, but just let me recall what you have often noticed, that while the different characteristics which make up a personality are all the time influencing one another (I am selfish, but my degree and my kind of selfishness are determined partly by my other characteristics), while the different characteristics, I say, are all the time influencing one another, at the same time they are being influenced by the whole personality as it is at any one moment. My personality as a whole is influencing my selfishness, my aggressiveness. Next year if my personality as a whole is different, it will have a different influence on the different characteristics which make up my personality.

It is the same with business unities. I have just given the example of the influence of general policy on departmental policies, but there is no point in an industrial plant where this is not seen. If two department heads form a good working team, the kind of team they make will influence the activities of each. At the same time, the activities of each are relating themselves to each other to form the whole. When you put it in terms of yourself and Jones in the next room, it seems easy enough to understand, and yet we have here one of the most profound truths of philosophy. However, while it may be easy enough to understand in case of yourself and Jones, it is by no means so easy to understand when relations become more complex. When we do understand this more fully, it will be a big step forward for business organization.

But both in my illustrations from the social level and from the personal level, I have run the risk of presenting this idea to you in an over-simplified form. To avoid this danger, let me take some actual instance and run over it quickly. I am going to take the conflict which often occurs between a marketing co-operative association and its members over the question of violation of contract, and I am going to express this conflict in terms of desire, thus:

THE MARKETING CO-OPERATIVES WANT:	THE INDIVIDUAL FARMERS WANT:
1. To get enough cotton or tobacco or whatever the commodity may be to control the market.	1. Higher prices and a stabilized market.
2. To get enough money to pay overhead.	2. Easier credit.
3. To keep the goodwill of the farmers, so that they will not only fulfill their contracts this time because they must, but will sign up next time.	3. To avoid certain disastrous consequences of not selling independently this particular year.

My chief point in this illustration is that the process of forming a unity here is not that 1, 2, and 3 on the left-hand side interweave, and 1, 2 and 3 on the right-hand side interweave, and then these two unities join. Nothing could be further from life than this, for the interweaving between the left-hand and right-hand sides is going on at the same time that 1, 2 and 3 on each side are unifying, and, moreover, is influencing very greatly the unifying of 1, 2 and 3 on each side of the line. No study of any social situation will be adequate if it does not take this into account.

I have been speaking of the nature of the interacting which constitutes a unity. While we have not time to go very far into this process, I want to pause to note one feature of it, what I have called the evoking, that each calls out something from the other, releases something, frees something, opens the way for the expression of latent capacities and possibilities. This is a very important consideration for business management, for you have to call out all the capacities of everyone in your organization before you can unite these capacities. Evoking, releasing, is the foundation of co-ordination. In other words, you have to catch your hare before you cook him.

It is because of this necessity that we are now emphasizing education in the plant, education of both workmen and executives. It is not because of some vague idea that it is better for everyone to be educated, but, taking co-ordination as the central point of organization, we say to ourselves: What is the quality of that which we are going to unite? That is the initial step—to look first of all to that which is to be co-ordinated.

The Emergence of the Synthesis

We now come to the third point of this paper. Every social process has three aspects: the interacting, the unifying, and the emerging. But our consideration of the interacting has shown us that the interacting and unifying are one. Shall we now therefore consider the emerging? We have already done that. Because the emerging also is part of the same process. Still I am not expressing myself quite accurately when I speak of it as *part* of the process. These three—the interacting, the unifying, and the emerging—are not parts of a process in the sense of steps in a process. There is one simultaneous process, and these three are aspects of that process.

"Emerging" is the word which is being used more and more every day by scientists to denote the novelty wherever it appears in evolution. Morgan has told us of emergent evolution, Spaulding of creative synthesis, Broad of emergent vitalism. Emerging and the emergent seem to be the words most commonly used. They signify at once the something new, the progressive feature in the process. And these philosophers and scientists agree that the emergent pattern, the complex emergent whole, is formed by the interacting, the relating, of the constituent factors. This, too, we see every day in business administration. In situation after situation we find that when we have a progressive and successful policy it has resulted from what a scientist has called an "interactive accumulation," what I have called integration. Let me give an example.

I want to say first, however, that when I use these expressions of the scientists, like interactive accumulation, emerging, and the rest, I hope you understand that I am not trying to put everyday truths to you in a learned form. I am using these expressions because I am interested—more interested than in anything else in the world—in these correspondences in thinking between scientists, philosophers, and business managers, because such correspondences seem to me a pretty strong indication that we are on the right track. If people studying relations from such totally different angles come to the same conclusions, it seems to me of the greatest significance.

To return now to the example I was about to give you of integration. A purchasing agent suggests buying a material which is somewhat inferior which he says will do just as well for the purpose it is to be used for, and he can get it at a lower price than what he has been paying. The head of the production department says that he cannot get satisfactory results with this material. Which is to have his way? Perhaps this very difference of opinion may make the purchasing agent begin a more systematic search for a material which will cost less and at the same time give results satisfactory to the production manager. This would be an integration. And I want you to notice that we should have here the three results which often follow an integration: both parties would be satisfied; the situation would be improved—that is, costs would be reduced without deterioration in the quality of the product; and there might in time be a still wider, a community, value, in this material being used throughout the industry for this particular purpose, and thus a reduction to the consumer eventually effected.

When I gave you the illustration of the dispute between father and son as to whether a certain grade of stockings should be sold for 87 cents or $1, I said we would speak of a possible solution later. This dispute reflects the whole irregularity, inconsistency, planlessness in price-fixing. Suppose father and son had recognized this, suppose this occurrence had led them to make some beginning toward getting retailers, wholesale merchants, and manufacturers to try to find some proper basis for price-fixing, and then some means to educate the public to understand the basis of price-fixing. In that case, the psychological aspirations of the son and the economic integrity of the father, might eventually have been satisfied; and besides satisfying the two parties concerned, there would have been an emergent value, the emergent value being a better business policy, a better social policy.

To end my third point and to summarize thus far: My first point concerned the total situation; my second the nature of the interacting which determines the total situation; my third, the evolving situation. We have come to see that reciprocal adjustment is more than mere adjustment; that it is there we get what the psychologist has called the "something new," "the critical moment in evolution." Everyone of us engaged in any form of constructive activity is looking for the plus values of our activity. As men who are interested in organisms, in unities (biologists, philosophers, social scientists, or whatever they may be) are interested in what is called by some the emerging, by some the overflow, by some the evolving, by some the appearance of new values —Professor Whitehead's philosophy is largely based on what he calls "the interplay of diverse values" and the "emergent values"—so in business management we find this same principle at work. We see that functional relating has always a value beyond the mere addition of the parts. A genuine interweaving or interpenetrating by changing both sides creates new situations. Recall what the president of the factory said in regard to the co-ordinating of his departments—that a genuine co-ordinating changed to some extent the two parts co-ordinated. *Functional relating is the continuing process of self-creating coherence.* Most of my philosophy is contained in that sentence. You can take that sentence, I believe, as a test for any part of business organization or business management. If you have the right kind of functional relating, you will have a process which will create a unity which will lead to further unities—a self-creating progression.

An understanding of this is of the utmost importance in settling labour disputes. If we want a settlement which will mean progress, greater success for our business, we shall try to include the values of both sides, which will give us more than the values of the two sides added together, will give us an emergent value. Our outlook is narrowed, our chances of success are largely diminished, when our thinking is constrained with the limits of an either-or situation. We should never allow ourselves to be bullied by an either-or. We want to learn how to make any human association most effective, most fruitful. The reciprocal influence, the interactive behaviour, which involves a developing situation, is fundamental for business administration as it is for politics, economics, jurisprudence, and ethics.

Before going on to the second part of my paper, to the question of control, let me take a moment to carry the correspondences I have been speaking of into still another field, for I cannot emphasize too strongly the significance of finding the same underlying principles in every field of human activity. We find in the arts—in architecture, in painting, in poetry, in music—that the fundamental principle is organization, is relatedness. I have been interested in that approach to the study of Greek art during the last decade which involves a mathematical analysis and hence rests on relations. In a recent book on poetry I read: "In so far as a poem is an organic unity, it changes its meaning, which is why it lasts to ever succeeding generations." As to music, I was much struck by what a friend said to me only last week: that while we think of the players in an orchestra as each knowing his part and of the conductor as having an awareness of the total process as an integrative unity, we must remember also that the players play best when the conductor is able to make each share his inclusive awareness. This is a rather subtle point, I think.

Besides the interest and significance of seeing our principle at work in the arts, I am also very much interested in the different degrees of sensitiveness to relations shown by different people. A biologist who had, among his assistants, a Japanese who made drawings for him said that a fish under the hand of this Japanese took on certain curves indicating movement, suggesting water. He did not seem to be able to draw a fish as the other young men did—just a fish.

I sometimes think we are all more sensitive to relations æsthetically than we are in our everyday jobs. In taking a railway journey a succession of pictures, that is, of wholes, passes before your eyes all day. You see flowers by a stream, cows in a meadow, a boulder at the foot of a pine. At the end of the day you have this accumulation of *pictures*, you do not think merely of fields and rocks and streams and trees. I believe this same sensitiveness in regard to relations is going to be our greatest asset in business management.

The Nature of Control—Dependence upon an Understanding of Unities

What has all this to do with the title of my paper, *Control?* Why have I talked so long of the nature of unities? Because we cannot understand control without understanding unities. I said that the chief problem of the organization engineer was acknowledgedly co-ordination. That simply means he cannot get control without unity. Put this in the plainest language of your everyday job. In order to control a certain situation, you have to get the co-operation of those fellow executives who are also concerned in that situation. The degree of control will depend partly on how far you can successfully unite the ideas of these men and yourself.

I find this the law on every level I have studied. Those biologists, psychologists, and philosophers I have mentioned in this paper whose most fundamental thinking is concerned with integrative unities, tell us of the self-regulating, self-directing character of an organism as a whole. They mean that the organizing activity *is* the directing activity. The interacting *is* the control, it does not set up a control, that fatal expression of some writers on government and also some writers on business administration. I cannot get up in the morning, I cannot walk to my work, without that co-ordination of muscles which is control. The athlete has more of that co-ordination and therefore more control than I have. On the personal level, I gain more and more control over myself as I co-ordinate my various tendencies. This is interesting to us from two points of view, not only as showing the operation of the same law on different levels, but because we are more and more using this knowledge in dealing with individuals in industry as well as to obtain effective group action. In fact, the two are more closely connected than is always recognized. When we have conflicts, or differences of opinion, between two individuals—employer and employee, or two executives, or two members of a board of directors— it is not only our task to try to reconcile these two individuals. We have to study each individual to see if there are not, perhaps, diverse tendencies warring with each other within the individual, for this internal conflict may be the very thing which will prevent a satisfactory settling of the conflict between these individuals. We have, moreover, to see what measures we can take to reconcile these warring tendencies, to resolve the internal conflict, in order that these individuals can enter into effective relations with each other. But we must remember, what is sometimes forgotten, that this is not an antecedent process; the two integrations are simultaneous. The conflict between A and B, or the integrating between A and B, may help A to unify the diverse tendencies in himself, may help B to do the same. These are not really two processes, but one; the individual would not be integrating his personality if he lived in a world by himself. It is exactly the same kind of a double process as that which I gave you in my illustration from the marketing co-operatives.

Not all psychiatrists who go into industry pay enough attention to this. They are going to adjust the individual, they say, but the very word "adjust" implies that the man is to be adjusted *to* something, and the simultaneous processes of internal and external adjustment, and their influence on each other, should be fully recognized.

I have said that on the biological level, growth is by integration, by the continuous integration of simple, specific responses. I have said that we see the same law in operation on the personal level; diverse tendencies are united into new action patterns. I have said that in the case of two individuals, that is, on the social level, here, too, we get control through effective integration. Authority should arise within the unifying process. As every living process is subject to its own authority, that is, the authority evolved by or involved in the process itself, so social control is generated by the process itself. Or rather, the activity of self-creating coherence *is* the controlling activity. We see this clearly in international relations. We shall never be able to make an international settlement and erect some power to enforce it; the settlement must be such as to provide its own momentum. A political scientist says in a recent book that authority co-ordinates the experience of men. It does not. It is just the other way around. Legitimate authority flows from co-ordination, not co-ordination from authority. This is implied in everything I have said here. Legitimate authority is the interweaving of all the experience concerned.

The intellectuals of the English Labour Party are making, I think, a grave mistake in not accepting this fundamental principle. They see the whole labour question in the fight pattern. G. D. H. Cole, in a passionate article in the *Labour Magazine* advocating the acceptance of Easton Lodge, which Lady Warwick had offered for a Labour College, ended with these words: "And education . . . will create in the hearts of our young workers a will to power . . . that will carry us on to victory."

You see, Cole is thinking in terms of the fight; but as we have been trying that for several thousands, or millions, of years, and it does not seem to be very successful, why not try another method? And another is indicated to us, indicated in the idea that one part can never get any lasting power over another, but that you can have self-direction by forming integrative unities. When employers and employees are willing to sit down together to try to solve their problems rather than to bargain on the basis of who possesses the greater economic power of the moment, then we shall be on the road to settling "the labour question." That genuine authority arises spontaneously within the process of building up an integrative unity should be the argument for employee representation, not that it is the "right" of the workman nor because it will ease up things for the employer.

I speak of the English Labour Party. We see in many places this same disregard of the fundamental principle of control as part of the essential nature of a unity. Many in the Consumers' League over-emphasize the "fight" with the manufacturers; they do not see that they will get their full share in controlling the situation only when they and the manufacturers join. In the very last circular I received from the Consumers' League, it is stated, "With the consumer lies the balance of power." I hope I do not have to pause and say why I think this all wrong. "The balance of power" is the phrase we hear in international disputes, in industrial controversy, and here in the mouths of the consumers as against the manufacturers. What I think the doctrine of this paper shows us is that a jointly developing power means the possibility of creating new values, a wholly different process from the sterile one of balancing.

I have spoken of government, of international relations, of capital and labour, of producer and consumer. In the study of business organization we are saying that authority is not all at the top, that authority goes with function, that what we are seeking in business organization is the method of obtaining a cumulative authority as the interweaving experience of all those who are performing some functional part of the activity under consideration.

Let us note, too, that if control arises within the unifying process, then the more highly integrated unity you have, the more self-direction you get. When bankers, manufacturers, workers, and consumers, learn how to form an integrative unity, then we shall have a large degree of social control.

I was much interested last summer in England in a small

occurrence which yet seemed to me to have a good deal of significance. I dropped my watch, and it stopped. I was leaving London the next day and wished to get it repaired at once, as I had no other watch with me. I took it to the repair department of a jeweller in Bond Street, and they said it would take ten days to repair it. I understood that it would if the usual routine was followed of sending the watch to a repair shop and letting it wait its turn. So I explained to them the urgency of the case and asked if they would give me the address of someone who did repairing. They said they did not know of anyone. I then walked the length of Bond Street going into those shops that had watches in the windows and asking the same question. They all made the same reply, that they did not know of anyone, but all offered to get it done for me. Now I do not believe this could have happened in America. I think it is because there has not developed in England a group consciousness of sellers. And when I was told in England, as I was, that retail selling is done better in America than in England, I thought to myself that I knew one of the reasons why. These men selling watches in Bond Street were thinking of the immediate profit of the few shillings they would make from repairing my watch; they were not thinking that whatever arouses confidence on the part of the buying public in those who sell is in the long run to the greatest advantage of the selling group. Here was lacking a consciousness of unity, and in so far there was lacking control in retail selling. There are many other reasons why retail selling is more advanced in America, but I thought this was probably one reason.

To sum up what I have said of control thus far: Control is part of a process, a process which we see on biological, personal, and social levels. Conscious control is the self-regulation of the biologist rising to consciousness. And conscious control is the dominant thought of the twentieth century. More and more do we hear that phrase from economists, jurists, historians, and sociologists. It is the chief contribution which our generation is making to the world. And we get control through co-ordination.

I have not entered on the *methods* of obtaining control through effective unities, as that is the whole problem of management and would take a whole series of conferences instead of only one conference. Overselling, for instance, is a lack of control through lack of co-ordination of the departments concerned, and you could give me a hundred illustrations. And we should remember that we must unify policies before we can unify activities. Suppose a department in our business is studying customers' demands. We shall never be able to co-ordinate that department successfully with the selling department unless the underlying policies of these two departments are the same.

Summary: Steps in Attaining Control

If there is not time to consider the matter of control in detail, let us at least note in a general way the steps to be taken in attaining control, using the terms of this paper. I shall take this as a means of summarizing the whole paper. As a summary, there will be some repetition.

The first step is to see the field of control. In any situation the total is complex, not single. Consider Italy at the present moment. While the most interesting thing about the situation is that one man is such a large factor in it, yet to understand the Italian situation we have to get together all that is influencing Italy, all that has gone to give Mussolini his power. But we have to go beyond finding the elements which constitute the field of control. We have to see the field of control as an integrative unity—that is, we have to realize that it is constituted not by certain elements alone, but by certain reciprocal activities.

If the first step in the understanding of a problem is an understanding of the field of control as an integrative unit, the second is the process of passing from one field of control to another. When we get to this point, we are so in the heart of the matter that I wish we were just beginning this discussion. If I elaborated this point, it would be along the line of what I have said of the emerging. I can only say here that when we understand this process, anticipation will not mean forecasting alone, it will mean more than predicting. It will mean more than meeting the next situation; it will mean making the next situation. One of the largest manufacturers in Milan said last July that he and a number of other Italian manufacturers were studying American methods of scientific management so that they would be ready to deal with the industrial situation when Mussolini's hand should be withdrawn. This means, in the language we are using this evening, that when that field of control is broken up, they are going to have a hand in making the next.

I cannot therefore wholly agree with those historians who say that the study of history should help us to predict situations; it should do more than this—it should help us to create situations.

This has enormous importance in business management. Many employers are being told that they should study the psychology of the workers so that in the next strike they will know how to win. I think their aim should be not to be able to *meet* a strike situation, but to *create* a strike-less situation. Again, consider the business cycle. It used to be thought that there was something fatalistic about the business cycle. Then business men began to study it in order to meet the demands made by these periodic fluctuations. The next step is to prevent the fluctuations. When, for instance, enough manufacturers see that the times of peak prosperity are not the times to expand—to introduce new lines of goods, new equipment, and so on—then perhaps business will not follow an alternation of peaks and slumps. I spoke at Oxford this autumn at a conference on business management,[9] and one of the papers was on forecasting, a very able and interesting paper, but in the discussion that followed I was much interested in the fact that few there had apparently got beyond the idea of forecasting as predicting. In America many of our business men are trying to do what Hoover has called flattening out the cycle.

[9] The Rowntree Lecture Conference, held at Balliol College, Oxford, October, 1926. (For details of the papers read by Mary Follett at the Conference, see the "Notes on the English Papers," Appendix II, p. 318.

How to pass from one situation to another is the point on which we most need light; it is to this that we should now direct our studies. We have been told a good deal by biologists, philosophers, and psychologists of how a unity, or total situation, is constructed; we do not know so much about passing from one unity to another or, to use the language of the *Gestalt* school of psychology, how to make productive configurations. A friend who is a political scientist has told me that he considers this one of the chief problems of the political scientist. For instance, shall the Social-Democratic Party in Germany join a coalition? Will that make a productive configuration? Will it make an effective total situation? We do not know and we do not know how to find out. But while the political scientists have not yet worked out any satisfactory tests or technique of thinking here, the fact that they are working at this problem, and the fact that it is the same problem in which many of us are most interested seems to me hopeful. There are two fundamental problems for business management: first, to define the essential nature of the total situation; secondly, how to pass from one total situation to another. I think we have answered the first fairly satisfactorily as being not inclusiveness alone, but also relatedness, a functional relating. We have not yet answered the second, but the mere fact of stating a problem is a long way toward its solution, and many of us are now trying to state the problem of control.

X

THE PSYCHOLOGY OF CONSENT AND PARTICIPATION

In the preceding paper we considered certain fundamental principles of human relations. I wish to take these principles as a test for the relations which I am asked to speak of in my remaining talks in this conference series,[1] namely, the consenting relation, the participating relation, the relation of arbitrator and conciliator to the group, of leader and expert.

"Consent" of the Governed Not an Adequate Expression of Democracy

We are to consider first the doctrine of the consent of the governed.[2] I do not think it will bear our present tests. Mere consent, bare consent, gives us only the benefit of the ideas of those who put forward the propositions for consent; it does not give us what the others may be capable of contributing.

When our evening centres were opened in Boston (for adults to meet in schoolhouses for education, for recreation, for citizen's meetings, and the like), I was chairman of the advisory committee to the school committee. I hoped that the centres would be started on a more or less democratic basis, that the people of each neighbourhood might be taken into the counsels of the director and plan and initiate their own activities; direct them, too, as far as was possible. I therefore talked a good deal about this during our first months to the directors of the various centres. One evening, on visiting one of the centres, the director came up to me

[1] See note, p. 183; this paper was presented in March, 1927.
[2] *Cf. Creative Experience*, Chapter XI, " 'Consent' Not the Technique of the Governed."

smiling and said, "We are doing in this centre just what you wanted us to. We get the members together at 9.50 (the time for closing was ten o'clock) and take a vote on questions." But this was not at all what I had wanted. I had wanted all the education and the responsibility involved in a consideration of these questions, and the greater interest, too, that would undoubtedly have been aroused; I had not been thinking of the mere voting. That seemed to me consent at its barest. Mere voting is a gesture of agreement rather than real agreement. We cannot obtain genuine consent by a vote any more than you can "declare" peace. That is what the Allies tried to do at Versailles. They tried to declare peace instead of opening the way for the process of peace achievement. They did not clearly enough see that peace is a process and an attainment. In the same way, genuine agreement is part of a slow process of the interweaving of many activities, and this is not consent but participation.

Many people are now getting beyond the consent-of-the-governed stage in their thinking, yet there are political scientists who are still advocating it. And, indeed, it is much better to have the consent of the governed than not to have it. In the case of what are called the backward countries, that is what we are asking for, for we recognize it as a first step. But we are also recognizing to-day that it is only a first step; that not consent but participation is the right basis for all social relations.[3]

Incidently, I should like to point out that what we often see in business to-day is the consent of the governors, which is rather a blow at the consent-of-the-governed theory. An under-executive makes a plan and carries it to the man at the head of his department for his consent. The man at the head of a department makes a plan and carries it to the

---

[3] *Cf. Creative Experience*, p. 198: "The theory of consent rests on the wholly intellectual fallacy that thought and action can be separated. The theory of consent rests on the assumption that we think with our 'mind' and we don't. Political leaders are supposed to put something before our minds to which we respond with our minds. Yet how often we see cases where we have not been able to persuade people, by our most careful reasoning, to think differently, but later, by giving them an opportunity to enter on a certain course of action, their 'minds' are thereby changed."

president for his consent. The president of one of the largest concerns in America told me that he spent most of his time in consenting to the plans which his executives made.

What Is Participation?

If, however, we say that we believe, not in consent, but in participation, we have then to define participation. Mere participation is not enough. You may bring together all the parts of a machine, but you do not have the *machine* until they are properly related. The chief task of organization is how to relate the parts so that you have a working unit; then you get effective participation. We concluded in the preceding paper, did we not, that democracy does not mean merely all taking part, that democracy should mean organization, the relating of parts, co-functioning? This should be the definition of participation. In a conference we have participation when we have related thinking, not merely voting, which only registers opinions already formed. The Minimum Wage Law in Massachusetts has one wise provision: it subordinates mere voting to the process of seeking means of agreement. I sat on a minimum wage board once where the labour members tried to force the vote prematurely, and the secretary of the board had to point out to them that they were asked to come there not to register views already held, but to see if some agreement could not be found between representatives of labour, of employers, and of the public. I found this to be the principle on which the trade boards of England are working, too. I shall speak of these further in the following paper.

Another instance of the recognition that participation must involve the interpenetration of the ideas of the parties concerned was when a workers' representative in a plant which had employee representation protested when an important executive absented himself from a meeting and sent in word how he felt about a certain matter, not giving the other side a chance to present its case before he reached a decision. This workman understood one of the fundamental principles we considered in our discussion of "Control," the advantage of the process of what we called interacting, whereby each gets something from the other.

Again, in the Fore River Shipbuilding Plant, the plan for employee representation provided for separate meetings of employee representatives at regular intervals, but after a three months' trial the employees asked for permission to abandon these meetings on the ground that they were waste of time, only the joint meetings being effective in bringing to light all the evidence necessary for reaching decisions.

Obtaining Participation

If participation means everyone taking part, according to his capacity, in a unit composed of related activities, we then ask how we can get participation. In three ways: by an organization which provides for it, by a daily management which recognizes and acts on the principle of participation, and by a method of settling differences, or a method of dealing with the diverse contributions of men very different in temperament, training, and attainments. As it would require much more time and space than we have at our disposal to consider the questions of organization or management in general, I am going to devote this paper to the third point.

There are three ways of dealing with difference: domination, compromise, and integration. By domination only one side gets what it wants; by compromise neither side gets what it wants; by integration we find a way by which both sides may get what they wish. Do you remember the example in the preceding paper of a possible integration between purchasing agent and production manager which might result in the decreased costs for that plant or even for the whole industry? In dissensions between executives it is never merely peace that should be our aim, but progress. We get progress when we find a way that includes the ideas of both or the several parties to the controversy. But this requires hard thinking, inventiveness, ingenuity. We should never think of integration as a foregone conclusion; it is an achievement.

This whole matter of participation, or ways of joining the various contributions of men, is much more important in business to-day than it ever was before, because we have more kinds of knowledge and experience to join. A man at the head of the industrial relations department in a large plant in England told me that one of his chief difficulties, in questions of promotion or dismissal, was knowing how to join the opinions of the foreman and the findings of the psychologist. These did not seem to add up any more than tables and chairs will add up. He was working out a rather elaborate mathematical system of ratings by which these two different kinds of knowledge and experience could be joined.

Again, think of an occasion like this: the staff man who is responsible for the care of machines tells the foreman that one of his machines needs attention, and the foreman does not agree. Such are the problems we meet daily. A salesman in a certain locality says he cannot get a higher price. One of the staff goes in there and decides that he can. The salesman says, "I certainly know my customers better than this man who has just come here." The staff man says: "His customers are hammering at him all the time, so of course he can't see the situation as clearly as someone from outside." How are these two opinions to be joined? Such questions have to be met constantly under the form of management we have to-day. It makes the subject of "participation" a much more intricate one than it was formerly. At the same time, it raises problems of extra-ordinary interest.

I have said that there are three ways of settling difference. Compromise has been the way usually taken; it has been, as a rule, the way most approved. Diplomats laud it, as do many arbitrators in industrial disputes. But more and more among executives who differ do I notice a very sincere attempt to get at something better than compromise, to get the advantage of both points of view. When we compromise, something is always lost. Moreover, we do all of us want our own way, want the way which seems to us right. I can get my own way by imposing my will upon others or by joining my will with that of others. To impose one's will upon others sounds so crude that there are few people who will confess to wishing to do that, but suppose that I am willing to dominate and to acknowledge it; even so, is it the process most likely to succeed in the long run? I think not, because the fellow executive on whom I impose my will, next time will try to impose his will on me. I think that the principle of integration rests on the most profound philosophy of the ages, and that it is also decidedly to our interest in the long run.

I want to say, incidentally, that I was much interested in England this summer in this to me rather amazing occurrence. Two people said to me at different times, "You have an expression in America which interests us over here very much—'in the long run'." I was astonished because I had never imagined that every nation had not the expression or its equivalent. Of course, the English are looking ahead just as we are, and yet I think it rather interesting that our expression "in the long run" had arrested their attention. If American business philosophy is to be known by its recognition of the "long run," integration should certainly be part of that philosophy, for emergent values, to use our expression arrived at in the preceding paper, come through integration. Professor Ripley has told us to focus attention on the only real things in life, those that lie ahead of us. Integration is securing the future.

To accept the philosophy of integration is to change somewhat our ideas of sacrifice, so long held by many. I put domination and sacrifice together as based on the same error. If I dominate you, I get what *I* want. If I sacrifice myself to you, you get what *you* want. I do not see why one way is any better than the other. The only gain would be if we could both have what we want. As I stressed in the previous paper, integration means three things: you and I both get what we want, the whole situation moves forward, and the process often has community value. I do not therefore think that my participation in any social process should be one of self-sacrifice, but one of self-contribution.

One of the best results of employee representation is that

in many plants where some plan of employee representation is being carried out, both employers and employees are coming to see that many decisions are not favourable either to employers alone or to employees alone, but equally favourable to both sides. A workman said to me, "I have sometimes felt in a conference committee a double responsibility, a responsibility to both sides." Such a feeling is the beginning of a consciousness of unity, and when you get a consciousness of unity, self-interest is a good thing, for then it means the interest of the group with which you have identified yourself. A man joins a union and now identifies his self-interest with his union, which in time of a strike may be quite against his immediate or personal self-interest. The next step is when the trade union joins with management to help solve industrial problems. Here again, self-interest takes on a larger meaning. The cry all over England to-day, from both employers and employees, is for better management. This is in itself a recognition of the interlocking interests of employers and employed. Why is the International Labour Office at Geneva one of the three agencies in establishing the International Institute for Scientific Management? Because it sees that scientific management will benefit workers as well as employers.

A formal recognition that group interest should take precedence of individual interest was given in a decision made last November by the impartial chairman of the conference committee in the fur industry. The dispute concerned a reduction in wages during the dull season. The impartial chairman decided not only that it was contrary to the agreement between the Associated Fur Manufacturers and the Furriers Union, but also that while it might benefit individuals, it was contrary to the best interests of both the union and the employers' association. He said: "A particular firm wishes to reduce wages in order to underbid other manufacturers in the sale of that article of merchandise; the particular worker wishes to underbid other workers. Both these points of view are contrary to the general interests of the industry, to the interest of the employers' association and of the union." And he added, "And it goes without saying that in a conflict between the needs of the organizations and the desires of the individual members or workers, the rights of the bodies are superior to the rights of the individual and must prevail." He might have said what, of course, must have been also in his mind, that it is not really a case of the interests of the organization against the interests of the individual, for in the long run what is to the advantage of the organization will be to the advantage of the individual.

I think people often identify themselves with the group interest, feeling consciously that it will be to their own interest in the end. Once I was being rowed, with a friend, across Lake Como on a summer day at noon. We were all good-sized people, it was an exceptionally hot day, and the rower became about the hottest looking man I ever saw. I summoned up enough Italian to try to express my sympathy for him, to deplore the heat. He looked at me in amazement and replied, "But it's good for the vines." Probably he had no vines himself, but he had identified himself with the community interest. It was not that he was willing to suffer for the good of all, he saw his own interest included in that of all, even although he probably could not have put it into words.

This sounds as if I were saying that people are incapable of anything but self-interest, but I hope you will not misunderstand me on this point. I am not pitting idealistic and materialistic conceptions against each other. I maintain that my conception of self-interest is an idealistic one. I heard it said once that in any group you should have an idealist and a materialist and thus both views would get full consideration. But I do not believe in that. It would raise the same dilemma as was raised in the mind of the daughter of the clergyman who was offered a bishopric. A friend of the family came to call and was received by the daughter, whom he asked if they had decided to accept the call. She replied, "I don't know. Father is in his study praying for guidance and Mother is upstairs packing."

It must be evident to you now that I do not look on self-interest as a bad word. Patriotism is self-interest of the noblest kind. We fight for our country because it is a larger self. How often we hear a man try to prove that he is "disinterested." How often we hear, "There's nothing in it for me." But why shouldn't there be something in it for him? To say that a man is "disinterested" is, I think, not to praise him, but, on the contrary, a grave reproach. Growth, development, means that we want things—and get them. To be sure, if when a man says he is disinterested in a matter he means that he is not going to make it a question of private gain when it should be a question of the public good, we can only heartily approve. But what I am urging is that we should be as interested, as self-interested, as possible, but only as members of the highest unity with which we are capable of identifying ourselves.

Let us note, too, a point in regard to sympathy, namely, that the sympathy of identification is very different from the sympathy from outside. I speak of this because it is often said that the coming together of employer and employee under plans of employee representation is going to make each sympathize with the other. I think this is true, but I think they will have the best kind of sympathy as fast as they can unify their purposes. The definition of sympathy given by most psychologists to-day is a feeling with rather than a feeling for. A recent writer, a psychologist, gives a good illustration in the case of a man losing his wife. He says that a friend who has also lost his wife will sympathize with him; a friend who has feared at some time or another that he was going to lose his wife will sympathize with him, but a little less; a friend who has never thought of the possibility, still less; and a friend who has never had a wife, much less still. In other words, this psychologist makes sympathy depend on similar experience. While realizing that sympathy may be born of the imagination, while realizing also that similar experience does by no means always produce sympathy, I should say in general that when purposes of employers and employees become so integrated that they make one purpose, then we have the most real, the most vital sympathy—a feeling with rather than a feeling for.

It is the same in regard to confidence. Everywhere in England I was told that the chief difficulty in settling the coal strike was a lack of confidence on both sides, that this was so marked that when one side acted in perfectly good faith, the other side was always suspicious and attributed every kind of a base motive. I do not believe that confidence will ever be attained except by making the aims of employers and employees the same. I had one amusing story told me of this lack of confidence. A man known throughout England for his efforts to improve the condition of the workmen, himself the head of a business, received a call from a labour leader. In the course of the conversation, he told him some of his ideas in regard to labour, what he thought could be done, what he himself was trying to do. At the end of the interview, when he got up to go, the labour man said, "I'm glad to have met you, Mr. B., I've enjoyed our talk, and I hope when you come to Huddlestone you'll come to see me —*my* hobby is china."

If participation means playing one's part in an integrative unity, if we want to get what each one has to contribute, what are some of the rules which we should lay down for our guidance? First, I should say, never, if possible, allow an either-or situation to be created. This is done when the "Yes" or "No" style of question is put to the group, as, "Shall this go into effect Thursday morning?" Such questions are often put in groups where the members are supposed to be participating (not merely consenting), as in committees or boards of directors. The objection to this way of opening discussion is that by presenting two alternatives, you by no means exhaust the possibilities of a situation; it means a greatly impoverished thinking, a diminution of your mental recources; it often paralyses thinking or canalizes thinking. Look at the college debate: Resolved, that so and so be done. That gives us at once a Yes or No question; we will do it or we won't do it. That is fatal to the best thinking. There are almost always more than two alternatives in a situation, and our job is to analyse the situation carefully enough for as many as possible to appear.

A Yes or No question is in itself a pre-judgment. Let me give an illustration. An association took up the question of taking part in Defence Day. Many thought they should show their patriotism, their willingness to serve their country. On the other hand, there were those opposed to all military demonstration; the pacifists wanted to commit the association definitely to an attitude of noncompliance. The question was put: Shall we co-operate or not?—a Yes or No question. But there might have been considered other alternatives: the possibility of hostile demonstration, the possibility of co-operating perfunctorily, registering reservations, or there might have been an integration. Between the men who like war and those who say, "You will never again see me in khaki," there are those who will do everything in their power to prevent war before they put on khaki. This association might therefore have agreed to try to influence public opinion by some demonstration against war, at the same time deciding to co-operate in the Defence Day demonstration, assuming that if war should come they would take part.

If you will look back over your experience on any committee, I think you will find that it is the for-or-against attitude which makes conflict, that when you put up an executive policy in the form of, Shall this be done or not done? you often find you have a fight on your hands. If we look upon conference as not primarily for voting, but for deliberation, discussion, the pooling of knowledge, judgment, and purposes, then the rule should be: Look for all the factors in the situation; guide your conference or committee so that two alternatives do not present themselves in the early stages of discussion; curb those who wish to vote the moment two clear-cut alternatives appear from out the discussion. Some people seem to think that discussion is merely to sharp-cut the issue, and that when that is done we are then ready to vote. Not at all. Postpone facing alternatives until more than two are brought out. If two are proposed prematurely, break them up, add others, and then the final alignment may be different from the first.

In short, we do not get full participation unless we avoid either-or situations. Suppose our competitors have cut the price of some article. If we ask in our executive committee meeting whether or not we shall cut under our competitors, we thereby create an either-or situation with all its handicaps, instead of trying to get from our executives some thinking on how to meet the situation in some other way, which is, of course, what we really wish, as that kind of competition has an obvious limit.

Rules for Guidance in Assuring Participation

We are asking ourselves if we can formulate any rules to guide us in this matter of participation, which we are taking to mean two things: the contribution of each individual and the co-ordination of such contributions. For co-ordination we need understanding and for understanding we need openness and explicitness. In the case of conflict, openness is absolutely necessary, for you cannot integrate differences until you know what they are. "Cards on the table" has become almost you might say the slogan of the impartial chairmen in the clothing industry. I think the success of these men is partly due to their refusal to take part in union politics and their insistence on having all the facts in the case laid before them.

Indeed, secrecy is being attacked from many quarters. What is called open business is advocated by many. Mr. John A. Cole, of the Lord Electric Company, says, in his paper on the National Agreement: "No association of capital or labour should be afraid to allow the other party to know the nature of the business transacted at its meetings. . . . The principle of having a union represented at our business meetings was tried out locally with most gratifying results."

Mr. Seebohm Rowntree, head of the Cocoa Works at York, gives a talk three times a year to representatives from the entire works, in which he lays before them the exact condition of the company. I was very fortunate in being in York on the day when Mr. Rowntree made one of these reports. It was one of the best speeches I ever heard, and it seemed to me that it must have a large influence in inspiring confidence, in arousing effort, in providing that invaluable incentive of understanding and also the feeling of being part of a group purpose.[4]

I said that there were two elements in understanding, openness and explicitness. I mean by the latter that we have to find out what we *really* want, ourselves and others, for you can seldom tell by the general phrases people use. Let me illustrate. We may say that a man "is taking a drink." Now of course a man is never "taking a drink." He is:

1. Quenching thirst.
2. Being sociable.
3. Drowning trouble.
4. Stimulating himself.
5. Acting from habit.
6. Defying the amendment, asserting his individual rights.

You see how inadequate it is to say that a man is taking a drink. He may be doing any one of these, or two or three combined, or all of them combined. We cannot understand our own desires or those of others unless we have taken the blanket expression which we customarily use for them and tried to find out what it means, unless we have broken our desires up into their parts and seen the relation of these parts to one another; for the essential nature of a unity is the relation of its parts, as I tried to make clear in the preceding paper.

I have said that participation rests on two foundation stones—understanding and co-ordination. The most important thing to learn about co-ordination is that it must begin at the bottom, not at the top. I think the success of the Baltimore and Ohio plan depends largely on the fact that

[4] I do not mean to imply that the advantage of openness in business has been recognized by more than a few, or that those few have carried it far even theoretically. Giving cost information to workers, for instance, has hardly been more than suggested. Most employers would think that impossible. (M. P. F.)

the joint machinery of co-operation begins at the very bottom. One of the fundamental differences between consent and participation is that consent is not part of the process, it comes at the end of or after the process. Participation is not only part of the process; it should begin with the beginning of the process. And let us clearly understand what we mean by that. It is, indeed, a commonplace that when differences between people grow instead of being smoothed out while they are in the incipient stage, reconciliation will be much more difficult—let your differences crystallize and you will probably find yourself with a fight on your hands. But while we all recognize that, we do not understand with equal clearness that any contribution I may have to make to an undertaking can be correlated with the contributions of the others more successfully if the opportunity is given early in the undertaking.

We have a very hopeful sign in the management of to-day in the opportunity often given to labour and management to confer and integrate from the beginning, before sides have crystallized, before problems have become grievances, before the conference has become a fight. There is a tendency to-day in many plants, even where employee representation does not exist, and far more so where it does, for foreman and workers or department head and workers, to have some sort of consultation about everyday matters as they come up. This under some forms of employee representation is made a formal or obligatory matter. Many foremen consult with the employee representatives, before inaugurating any new practice. They thus not only often get the benefit of suggestions from the workers, but also they can anticipate objections and avoid collective resistance. On the other side, the workers come to appreciate the foreman's difficulties, the problems connected with the department, or often, indeed, problems connected with the running of the whole plant. No one who has watched participation in the early stages can doubt its advantage.

What we want, then, is co-ordination from the bottom and all along the line. This is successful organization engineering.

We are trying to work out a system of decentralization combined with a satisfactory system of cross-functioning so that the participation I am speaking of may be a continuous process.

The English Labour Party is, I think, making a mistake in asking for what they call "independent control." It is true that the National Union of Railwaymen in 1917 and the Miners' Federation in 1918 asked for "joint control." This has been the official demand of the English Labour Party, but speech after speech indicates that they do not mean by that what we are calling this evening "joint control," for over and over again we hear the demand for "independent" control, "independent" power. And that means, exactly as the phrase implies, that labour should be given a certain authority in its capacity as labour, and that this authority should, in the later stages of management, be joined to the authority exercised by management. This seems to me to rest on a wholly unsound principle of organization.

Participation in the early stages should begin even with the preliminary fact-finding. Mr. Laski in his last book[5] talks about "independent investigation," and suggests that the Miners' Federation of Great Britain should "independently" study the problem of safety in mines, and he speaks of "the vast and unequalled body of experience" on which they have to draw. I want to use that body of experience, but in *joint* investigation, for it is usually too late for that experience to be integrated with that of the managers by the time the separate reports are finished. When we have the two finished reports of "independent" investigation, the stage is set for a fight—of some sort.[6]

[5] This is probably a reference to *The Foundations of Sovereignty and Other Essays*, Harold J. Laski, London, 1922.

[6] *Cf. Creative Experience*, p. 15: "From my experience of Minimum Wage Boards, I see that there is possible a co-operative gathering of facts which is more useful to the resolution of conflict than for each side to get them separately and then try to integrate them, for when each side gets them separately there is a tendency for each side to stick rigidly to his own particular facts. On one occasion when the employees were bringing figures for a certain item, that of clothing, in the cost-of-living budget, and the employers another set, and the representatives of the public still another set, a sub-committee of three was appointed, one from each of these groups, to collect the facts jointly. The figures brought in at the next meeting, thus co-operatively gathered, were accepted by the Board and the rest of the discussion based upon them."

In America we are alive to this difficulty. In the conference committees in the clothing industry a great point is made of the necessity of joint investigation. And Mr. Burton[7] tells us that joint fact-finding has become a characteristic procedure under employee representation plans. He says:

Joint fact-finding on a large scale has been a noteworthy accomplishment under the employee representation plan of the Pennsylvania Railroad. Agreement on facts as the basis of discussion is encouraged at every step. . . . As originally drafted jointly by the management and general chairman representing the employees in the engine and train service, the procedure outlined for referring matters beyond the official first hearing of the case prescribed that there be 'a joint statement of agreed on facts,' . . . and the representation plans adopted later by other branches of the service in the Pennsylvania Railroad embody the same provision."

I suppose we have all seen cases where, business conditions being such that management considered wage reductions necessary, agreement on the part of the workers was obtained not by discussion and persuasion, but by a joint study of the facts underlying these business conditions.

The time is coming, I believe, when the advantage of joint investigation of facts as a basis for public policy will become so clear that the public will insist on it. Suppose the engineers tending to believe in the desirability of "giant power" developed for public service and the engineers tending to look at the advantage of private utility companies should join in their investigations; might we not then hope to get a report we could trust?

What Participation Is Not

Let us look at some of the things participation is not. I mean participation as we are now defining it, not mere taking part, but functional relating. It is not fighting. Many have thought that the most we could do for the industrial struggle was to set a fair field for the fight. But according

[7] *Employee Representation*, E. R. Burton, Williams and Wilkins, Baltimore, 1926, p. 191.

to the fundamental principle we are now considering, that would not be the most fruitful way of managing human relations.

Take, again, collective bargaining, which is constantly being put forward as the right relation between capital and labour. While I think it has been a necessary step on the way, and while, indeed, it is to-day exactly as necessary as ever, while I am sure that a grave mistake has been made when arrangements between employers and employees have not given the unions the chance to use through collective bargaining what economic power they had, still, collective bargaining rests on the balance of power and results in com-promise, both of which I think we are going some time to outgrow. I think, indeed, that there are a good many people to-day who are thinking of employee representation and of union-management co-operation as developing in such a way that there will be a step beyond collective bargaining, are thinking of them as resting on the principle of functional relating.

We have a clear recognition of this in the growing appre-ciation of the fact that labour can make constructive con-tributions to management. Mr. William H. Johnston, president of the International Association of Machinists, distinguishes between what he calls the protective and the constructive function of the workers. Under the former, he lists the negotiation of wage rates and working rules and the prevention of injustice to workers. Of the latter, he says that the unions should help management in its service to the public.

One of the most interesting things that happened in America last year was the fact that Mr. Green, president of the American Federation of Labour, in three public speeches, offered the services of the unions to help solve the problems of management. Indeed, we see in many places this change in the attitude of labour. A few years ago the Amalgamated saw its activity as confined to fighting the owners of the clothing industry, but look at some of their activities of recent years: they have succeeded in introducing employment insurance, they have financed a clothing factory in Russia, and they have a local bank. Mr. Burton, in his study of employee representation,[8] has given a good many interesting examples of the contributions made by employees in the telephone companies associated with the American Telephone and Telegraph Company since the system of joint conferences has been introduced.

In the Baltimore and Ohio plan the unions are recognized as constructive factors in railroad operation. The plan provides for *continuous* co-operation, not merely when a grievance arises or when labour wishes to make some demand on management, and it is understood that unions and management are to work together for improved railroad service, elimination of waste, and better operating efficiency; also for improving working conditions, stabilizing employment, and sharing the gains of co-operation.

In England we have many interesting examples of constructive contributions made by labour to management. It seems a pity that a man with so much influence in the English Labour Party as G. D. H. Cole should say: "The whole shop steward movement and all the movements associated with it are . . . forms of machinery . . . to make [the workers'] grievances more articulate." This is not fair to the shop steward movement, for I myself know shop stewards in England who are as capable of making contributions to management as many on the managing staff of those firms, and are being increasingly given the opportunity to do so.

Whenever the workmen are taken into counsel, I think it should be made clear to them that the aim is not merely industrial peace, to avoid strikes, nor to anticipate the union organizer, that is, to create some internal machinery which will make union affiliation seem unnecessary; that it is not merely to adjust petty grievances more expeditiously, nor is it merely a sop, or a way to get the managerial policy across, or even to provide a better field for collective bargaining, and certainly not a matter of altruism; but that it is in order

[8] *Op. cit.* See p. 225.

to get every bit of knowledge and experience the man in daily touch with the processes and details of the business has gained. A workman said to me, "The directors want to satisfy us as far as they can on a sound business basis." He thought that he was praising his directors, but this, of course, should not be the aim of the directors, merely to "satisfy," and that should be made clear to every employee. The success and progress of any business will depend largely on its ability to get his fullest contribution from every man in office or factory, store or bank.

Summary

In summary and in conclusion, there are three chief problems of organization engineering: how to educate and train the members of an organization so that each can give the most he is capable of; secondly, how to give to each the fullest opportunity for contribution; thirdly, how to unify the various contributions, that is, the problem of co-ordination, confessedly the crux of business organization.

I should like to quote Mr. Dennison on all these points. In regard to the first he says:

"We should analyse our material—men and women—to discover their deeper and their more superficial characteristics and, while making the most of what they are, we should try to find ways to develop them into still higher units of service."

In regard to my second point he says:

"The managing ability of all employees is a great untapped source of social wealth. For, based upon order-giving, our organizing so far has been planned to do without and to suppress the managing possibilities which lie in small degree in each of large numbers of men."

In regard to my third point he says:

"Organization as an engineering project will plan so as to arrange the influences about its members that every possible bit of their abilities shall be brought out and aligned into the main direction of effort of the whole organization."

That last phrase is what this whole paper has been written to show. If we have got beyond mere consent, so also we have got beyond mere participation. Our contribution is of no value unless it is effectively related to the contributions of all the others concerned. This is a problem which needs the best efforts of our best organization engineers. For the "will to integrate," as it has been called, is not enough. Integrative unity willed with ardour will not unfold itself before our eyes. By willing ends we do not automatically will means. The success of organization engineering depends on its treatment of the problem of participation, of functional relating. To draw out the capacities of all and then to fit these together is our problem.

Have we stated our problem in accordance with the fundamental principles we considered in the preceding paper? I believe we have, for those principles were evoking, what we are calling here drawing out the capacities of all; secondly, reciprocal interacting and integrating, what we are calling here co-ordinating; and finally, emerging, which, translated as business progress, is the aim of organization engineering.

XI

THE PSYCHOLOGY OF CONCILIATION AND ARBITRATION[1]

I THINK we should decide at the outset what, in a general way, we are going to make the term "conciliation" cover, since there is some difference of opinion about this. Many include employee representation, joint committees, and one man goes so far as to include the plant magazine, since, he says, its object is conciliation. It seems to me best, however, merely to take that machinery provided within the industry or by the State which is called machinery of conciliation or mediation. The purpose of such machinery is the settling of disputes, whereas many of us hope that some day employee representation and joint committees will have a larger function. Indeed, they already have in some instances.

Distinction between Conciliation and Arbitration

In regard to the difference between conciliation and arbitration, while in practice it is often difficult to draw the line, in theory the two are wholly different. The principle of arbitration is that of an adjudicated dispute; the arbitrator, a man or a board, hears both sides and gives the decision. In cases of conciliation, an attempt is made to bring the two sides to agreement. It is encouraging that conciliation is pretty generally recognized to be a more satisfactory way of settling industrial disputes than arbitration. In many cases arbitration is resorted to only when conciliation fails.

Most of our states have some conciliation or mediation machinery. The machinery provided by the United States for the settlement of industrial disputes in general is the Conciliation Service in the Department of Labour. From

[1] See note, p. 183; this paper was presented in March, 1927.

1921 to 1925, 2,000 cases involving 2,500,000 workers were referred to the United States Conciliation Service, and in 87 per cent. of the cases settlements were reached.

In May, 1926, an act was passed in regard to the settlement of disputes between railroads and their employees, and here conciliation is to be tried first, and arbitration only if that does not succeed. Section 7 reads:

"Wherever a controversy shall arise between a carrier or carriers and its or their employees which is not settled either in conference between the representatives of the parties or by the appropriate adjustment board or through mediation, in the manner provided in the preceding sections, such controversy may, by agreement of the parties to such controversy, be submitted to the arbitration of a board of three persons. . . ."

I quote that merely to show that arbitration is to be resorted to only after other measures have been tried first.

In Germany, the arbitration decrees of 1925 seem to combine arbitration and conciliation, but arbitration is provided for only when conciliation fails. The procedure is as follows. First, the impartial chairman appointed by the Government calls a conference of the two parties and attempts to bring them to an agreement without calling an official session of the board. An agreement concluded in this manner is in no way different from any other voluntary agreement concluded by direct negotiations. Should this effort of the chairman fail, it becomes his duty to organize an arbitration board consisting of two members from each party and presided over by himself. This board, although called an arbitration board, also acts as a mediation agency, and only after a second effort to bring about a voluntary agreement between the parties has failed does the board make a proposition of its own. This is not, however, compulsory unless the parties have agreed beforehand that the decision shall be binding.

In the same year, 1923, an act was passed in the Netherlands for conciliation and arbitration of labour disputes, which also provides for arbitration only after mediation has failed. The act provides that when a dispute occurs involving not less than fifty workers, the Government, on receiving notification from the mayor of the commune concerned, shall appoint a conciliator to mediate between the parties. The parties themselves or a trade organization may also appeal to the Government conciliator. If the Government conciliator does not succeed in settling the dispute, he may recommend to the parties to appeal either to a conciliation board constituted by him or to an arbitration board. Arbitration awards are binding. The law seems to have been successful in operation. The Government conciliators have settled many disputes satisfactorily.

In England, the Conciliation Act of 1896 has been superseded by the Industrial Court Act of 1919. This act establishes a permanent state arbitration tribunal. This is a semi-judicial body. The procedure is one of pure arbitration; there is no attempt at conciliation. Three members usually take a case; they receive evidence from both sides and issue the award.

The trade boards, on the other hand, are not arbitration boards. The chairman, who is always one of the three independent members, is, and is said to be, a conciliator, not an arbitrator. They are not supposed to have, and do not have, the attitude that they are adjudicating a dispute. They consider that what they are for is to get the two sides to come to agreement. The Minister of Labour very kindly allowed me to sit in with one trade board last summer, and in that one the effort undoubtedly was not only to find an agreement which would be equally satisfactory to both sides, but one to which both sides had themselves contributed.

There is other conciliation machinery provided by parliamentary acts, but I have spoken of that most in use.

Advantages of Conciliation over Arbitration

As conciliation is generally considered a better method than arbitration, as many industries or firms have inaugurated conciliation machinery, let us consider why conciliation is better than arbitration. First, since arbitration is often thought of as a judicial process, where the arbitrator decides that one side is right and the other wrong, the side against whom the award is made will always bide its time, will always try to acquire power, as against the other side, so that it may conquer another day. No external settling of the conflict will be successful in the long run.

The most usual view of arbitration, however, is not that an arbitrary decision is given for one side or the other. It is generally taken for granted that an arbitration decision will be a compromise. But more and more people are coming to agree that compromise is not the best way of settling disputes. Someone in England said to me: "The principle of arbitration is to split the difference, and that makes both sides suspicious. It is too easy. They feel no confidence that a well-grounded decision has been arrived at." In an article in an American magazine I find the same view expressed: "Arbitration is not fair because the decision is usually a compromise decision." Another American writer says that arbitration does not establish justice because third parties, not being so well informed on the matters under dispute, adopt the method of splitting the difference.

But if the charge of compromise can be brought against arbitration, it can be brought against conciliation, too. There is, however, an essential difference between the compromise of arbitration and the compromise of conciliation: in the one case you have an adjudicated compromise; in the other, an internally adjusted compromise, a compromise to which both parties agree, to which both parties have perhaps contributed. But whenever I seem to draw the line sharply like this, please remember that these two are always shading into each other. Many a so-called arbitrator sees that there is something better than compromise; many a conciliator has never thought of anything beyond.

Another objection to arbitration, and one strongly voiced by the unions, is that it does away with negotiation, deprives the workers of part of their bargaining power. The new arbitration machinery in Germany has been severely criticized by the trade unions on this ground, that the strong trade unions are hampered by State intervention in their exercise of collective bargaining. Yet it seems to me that arbitration often, or perhaps usually, takes into consideration the strength of both sides. A case occurred in the Pennsylvania Railroad about two years ago where it was pretty evident, during arbitration on a question of wages for a certain class of employees, that what they obtained by arbitration was due to the fact that they were strong enough to enforce a wage increase without the arbitration board. In a dispute in Germany I saw a similar instance of the award following the strength of the union, only in this case the union was not strong and the award was not favourable to labour. One of the trade-union representatives accused the government official conducting the case of partiality. He replied: "Are your unions strong enough to propose better wages than I propose?"

After the Canadian Act for investigation and conciliation in industrial disputes had been in existence for some years, I was rather amused one day, in reading the testimony of a large executive in its favour, at the grounds upon which he based his opinion. He said: "The act gives us time to consider the condition of the labour market, and to find out whether, if the men strike, they will win. That's the beauty of the act."

It is my opinion, founded on my observation of industrial disputes, that whether we have an arbitration board or a mediator, or whatever the machinery is for settling disputes, the balance of economic power of the moment has a great deal to do with the decision.[2] But at the same time it is also my opinion, and I have been confirmed in this by one of our most successful mediators, that the effort on each side to get its own way through the use of its economic power has decreased in some industries where the confidence between

[2] *Cf. Creative Experience*, p. 175: "When the arbitrator of industrial disputes tells you that the first thing to be done is to find out what both sides represented at the conference will accept, it is wise to see just what that means. It means that integration occurs in the sphere of activities rather than of ideas. Business men try to make agreements court-proof, but a finesse in wording your agreement is not what nails it down as an agreement. Unless it is heartily ratified by both sides, it seldom lasts."

employers and employees has been gaining ground. There seems to be an ever-increasing wish to settle a dispute—some say "fairly"; Professor Ripley says according to "logic"; I should say by an attempt to integrate the desires of both sides.

Ramsey Muir, Editor of the *Weekly Westminster*, says: "What is breaking down in industry is what has already broken down in international relations . . . the system of . . . the balance of power." At the same time, arbitrators in industrial disputes tell me, "It always comes down to one thing, the balance of power." Both are right, of course. The balance of economic power at the moment is the chief factor in settling most industrial disputes. But Mr. Muir is also right, for there are many signs that this is changing.

The chief objection to arbitration is that while arbitration boards hear the evidence from both sides, arbitration pure and simple does not allow for a process of interchange of ideas between the two sides which may lead to modifications and changes on the part of both sides. Hence people come to it in the wrong attitude. If the award is to be given to one side or the other, or even if a compromise is expected, the members on each side have to make out a case for their side. They do not come in the attitude that the other party may have something to say that is worth hearing. In a conference where conciliation is the object, you can actually watch (you must often have done so) the changes going on in the minds of those present while the conference proceeds. You must have seen an interpenetrating of ideas. A Canadian who had watched the administration of the Investigation and Conciliation Act already referred to said: "The most obvious virtue of the act . . . lies in bringing the parties together . . . where a free and frank discussion of the differences may take place and the dispute may be threshed out."

I was interested in England to hear one man, who complained of the industrial court which I mentioned above, say he did not consider that it followed the proper procedure because "the parties never get in touch with each other in the industrial court." Another man, a chairman of one of the trade boards, said to me: "If one side is standing out for sixpence an hour and the other for a shilling an hour, it is of no use to decide on ninepence; you have got to carry the members with you." This was a pronouncement against compromise and also a recognition that the parties must themselves take part in the adjustment, that it cannot satisfactorily be made for them. In pure arbitration the only task recognized is that of deciding *between*, not of bringing the two parties *together*. The conciliator or mediator, on the other hand, tries to energize the two parties to the controversy to reach their own decision. Unless both sides are satisfied, the struggle will go on, underneath if not openly. We see again and again that unless an agreement is heartily ratified by both sides, it seldom lasts. Business men, of course, always try to make their agreements court-proof, and yet we know that it is not our subtlety in wording our agreement which nails it down as an agreement.

I have spoken of the prime necessity of bringing the parties together. A mediator may recognize this necessity and yet be thwarted by the parties objecting to the meeting. He then has to exercise some ingenuity. A strike in Boston occurred a few years ago where feeling ran so high that the two parties refused to meet each other. Three connecting rooms were taken at an hotel. The representatives of the manufacturers occupied one room with one mediator, the representatives of the workers another room with the other mediator, and the middle room was kept for consultation between the mediators, who ran backwards and forwards making explanations, clearing up misunderstandings. The case was settled before the conference broke up, and certainly in that case the credit was given to the mediators. I shall touch on this again, that is, on the influence mediators may exert, when we consider leadership. The subject of this conference merges into the next, for nowhere have we better examples of leadership in the best sense of the word than we have had in the case of certain mediators who led the two parties to make their own decisions while encouraging and directing that process.

In speaking of the difference between arbitration and conciliation, I have used the expression "pure arbitration." I have had to do that because we have so many different methods followed in arbitration. It all depends on the man in charge. Mr. William M. Leiserson, while with the clothing industry in Rochester, called himself an industrial *judge*, as I think most of the impartial chairmen in the clothing industry do. In the fur industry, the conference committee is even called an industrial court. The chairman of this committee told me that the reason the impartial chairmen in the clothing industry were looked upon as judges was that the men and women in the clothing industry were Jews and that the Jews had always held judges in high esteem; they looked up to them as above kings. He said: "You remen.ber all that, of course, from the Book of Judges in the Bible." I am afraid I have forgotten the Book of Judges, but I think this an interesting point.

Nevertheless, I think both this chairman and Mr. Leiserson —and this could probably be said of most of the impartial chairmen in the clothing industry—act as judges and conciliators and educators. They try to bring the parties themselves into agreement, an agreement based on an enlarged understanding of each other and of the whole situation.

Again, I think the success of Professor Ripley, while official arbitrator during the War for the Adjustment Commission of the Shipping Board, was due largely to the fact that he was alive to the limitations of arbitration and compromise. He had often, to be sure, to make compromise decisions, but what he always tried for was the integration of the two sides. Indeed, in regard to one case, he stated: "My final decision was midway, but mind you—and this is the point—it was not a compromise; it was sheer logic."

Mr. D. L. Hoopingarner, in an article on "Arbitration" in the *Harvard Business Review* of April, 1926, states: "There are concrete evidences that co-operative control and joint relations on the basis of common conference are coming more and more to be recognized as the most successful methods and coming to play a greater and greater part in arbitration itself. . . ."

I think we may say that the most successful arbitrator is one who does not "arbitrate," but who gets the parties in the controversy face to face and helps them to work out the decision for themselves, helps them to larger understandings, to reciprocal modifyings and adjustments.

Probably one of the reasons that arbitration has been accepted is that as a judicial process it is one we have long been accustomed to in the courts; but we should be careful not to follow too closely a judicial precedent from which the courts themselves have begun to move away. It is noteworthy that in legal procedure to-day, the purely judicial process is giving way in two directions. First, there is a tendency now to try to get people to make their own adjustments to each other, as in the conciliation courts. Secondly, there is an attempt, instead of pronouncing judgment on the individual, to direct his activities so that he shall find a more successful way of living. We have the probation system, the indeterminate sentence, the juvenile courts. Here is a recognition, conscious or unconscious, that men are changed by what they *do*.

The search in the settling of disputes should always be for the best future activities of the parties concerned. This very fundamental psychological principle is accepted by most conciliators. An impartial chairman in the clothing industry said to me: "The courts are concerned with what *has* happened; our problem is always what is going to happen afterwards." Another man said to me, "Arbitration looks to the past, conciliation to the future."

If I have seemed to speak against arbitration as a method of settling industrial disputes, it must be understood that I believe in it unless a better way can be made to work, as I am entirely in favour of it for international disputes— until we find a better way.

The Importance of Determining "What is Right"—Getting an Integration

There is one thing that we often have to face in discussing the ways of settling disputes, and that is the wish of many, not merely for a settlement, but for some pronouncement as to what is "right" and what is "wrong." Mr. Leiserson gives an instance where the unions had questioned a discharge. He decided that the man should be re-employed, but without pay for lost time, and that he should be put into another shop. The man violently objected to this decision. He said: "What I want to know is, am I right or wrong? If right, I should be reinstated with pay. If wrong, I should be discharged."

Another instance of the demand for what is right was given me in England by the Secretary of the Trade Boards. In a certain trade board the proposals in regard to wages were getting nearer and nearer until they were only a penny apart. The chairman of the board, a Scotsman, went to the secretary and said: "I don't think you need worry; the two sides seem to be going to settle it." "But," said the Scotsman, "suppose they do agree on a figure; it won't necessarily be the right figure. You English care about nothing but compromise; we care about what is right. You English care for nothing but coming to agreement." And the secretary telling me this story added: "It is always so with the Scots. They fight for a principle; they will not give way. The Scotsman will die for a principle." This, coming from an Englishman, interested me, and I could not quite make out whether it was said in praise or as a reproach. But I should have said to the Scotsman: That is exactly what we are after, to find what is right; but we have to consider what the employees think right and what the employers think right.

This same disregard of the difficulty of discovering what is right is found in those writers who say that questions of fact can be decided by arbitration, but that other questions must be mediated. This position was taken some years ago in an article in the *Taylor Society Bulletin*. The writer said: "As to conditions of work, experience so far tends to show that all questions are arbitrable; namely, they are capable of being decided by an impartial third party on the basis of the facts presented. Questions of pay, on the other hand, are still so unsupported by scientific, basic facts as to be a matter of conciliation rather than of arbitration." I do not agree with this because the interpretation of facts, the relation of facts, still leave room for legitimate disagreement.

It seems to me that it does not make any difference whether we talk of arbitration or conciliation or of an impartial chairman or mediator or industrial relations expert; the most satisfactory way of settling disputes is to get as near an integration as possible. I will give two illustrations of integration in a wage dispute, one in England, one in America.

The workers on a trade board demanded 1*s.* 6*d.* an hour. The employers said that they would give only 1*s.* Neither side would move. But one of the independent members said to the workers outside (the discussion had assumed that they were talking about the twenty-one-year age): "Would you agree that this one-and-six which you are holding out for should not apply until the twenty-five-year age?" They said they would. (It was, in fact, more complicated than this; the proposal was that there should be different figures for the different ages between twenty-one and twenty-five.) Now this was nearer an integration than a compromise. The 1*s.* 6*d.* against the 1*s.* created what we have called an either-or situation. Nothing could be done as long as they stayed within that situation. Only when someone thought of a way which included the essential desires of both sides could agreement be reached.

I take my American example from one of the cases settled by the National Adjustment Commission during the War. The case had to do with the right of the Steamship Pier Office Employees' Association, affiliated with the International Longshoremen, to recognition by the steamship operators. The employers contended that these men so directly represented them, especially through their supervision over the manual labourers handling freight, that they refused to recognize the union. The men insisted on their right of collective bargaining. The arbitrator considered that the employers were right in regard to the men at the top of this class, but that the rank and file did not thus "represent" the employers. This decision was not a compromise, for it fully satisfied both sides. It supported the employers' contention of freedom from union domination for their representatives, and at the same time left to the large majority in that class the protection of the union, which they badly needed.

I have said that integration is the best way of settling controversy, and perhaps that implies that the chief qualification of arbitrator and conciliator should be that he himself be able to find an integration, usually a pretty difficult task. Probably the main reason why we do not have more integration is that it requires much more thinking on the part of arbitrator or mediator. You remember, perhaps, the careless newspaper reporter who spoke of Mr. Brown's job of "meditation." Putting that one extra letter in "mediation" got him pretty near the truth of the matter. Moreover, besides finding the integration, the conciliator has to see just the right moment in the proceedings to propose it. He can sometimes do even better than this and lead the parties themselves to see and suggest it. All mediators tell us that the best way to bring two parties together is by informal preliminary conferences with both sides. I have seen this myself in the case of Minimum Wage Boards on which I have sat in Massachusetts. It was very marked in the Nash-Hillman controversy.[3] Unless those chiefly instrumental in settling that dispute had conferred many times with each side separately, it is doubtful whether the final joint conferences would have been successful.

All the mediators with whom I have talked personally, and the shop stewards, too, have told me that their chief difficulty is in finding the solution which seems just to both

[3] See pp. 179–81.

sides and at the same time gives those representing the workers a chance to go back and make their constituents feel they have won something for them. One of the ablest industrial relations counsellors I saw in England told me that he had to exercise more ingenuity in this than in any other part of his job. This opens up a number of problems for us.

I should like to try to express the job of the mediator in the terms of our discussion of "The Psychology of Control," when we were trying to lay the foundations for these three remaining talks. I want to see whether we can apply our idea of control as resting on integrative unities to the subject we are discussing. In my talk with mediators I have often noticed that that is exactly their aim, to create a unity of the demands of workers and employers.

A mediator from the West, I suppose one of the ablest in the United States, described his methods to me in this way. He said: "Suppose A, B, C, and D to represent the demands of the workers. First of all, I find out the weight they give to each. Perhaps I find that they will go to the stake for A and B, but that they do not care so much for C. Then I examine the demands of the employers as expressed by A, B, C, and D. Perhaps I find here that C is the point upon which they are determined never to give way." And he added: "Over and over again, I find that what the employer will fight the hardest for is not what the workers are willing to go to the last ditch for. I thus am able by this analysis to unite A, B, C, and D differently from the way they were united by either workers or employers." What is this but stating, in the terms we used previously, that he succeeds in making a different total desire on each side by changing the relation existing between the constituents of these total desires, or rather, by showing what the relation really is, by showing that a different pattern or configuration is made by this different emphasis of values? And what is this but leading the way to the next step, the changing of the united desires of employers and employees, here again a new pattern, an emergent value? This is better than arbitration,

arbitration in its strictest sense, because arbitration decides *between* values; it is not creative of new values.

Another mediator expressed what I think is essentially the same idea in this way: "The two parties come together. There comes a moment in the negotiations when a new relationship between them is born. I am the midwife to that birth."

The Minister of Labour told me in September, when I was in England, that a very interesting conciliation process was going on in the shipbuilding industry, and he offered to give me the opportunity of learning about it. I am going to describe that case very briefly to you, as it illustrates an important point and one I have not yet touched on in this paper.

Early in 1925, a contract for five large motor boats was placed with a German firm. This was a big blow to the British firms. On their own initiative, therefore, they suggested to the unions that they should have a joint conference in order to discuss the whole situation. At the first meeting, employers and unions agreed on a joint inquiry into the position of the industry with special regard to the ability to meet foreign competition. They split the inquiry into two sections: costs within the control of the industry and costs outside.

The first thing they considered under the first section was hours, wages, and conditions of work in England and abroad. They found that some of the Continental countries, while having nominally a forty-eight-hour week, in a number of instances had it extended to fifty-four. Their conclusion on this point was to approach the Government to see whether they could get hours on the Continent shortened to compare with the forty-seven hours in England. They probably had in mind some sort of a convention through the International Labour Office. On the subject of wages, they came to no definite conclusions; they merely gave comparisons.

They did come to conclusions on the questions of interchangeability and demarcation, and it is chiefly because of these conclusions that I am giving some account of this case. The lines of demarcation are rigidly drawn. The craft unions have allocated to themselves certain branches in the trade and do not like to see others encroach on their preserves. But in shipbuilding much can be done by more than one craft. Some things can be done equally well by joiners and by shipwrights. Some of the work which the boiler makers do can be done by the shipwrights. Some of the work of engineers and plumbers is interchangeable. Questions are always arising on demarcation.

The committee considered this question and came to three conclusions.

First, the custom has been that if one class starts a piece of work, that class should finish it. They came to the conclusion that another class capable of doing it might finish it if conditions made that seem desirable.

Secondly, there are the cases where the work may not distinctively belong to any one class, but by custom is performed in one yard by one class, in another by another. The committee came to the conclusion that if it was a case of work not belonging distinctively to any one class, any one competent should be allowed to do it.

Thirdly, they came to the conclusion that when there is a definite shortage of craftsmen in any one class, men in another class capable of doing the work should be allowed to do it. This referred mainly to joiners and shipwrights because there was a shortage of joiners, and shipwrights are of course capable of doing their work.

The second part of the inquiry was concerned with costs outside the industry.

First, considering some charges higher than they should be, they recommended that the Board of Trade should be asked to investigate rings and price-fixing associations.

Then the question of local rates came up. The shipbuilding centres have been hit hard and poor relief has gone up. Poor relief is a charge on the district, so the industry gets hit in this way.

They next considered the social services: health insurance,

244

employment insurance, the new Pension Act. Quotations were given as to the contributions made by employers, employees, and the State respectively, and it was found that the State pays less than the industry. The conclusion they came to on this point was that it would be a more equitable distribution if the State paid more than the industry.

Then they considered cost of living, and wished the Government to consider whether the Food Council could do anything to keep prices down.

They considered public charges, and thought pilot charges, dock charges, harbour dues were rather high, and that the question of these charges should be taken up locally.

Finally, they protested against the discontinuance of facilities under the Trade Facilities Act. By this act, firms can get the assistance of the Government in getting loans at a lower rate of interest. It was the Government's intention to discontinue such assistance. Against this they protested.

Another matter taken up was the question of some continuous conciliation machinery for settling disputes. They came to agreement with some of the unions in regard to this, but not with others.

This, in general, is the outline of the Report of the Joint Committee. They had, as a matter of fact, come to feel, through their investigations abroad, that the German firm had not given an economic price for the contract, and that was confirmed by certain financial troubles which the firm underwent later, but the fact that the English firm had lost these contracts still acted as a powerful incentive to a joint effort of employers and employees to reduce costs.

After the report had been accepted by the joint committee, each side—shipbuilding federation and trade union—had to consider it. The federation accepted it at once. The trade unions took more time about it because they had to refer it to all their executives. When I left England in October, it had been accepted with some reservations, and there was to be a further conference between representatives of the federation and representatives of the unions on certain questions.

The interesting thing to me about this case was that the losing of these contracts made both sides see that their interests were more nearly identical than they had thought. When they discussed costs outside the industry, both sides saw that they were equally affected by these. When they discussed hours, labour saw that the number of working hours in a day did not depend on the selfishness or unselfishness of employers, that large problems were involved in this question, that unless international agreements were made they might have to pay dearly for their forty-seven-hour week. Above all, in regard to interchangeability and demarcation labour saw that the present arrangements were increasing costs and that unless this matter could be put on a more rational basis, it might be one of the causes of their losing the contracts which gave them employment. It was the fact of actually losing large contracts which brought the two sides together.

The lesson to be learned from this case in regard to the subject of this paper is, I think, that it is the duty of arbitrator or conciliator, as it is of management itself, continuously day by day and not merely when disputes arise, to show to labour the common purpose for which all are working. At the same time, we must bear in mind that no statement of a common purpose will carry conviction unless those uttering it have a purpose which truly includes the advantage of all, and unless they are sincerely working for the accomplishment of that purpose. Conciliation and arbitration are not merely temporary expedients. They give us an opportunity to justify that reputation for long views which Europe is attributing to us. A recent writer says: "Foresight is the last gift of gods to men." We do not claim that gift, but we can surely try to base our business policies on more than the expediency of the moment, we can try to make every conciliation pave the way for a larger conception of business relationships.

XII

LEADER AND EXPERT[1]

In my discussion I shall mean by leadership that shown by foreman, head of a department, chief executive, or that found in many other places. For instance, in a committee it may not be the one holding the highest official position who is the leader.

Changes in the Conception of Leadership

Leadership, however, is such a vast subject that I have limited myself to the changes in our ideas of leadership, which have come about in two ways: through certain changes in some of our fundamental conceptions of human relations, and also through some of the more recent developments in management. Take the doctrine of "the consent of the governed." When that had greater sway over us than it has at present, the leader was the man who could persuade others to consent. To-day, persuasion, as mere persuasion, is taking a less dignified place in human relations. Now that we are recognizing more fully the value of the individual, now that management is defining more exactly the function of each, many are coming to regard the leader as the man who can energize his group, who knows how to encourage initiative, how to draw from all what each has to give.[2]

Moreover, we have now to lay somewhat less stress than formerly on this matter of the leader influencing his group because we now think of the leader as also being influenced by his group. One of our chief justices said to me once that he considered this reciprocal relation the main characteristic

[1] This paper was given in two successive Bureau of Personnel Administration annual conference series (April, 1927, and November, 1927), and so appears in two of the resulting volumes, first as the final one of the four which Miss Follett gave in the series entitled *Psychological Foundations of Business Management* (see note, p. 183) and again in *Business Leadership*, Henry C. Metcalf, *Editor*, Isaac Pitman & Sons, 1930.

[2] *Cf. The New State*, Chapter XXV, "Leaders or Bosses?"

of leadership. I think it is one of the best examples of what I have elsewhere called circular response. The currents go both ways. The channels should be kept open for this continuous flow to go on all the time. When it gets dammed up, effective leadership stops. That is, we should think not only of what the leader does to the group, but also of what the group does to the leader. Any of you who have watched in joint committees of management and labour the influence which his constituents exert on the workers' representative, will understand the importance of this.

Again, our idea of power is changing. Men have long worshipped power; the power of arms, the power of divine right —of kings or priests—and then in the nineteenth century the power of majorities. Our conception of democracy is only to-day beginning to free itself from that taint. And the reason that it *is* freeing itself is that our idea of power is changing. Power is now beginning to be thought of by some as the combined capacities of a group. We get power through effective relations. This means that some people are beginning to conceive of the leader, not as the man in the group who is able to assert his individual will and get others to follow him, but as the one who knows how to relate these different wills so that they will have a driving force. He must know how to create a group power rather than to express a personal power. He must make the team.

In a recent book on government this sentence occurs: "Men who have once tasted power will not, without conflict, surrender it." But one of the most interesting things I find in recent business organization is that fewer officials than formerly—higher or lower—are "tasting power." Of course, there are plenty of men who love power, who love to use power, but the form of organization toward which business is tending to-day discourages this.

When I speak against the autocratic view of leadership, however, I am often met with the remark, "But men like to be led." And these people have good psychological backing for such a statement. One psychologist speaks of the "instinct of submission," another of "the psychic urge to submit to

248

authority." But I do not agree with these psychologists; in fact, I do not quite know what all this means. If it means merely that we are all lazy, I certainly agree to that. But I do not see that our liking to be led constitutes any reason that that desire should be encouraged. You may have a child who prefers that you make his decisions for him, but the essence of parenthood, as of teaching, is that children should be made to take responsibility as fast as they are able to do so. We have all to learn to take our share of responsibility or get out of the game. The leader should make us feel our responsibility, not take it from us. Thus he gets men whom it is worth while to lead.

But the time is fast disappearing when we need ask ourselves whether we believe in an "autocratic" or "democratic" leadership, for we are developing something that is neither, something that is better than either. Business men are quietly, without much talk of theory, working out a system of organization which is not democratic in our old understanding of the word, but something better than that. It is a system based neither on equality nor on arbitrary authority, but on functional unity. I am speaking, of course, only of the more progressively organized plants. In these it is impossible in many instances to tell whether Smith or Brown is boss, because in some things Smith is boss over Brown and in some things Brown is boss over Smith. But we have not as yet any wholly agreed-on technique for this relation. That is why I think business management by far the most interesting human activity at present, because we are pioneers, because we are working out something new in human relationships, something that I believe goes to the very bottom of the whole question and is going to be of great value to the world.

Let me give an example of what I mean by one man or department not being "over" another. I have taken it from a rather amusing occurrence during the War, but all of you who are operating under some form of functional management could give me many instances of this same kind. In the beginning of the War, the Quartermaster at Washington had fourteen geographical divisions under him, with a quarter-master over each. Then there was set up a commodity department with eleven divisions—food, fodder, leather, and so forth. Much confusion followed. The men at the head of the geographical divisions could not realize that the commodity department could do what it had to do—in regard to setting policies and standards for price, quality, and the like—without interfering with them. And it was equally difficult, on the other hand, for the commodity department to realize that the quartermasters at the head of the geographical divisions could do their job without encroaching on the prerogatives of the commodity department.

The plan worked as badly as possible. At last the eleven heads of the commodity divisions and the fourteen heads of the geographical areas were brought together for discussion. At the end of four days nothing had been accomplished, and all seemed in despair that anything could be accomplished. At the next meeting, the chairman, the Quartermaster at Washington, said something like this: "I have an agreeable surprise for you. You are probably thinking that we shall have to stay here four days more, but I am going to dismiss you in ten minutes. I herewith divest the fourteen and the eleven heads of every bit of authority and power over their territory and commodity except what they can peacefully enforce. When you bring me a dispute to settle, I shan't do what you will expect me to do, I shan't decide who is right and who is wrong. I shall decide who is pig-headed and I shall fire him."

I am told that this worked like a charm. This was forcible integration, and it was evidently accomplished by a man with some power of leadership; but the reason I am telling this story is that it illustrates one of my main theses in regard to business management, namely, that when differences are integrated instead of each side to a dispute claiming right of way, that is when we have control of the situation. Perfect control is never got except through unity, as I tried to show in the first paper in this group. This was what the Quartermaster meant by saying he would fire the one that was pig-headed, namely, that they must learn how to integrate their differences, not run to him to find out who was "right." Seldom is any side right in that absolute sense. The reason this conference was in the end successful was that all were made to understand that neither commodity department nor geographical divisions had the chief direction; in some instances one was boss, in some instances the other.

I am speaking, you will remember, of recent changes in our ways of thinking which affect our conception of leadership. Another change in our ideas is that connected with checks and balances.

"Checks and balances" was a fundamental part of our thinking a hundred years ago. Whenever we gave power to any official, we immediately provided some check upon it. Some of you feel that the theory of checks and balances still prevails in industry. While that is true, I do not think it is as universal as formerly. I was talking with a man connected with a bank who told me something of the machinery of his organization, and when he got to the subject of loans he mentioned the different officials who had to pass on the larger loans and he said, "This is in order to get their combined judgment." I felt sure that a few years ago he would have said that several men passed on large loans in order to be a check on one another. To-day, however, it seems to me that the tendency is not to check leadership, but to encourage a multiple leadership.

And please remember that in all this I am talking merely of tendencies, of certain trends, of occasional signs, which seem to me significant. It is a difficult moment to give a talk on leadership, because we are in a transition stage in our thinking on that subject. I say I am talking merely of tendencies, but I could give you a number of instances where I think this is going on, plants where they are deliberately trying to develop leaders for the sake of combining their powers, not so that they shall be a check on each other.

But at a meeting of the American Management Association, one of the speakers spoke of the three departments in the insurance business—selling, claims, and underwriting—

and said that they were checks upon one another. As we see this same idea expressed again and again in many places, I am not asserting that we have got rid of it. I say merely that I see signs of a change, and I think that change will be still another step toward that unity which many of us think the chief essential to business success.

Very closely connected with this matter of checks and balances is the change in our attitude toward the veto. Few executives use it as it was once used. An editorial in the *Taylor Society Bulletin* says: "The general manager's first reaction to red-ink balances was to cut expenses right and left—sometimes ruthlessly and unwisely. . . . Now he spends hours with department heads sharing with each the responsibility for policies and plans, and bringing them together in new co-operative effort."

Another idea that is changing is that the leader must be one who can make quick decisions. The leader to-day is often one who thinks out his decisions very slowly. Moreover, as Mr. Dennison says, "In the steady running of an organization, the frequent need of great speed of decision is a symptom of lack of sufficient advance thinking."

Again, the idea of leadership itself is changing. The leaders of the trade-union movement were formerly men of aggressive personality, those who could put up the best fight with employers, those who could build up the best defence organization. That is not so true to-day as it was even a few years ago. I noticed that very much in England last summer. Aggressive as some of their leaders to be sure are, many, particularly some of the shop stewards, are gaining their power in their own ranks through their constructive ability, through their ability to solve problems rather than merely to fight.

We find the different conceptions of leadership reflected often in definitions of management. In an article in a business magazine I saw it stated that management is the way you manage an unruly horse. Another writer says that the leader is he who can drive a team. Others say that managing is manipulating men. This is not the way I am defining management or leadership to you. Some years ago, about ten I think, I went to the president of an industrial concern and asked him if I could make some visits to his plant, telling him that my object was to make some studies in group action. You can imagine that I had not expressed myself well when he replied: "You go ahead, you can have all the facilities you want in my place. You teach me how to manipulate groups and I'm in your debt." But that was not to be the object of my study—to learn how to "manipulate" groups. And I do not think that this conception can last long now that everyone is studying what they call applied psychology; for if employers can learn how to manipulate employees, employees can learn how to manipulate employers, and where are we then?

The Part of the Expert in Decision-Making

A change in organization which is affecting our conception of leadership very fundamentally is the different attitude we now take toward the expert.[3] The expert's information not only forms a large part of the executive's decision; it is becoming an integral part of the decision-making machinery. This comes from two causes chiefly. We have experts on more matters, and the expert is taking a different place in the organization. I say we have experts on more questions. For instance, we used to have experts for the mechanical side of industry; now we have experts for the personal side also. If the chemist or the engineer told an executive a certain purely technical fact, the executive would never have replied, "My opinion about that is different." All were aware that it was a question not of opinion, but of technical fact. In regard to personal questions, however, it was thought to be perfectly legitimate for everyone to have his own opinion, even on purely technical matters of measurable fact. That is changing to-day as we are gaining a larger knowledge of the sciences dealing with human beings, as we are becoming more willing to accept such knowledge and are applying it more widely.

[3] Cf. *Creative Experience*, Chapter I, "Experience and the Expert."

Then the fact that large businesses have their own experts inside the plant makes a different relation between expert and executive. It is giving us, for one thing, a different conception of advice. There is a change going on in this direction which will probably eventually give us a new vocabulary. We used to think that the various heads gave orders, that the different experts gave advice, but a new relation has entered in of recent years; there is something emerging which is neither orders nor advice. For instance, a staff man may be responsible for seeing that machines are taken care of, but the line man takes care of them. Now suppose the staff man tells the line man that a certain machine needs attention. Is that an order? No, because the line man does not take orders from this man. Is it advice? No, because one of the characteristics of advice is that it can be rejected, and this cannot be rejected without taking it higher up. To be sure, we use the word "requisition," but that has not yet been defined with sufficient clearness.

Again, I have often heard the question asked whether the employment manager should give advice to the line executives in regard to hiring, transfers, dismissals, or whether he should have final authority. What is being actually worked out is something different from either. Most of us do not believe in the employment manager's having final authority. Yet I cannot say, as so many do, that he is merely to give advice, for his opinions are being given more weight than mere advice in the ordinary acceptance of that word.

The ordinary use of the word "advice" involves a take-it-or-leave-it attitude. If I should ask one of you to give me your advice about something in my life, we should both of us have a take-it-or-leave-it attitude about what you might say. That is, I should not feel any obligation to take your advice and you would not expect me to. It would be advice from outside, advice unrelated to the currents of my life. But those who give advice in business to-day are usually such an integral part of the organization that one cannot have the take-it-or-leave-it attitude toward their suggestions. It seems to me that our present methods of management have given us new interrelations of duties and responsibilities which have not yet found a place in our vocabulary or in our philosophy of management. What we are trying to do is to find a method by which advice does not coerce and yet enters integrally into the situation.

I read recently in a book on management: "The research department makes suggestions to the manufacturing department. The head of the manufacturing department has the right to veto these suggestions." Well, technically he has, and practically he frequently does, and yet the word "veto" does not accurately express the relation which is being worked out between executive and expert.

Moreover, the separation between advice and decision cannot be a rigid one, since pure information is seldom given by expert to executive. Most experts both interpret facts and relate facts, and decisions are largely determined by the interpretation of facts and the way in which they are related. While information comes to the expert as fact, it usually leaves him as opinion. The head of a business said to me: "I don't know that we can get any pure information except from reports like Babson's, and when you get opinions, that makes the man who gives them to a certain extent a part of management."

At the same time, it is true that most of us in this country want to keep distinct the executive function and the function of the specialist. I know a town in Massachusetts where they put an engineer on the Water Board, and one of the members of the board said to me: "Everything goes wrong; he can think of nothing but engineering problems."

On the other hand, in Germany, in the German municipal system, the experts, the specialists in the various branches of administration, have the authority. They can go ahead and do things. The elected council may criticize, may demand explanation, may in the last resort reject, but it is essentially the business of the specialists to say what ought to be done and how it should be done.

As the relation between specialist and executive is one

which we are at present trying to work out, we cannot yet dogmatize on the subject, but I think we may say that while the executive should give every possible value to the information of the specialist, *no executive should abdicate thinking on any subject because of the expert.* The expert's information or opinion should not be allowed automatically to become a decision. On the other hand, full recognition should be given to the part the expert plays in decision making.

One of the speakers at an American Management Association Conference said: "The executive may get all the help and advice he wishes, but the responsibility for a decision rests with him." While this is theoretically true, yet in those cases where the executive gives way to the specialist (you must have seen this often in committees, as I have), both executive and specialist feel that the specialist has a large share in the responsibility. (I am not, of course, speaking of legal accountability.) I think our problem should be stated in different terms: it is to find a way by which the specialist's kind of knowledge and the executive's kind of knowledge can be joined. I have seen it stated that the specialist has the knowledge and the executive the wisdom, but I cannot agree to that. They have different kinds of knowledge and experience.

I have often spoken to you of the advantage of integration in settling disputes over any other method. Some of my hearers have thought that too Utopian a method to be worth trying. I should like to point out here that when there is a difference of opinion with an expert we take that method without realizing that we are doing so. Let me try to make this clear by a very simple illustration. An electrician comes to wire my house for electric lighting. I say that I want it done in a certain way. He says that there are mechanical difficulties about doing it in that way. I suggest another way. He says that the laws of the State in regard to fire safeguards do not permit that way. Then he tells me how he thinks it should be done. Do I accept his suggestions? No. Because I have a very decided objection on account of æsthetic reasons or reasons of convenience. We continue our discussion until we find a way which meets the mechanical difficulties and the laws of the State and at the same time satisfies me.

Now, I believe the reason that we integrate so often with the expert without knowing that we are doing such a difficult thing as I am told integration is, is that we do not usually think of our relation with the expert as that of a fight. We *expect* to be able to unite a difference of opinion with the expert. We have gone to him for that purpose. We recognize that he has one kind of knowledge and we another. This kind of integration we see often in committees in a plant or business. The president or vice-president is apt neither to give in to some plan presented by a specialist nor to veto it. They usually integrate their different kinds of knowledge, and this is because president and specialist seldom meet to fight. They meet *in order to integrate* and therefore they do it.

Leadership a Problem of Relating—Organizing—Experience

In considering the relation of executive and expert, it has occurred to me that perhaps we ought to make a distinction between leadership and decision-making. It seems to me that the leader has not always the largest share in decision-making, and yet he may not thereby be any the less the leader.

It seems rather as if decisions in the better organized and more progressive industries tend to be determined largely by the people with the special knowledge required for the special problem. If the psychologist, the employment manager, the general manager, and the president meet to decide on some plan the psychologist may have for tests or training, the decision is likely to be made largely in accordance with the psychologist's suggestions because he has the special knowledge on which the plan they are considering is based. Or in a committee of department heads and president, a plan of the merchandising manager may be accepted. This plan may be modified or changed by suggestions from the others, yet the decision made may be due chiefly to the merchandising manager. And yet I do not know that that necessarily makes him the leader of that group. The leader in both these instances may have been the chairman who brought them to a mutual understanding, who showed them how to make the necessary reciprocal adjustments, who brought out unexpected strength and knowledge from the different members of the committee. Or it may have been the president who, while he had not the special knowledge of the psychologist or the merchandising manager, had more knowledge of the plant in its entirety, its policies and plans, and could fit all the special knowledge into a larger view of the whole. Or it may have been some other member of the committee who had pre-eminently this particular ability.

I believe we shall soon think of the leader as one who can organize the experience of the group, make it all available and most effectively available, and thus get the full power of the group. It is by *organizing* experience that we transform experience into power. And that is what experience is for, to be made into power.

You will have gathered by this time that my key word of organization is relatedness. Unrelated experience means partly wasted experience. For instance, society needs the experience of the consumers in solving some of our industrial problems, but we must find some way of joining it to the experience of producers. At present, producers and consumers are in separate associations. The organization of experience is the problem of industrial, of political, of our everyday life. A woman once said to me, a woman very well known in this city, "The trouble with me is that I don't organize my experience." What she meant obviously was that having a very full life, connected with very important undertakings, she had a great deal of experience, but that she did not relate these different experiences in a way to get the most out of them, that she did not discriminate between their different values, subordinate some to others, see what they meant all together. This is the same with a group. Just exactly as my own life is more successful as I learn how to organize my experience, so will the group be more successful as it learns how to do this. And the organization of experience is the task of the leader in any business or industry.

This view of leadership is not lessening the power of the leader; it is vastly increasing it. Or perhaps I should say that a different kind of leader is developing. This is very markedly shown in the trade unions which are now employing statisticians, accountants, expert fact-finders of all kinds. The leader in these trade unions is now tending to be one who can use these facts, who can put them all together and see what they amount to. We see this everywhere. The higher railroad officials may not understand railroad accounting, design of rolling stock, and assignment of rates as well as their expert assistants, but they know how to use this knowledge, how to relate it, how to make a total situation, an integrative unity.

In considering those changes in our thinking which are influencing our idea of leadership, we find there has been one very marked change recently. Only a short time ago people were telling us that leadership was an "intangible capacity," also that if you were not born with this capacity, you could never acquire it. We are coming to think now that executive leadership can in part be learned. This is the point about leadership I like most to emphasize, for unless this is true, there is not much hope for men in subordinate positions being able to rise, and also, if it were not possible for men to learn to be leaders, our large, complex businesses would not have much chance of success, for they require able leadership in many places, not merely in the president's chair.

An article in the *Boston Herald* gave the results of several interviews with business women, aimed at finding out what these women considered the essentials of business success. One of the questions asked in the interviews was whether they thought hard work necessary to success, and the way the question was put seemed to imply that perhaps a compelling personality was all that was necessary. Such a question must have come out of the old notion of leadership. I most certainly believe that many personal qualities enter into leadership—tenacity, steadfastness of purpose, power of forceful expression, depth of conviction, tactfulness, steadiness in stormy periods, and so on and so on—and yet we must be careful of that old superstition about leadership which said, "Leaders are born, not made."

When I say that I believe that leadership can be studied, I mean that it is part of the study of organization and management. The leader must learn his place in the organization, his relation to all the other parts. An organization engineer told me that he was hired for a three months' job in a business, and when he left, the head said to him: "Well, you've done this much for me, at any rate. I used to raise hell with everyone and now I know who to raise hell with."

The Main Functions of the Chief Executive

In the light, then, of what we have thus far considered, what are the main functions of the chief executive? If functional unity is the chief task of management, if the organization chart provides primarily for this, still it is to the chief executive more than to any other one person that we look to make the organization chart a going affair. While he may have a planning department, an organizing secretary, an economic adviser, a psychologist, experts of many kinds, and his department heads, too, are of course specialists, and while more and more we are expecting co-ordination to take place below the president's office, while we do not think of the president as holding together an aggregate of unco-ordinated authorities, still there is much he can do. Many a department head has a tendency to play a lone hand if not prevented. Again, he can often see that departmental or divisional policies do not get crystallized too quickly before it is discovered whether they are in accord with one another or with general policy. This is difficult if the plant is large, but the form of organization should be such as to keep this in view. Moreover, there are many matters which come to the president because of dissensions among executives. He should know how to integrate such differences. Also he should know how to give actual existence and official status to incipient integration. But while one of the jobs of the chief executive is to resolve differences that it has not been possible to integrate anywhere down the line, yet he should never be thought of as an umpire or arbitrator. If purchasing agent and production manager bring him different conclusions, his task is not to decide *between* them, but to try to unite the three different kinds of experience involved—that of purchasing agent and production manager *and his own*.

One of your New York writers on management would not agree with me on this point. He says explicitly that the chief executive should act as arbitrator, that if he did not, the heads of departments would settle their disputes by bargaining with each other. I agree with this writer that the chief executive should try to prevent this, but I do not think the method should be that of arbitration in its stricter sense of adjudication. He should try to find a solution which will include all, or as many as possible, of the different values involved in the varying opinions. Moreover, we should never forget that the chief executive does not judge from outside. He has to weld together the functions of critic, judge, and active participator. In other words, if we say that he passes *on* a situation, we must remember that he is *in* that situation. We should be careful not to use language which puts him outside that process of management of which he is an integral part.

The chief executive's main job may be co-ordination, but you cannot integrate the parts of your business successfully unless you have your purpose clearly defined. The chief executive should be able to define the purpose of the plant at any one minute, or rather, the whole complex of purposes. He should see the relation of the immediate purpose to the larger purpose. He should see the relation of every suggestion, of every separate plan, to the general purpose of the company. He should, as he considers each problem brought to him, scrutinize the proposed solution in order to see if it will promote the major purposes of the company. Moreover, he should always be able to summarize the purposes of the company and say how far the company is reaching them and how far not. The president's report should summarize present achievements and should always include what is still unachieved, what all are to work for in the coming year. It should encourage to further endeavour and it should never be vague as to what that endeavour is to be directed toward. It should not only inspire to do, but to do certain things. Above all, he should make his co-workers see that it is not *his* purpose which is to be achieved, but a common purpose, born of the desires and the activities of the group.

The best leader does not ask people to serve him, but the common end. The best leader has not followers, but men and women working with him. When we find that the leader does less than order and the expert more than advise, sub-ordinates—both executives and workers—will respond differently to leadership. We want to arouse not the attitudes of obedience, but the attitudes of co-operation, and we cannot do that effectively unless we are working for a common purpose understood and defined as such.

I am speaking at this point of the chief executive, but everything I am saying applies to all leaders. And, of course, sub-executives should be chosen with that idea primarily in mind, namely, whether they have the power of leadership, and one of the tests of that should be whether they have the power of making purposes articulate. I am convinced, and I cannot tell you how strongly I feel this, that one could get much larger output from the rank and file throughout a factory if they had some idea of what they were working for, of what it was all about. If you think that the foreman is not the man that you could expect to be able to do this, and I myself should not expect it of him, then there should be someone in the department who could connect the work of the girls or the men with the major purposes of the plant or the industry. They need not feel, as most of them do now, that they are mere bits in a huge machine. Their individual worth, their own wills and aims, could, I am sure, be made to find a place in the purposes of the industry in which they are working. When employers see the relation between this and output, then something will be done about it.

I have not spoken of the leader's part in the formation of

purpose and in the improvement of purpose, for the same reason that I have not allowed the word "policy" to come into this paper. The consideration of these subjects, involving the relation of the chief executive to the directors, would take us too far afield.

If we find that the task of the chief executive is to articulate the purpose which guides the integrated unity which his business aims to be, if it is his task to understand everyone's place in that purpose and that unity, there is another task which no leader ever forgets without disastrous consequences; namely, that each unit has to be fitted into a whole which is constantly changing, that is, into an evolving whole. In business we are always passing from one significant moment to another significant moment, and the leader's task is pre-eminently to understand the *moment of passing.* This is why the leader's task is so difficult, why it requires great qualities—the most delicate and sensitive perceptions, imagination and insight, and at the same time courage and faith.

A business man, the president of a large company, once told me that I would not make a good business woman because I had not enough faith. He did not, of course, mean religious faith, he meant faith in my own purposes, that I wanted to safeguard myself too much, that I would trust only the present which I could see, not the future which I could not see. This was in regard to some committee work we were doing together. I thought then that he was wrong, not about me necessarily, but about the course he wanted to take in the matter under discussion, but I have come to think he was right in the matter, as I have come to understand the fundamental principles underlying what he was saying.

This insight into, and faith in, the future we usually call in business "anticipation." In defining anticipation in an earlier paper, I said that it meant far more than *meeting* the next situation; that it meant *making* the next situation. So the leader should be able to do more than predict; he should be able to control. The highest-grade decision does not have to do merely with the situation with which it is directly concerned. It is always the sign of the second-rate man when the decision merely meets the present situation. It is the left-over in a decision which gives it its greatest value. It is the carry-over in the decision which helps develop the situation in the way we wish it to be developed.

The ablest administrators do not merely draw logical conclusions from the array of facts of the past which their expert assistants bring to them; they have a vision of the future. To be sure, business estimates are always, or should be, based on the probable future conditions. Sales policy, for instance, is guided not only by past sales but by probable future sales. But the leader must see *all* the forward trends and unite them. Business is always developing. Decisions have to anticipate the development. You remember how Alice in Wonderland had to run as fast as she could to stand still. That is a commonplace to every business man. And it is up to the president to see that his executives are running as fast as they can. Not, you understand, working as hard as they can—that is taken for granted—but anticipating as far as they can.

I told you in one of my papers that the English were calling the phrase "in the long run" an American expression. We should try to live up to this opinion of us, and it is to the chief executive especially that we have a right to look for our long views. Some years ago the heads of a number of firms in Boston met to consider all-day closing on Saturdays in July and August. At that time they could not agree about it, but a woman at the head of a string of restaurants in Boston described the meeting to me, and she said she could have told beforehand who would be in favour of the proposition and who against. Those in favour would be, and were, she said, those who appreciate the value of the long view, who understand that whatever is good for the community is good for your business in the long run. I must add that I think she showed herself particularly able to do this when she voted in favour of all-day closing on Saturdays, for if you cannot buy a dress or a carpet on Saturday you will simply buy it on Monday and the merchants will lose nothing; but you cannot eat two luncheons on Monday! Therefore she might have thought that she stood to lose by this project if she had not been convinced of the soundness of the principle that what is good for the community is good for business "in the long run."

I am not advocating Saturday closing. I am merely saying that I believe that a business will not long be successful if it runs counter to the good of the community. I believe that the good of the community and the good of one's business are synonymous and therefore the leader should try to understand what is the good of the community.

It is pre-eminently to the chief executive, then, that we are to look for long views. We look to him to open up new paths, new opportunities for the development of individuals, of groups, of the whole plant. He should see not only larger situations, but situations of greater value to all concerned. This means a power of fine discrimination. "Growing with the business" has subtler meanings than we usually realize.

It is obvious that the job of the chief executive is not easier because he has now so many "facilitating services," his planning and co-ordinating departments, his many experts of many kinds. It is, indeed, much harder. It requires a higher order of intelligence and more training to be the head of these intricate, highly organized units. Moreover, we have been speaking only of the leader's relation to the internal affairs of his group. We must remember that a group had always two aspects—its internal relations and its external relations. As the President of the United States is concerned, not only with the affairs of the nation, but has also to consider the relation of the United States to other nations, so it is with the chief executive. As he is responsible for those internal adjustments which make for the effective operation of his plant, so is he responsible for relating these to all the outside forces which are affecting the operation of the industry. I have said that we get control through unity. The great leader is he who so relates all the complex outer forces and all the complex inner forces that they work together effectively.

I have given co-ordination, definition of purpose, and anticipation as three of the functions of the chief executive, and I have said these are the functions of the leader wherever found, whether in the president's chair or down the line. The leader may even not be the head of a department or division. In a committee, the man tends to lead who can see all round a situation, who sees it as related to certain purposes and policies, who sees it evolving into the next situation, who understands how to pass from one situation to another. I want to emphasize this point, that leadership appears in many places, because what I find in regard to leadership when I go into plants is so very different from what I usually find in speeches or articles or books on the subject. Forgetting the actual practice, which most of these speakers and writers must be more or less familiar with, they hark back to some preconceived idea of leadership.

For some weeks I was allowed to sit in with the co-ordinating committee of a plant. One of the most interesting things about that committee was the way in which the leadership was sometimes with one person and sometimes with another. Sometimes, I think I may say usually, it was with the chairman, but sometimes it was with a specialist, and sometimes, rather often, it was with a certain man in that committee who seemed to have an unusual power of grasping the situation as a whole, and also that extra-ordinary gift of identifying the conditions which would lead them most effectively from that situation to the next. The leader of the highest order understands the evolving present, the present that is at the very moment in process of change.

I am especially interested in the subject of leadership in connection with sub-executives, for I believe that there is more capacity for leadership among under-executives that is utilized by our present forms of organization. I believe that that should be one of the aims in further developments in organization, namely, to provide opportunities for utilizing more fully the capacities of under-executives, rather than that they should wait until they get into some higher position before they can use their capacities 100 per cent.

Summary—The Leader's Relation to the Fundamental Principles of Organization

I want to summarize this talk by taking the principles which I gave you in our discussion of "Controls," and which I consider the fundamental principles of organization: namely, evoking, interacting, integrating, and emerging, and ask what part the leader has in all these.

Under evoking, we shall all agree that it is one of the leader's chief duties to draw out from each his fullest possibilities. The foreman should feel responsible for the education and training of those under him, the heads of departments should feel the same, and so all along up the line to the chief executive. In fact, several men at a meeting of the American Management Association voiced their conviction that "leader" and "teacher" are synonymous terms. If we are coming to think that the leader is not the boss, but the educator, that seems to me an indication that business thinking is taking a long step forward. Our old idea of leadership was that of being able to impress oneself upon others. But to persuade men to *follow* you and to train men to work *with* you are conceptions of leadership as far apart as the poles. The best type of leader to-day does not want men who are subservient to him, those who render him a passive obedience. He is trying to develop men exactly the opposite of this, men themselves with mastery, and such men will give his own leadership worth and power.

I say that it is the part of the leader to educate and train. He must know how to do this. He must himself understand, or get others who understand, the scientific methods which have lately been applied to production, to marketing, to office management, to finance, and, perhaps more important than all, the scientific methods which psychology is giving us for the understanding and controlling of human relationships.

Our second and third principles were interacting and integrating. The leader is more responsible than anyone else for that integrative unity which is the aim of organization. As our business undertakings are not only becoming vast in size but also more complex in character, the success of these undertakings depends on their parts being so skilfully related one to another that they function effectively as a whole. The leader should be leader of a coherent group, of men who are finding their material welfare, their most effective expression, their spiritual satisfaction, through their relations to one another, through the functioning of the group to which they belong. If the old idea of leader was the man with compelling personality, the idea to-day is the man who is the expression of a harmonious and effective unity which he has helped to form and which he is able to make a going affair. We no longer think that the best leader is the greatest hustler or the most persuasive orator or even the best trader. The great leader is he who is able to integrate the experience of all and use it for a common purpose. All the ramifications of organization are the ways he does this; they are not set up to provide a machinery of following.

The fourth fundamental principle of organization which I gave you was what I called the emerging, because that is the expression so much used to-day to denote the evolving, the creating of new values, the forward movement. It is the word with most significance in modern literature. Scientists are using it to describe evolution—emergent evolution—and the business man is as interested as the scientist in the emerging. As a certain psychologist speaks of those moments in creating when evolution turns a corner, as Huxley spoke of the mystery moments in evolution, so the leader in business is one who understands the creative moment in the progress of business, who sees one situation melting into another and has learned the mastery of *that* moment.

To sum up my summary: the leader releases energy, unites energies, and all with the object not only of carrying out a purpose, but of creating further and larger purposes. And I do not mean here by larger purposes mergers or more branches; I speak of larger in the qualitative rather than the quantitative sense. I mean purposes which will include more of those fundamental values for which most of us agree we are really living.

I hope you do not think that I am taking a rose-coloured view of business. Indeed, I am not. I am perfectly aware that in most plants the attitude is, "I'm the boss. You do what I say." But, aware as I am of that, at the same time I see signs of something else, and it is on these signs that I am placing my hopes.

If any of you think I have under-estimated the personal side of leadership, let me point out that I have spoken only against that conception which emphasizes the dominating, the masterful man. There is much in what is called "the personal view of leadership" with which I heartily agree, but I began by saying that I was going to limit myself to-night to certain changes in our ideas of leadership which have come about through recent changes in organization and management. So please remember that I do not undervalue the personal side of leadership; indeed, there is much in this paper, by implication, on that side. But since business management to-day depends so largely on organized control, what I have tried to do this evening particularly is to find the leader's part in that intricate system of human relationships which business has now become.

Our generation is, I think, contributing something to the history of thought in this matter of human relations, and it seems to me that business men have the opportunity, and that some are indeed using it, to share largely in that contribution. Academic people may hope that what they are teaching will be followed by their students, but business men can actually themselves put into practice certain fundamental principles. They may be making useful products; in addition to that they may be helping the individuals in their employ to further development; but even beyond all these things, by helping in solving the problems of organization, they are helping to solve the problems of human relations, and that is certainly the greatest task man has been given on this planet.

XIII

SOME DISCREPANCIES IN LEADERSHIP THEORY AND PRACTICE[1]

The Theory of Leadership

WHAT is the accepted *theory* of leadership? In general, we may say that the leader is usually supposed to be one who has a compelling personality, who wields a personal power, who constrains others to his will.

This has been the theory of the past and is still to a large extent the theory of the present. Certain psychologists, in their wish to facilitate the discovery of leadership qualities, are working at tests which are expected to show what they call "ascendancy traits." I think that these psychologists are doing valuable work and that their tests will probably enable them to discover those who possess ascendancy traits, but I do not think that these traits are the essential qualities of leadership. Indeed, not only do ascendancy traits not always indicate leadership, but, on the contrary, they often militate directly against leadership. I knew a boy who was very decidedly the boss of his gang through all his youthful days. That boy is now forty-five years old. He has not shown any ability to rise in his business or any power of leadership in his community. And I do not think that this is in spite of his "ascendancy traits," but because of them.

A few years ago two psychologists carried on some rather elaborate tests for the measurement of aggressiveness. I have no doubt that these tests disclosed, as the conductors of the experiments claim, the trait of aggressiveness, but what I question is their assumption that aggressiveness is necessary

[1] This paper was presented on March 8th, 1928, and reprinted from *Business Leadership*. See note, p. 247.

to success. They define aggressiveness as abundance of self-assertion and pugnacity combined with a lack of fear, and then add: "We may say with only slight qualification that, other things being equal, the measure of a man's aggressiveness is the measure of his chance of success." Surely this is an over-estimate of self-assurance, pugnacity, and lack of fear.

We have just had an interesting example of leadership in Charles Evans Hughes' influence at the Pan-American Conference. One reporter spoke of Mr. Hughes' ability to influence the Conference profoundly by quiet advice and suggestion, and thought this power due chiefly to his intimate knowledge of Latin-American affairs and of the phases of the continually changing situation developing in the Latin countries, to his large knowledge of history, and to his mastery of international law. Another article on the Conference stated: "By common consent, Mr. Hughes dominated every scene in which he figured importantly; not with the mien of superiority, but that of the friendly adviser who knew his law and his Latin America."

Consider another interesting study in leadership, that of Platt, famous boss of the New York Republican machine. The way he influenced local, state, and national politics throws much light on our subject. His leadership depended largely on his ability in organization, his cleverness in using people, and his power of harmonizing conflicting interests. His genius for political organization is shown throughout his career. In regard to his astuteness in using other people, we are told by his biographer: "Platt did not have a great deal of physical energy, but his chief-of-staff, 'Ben' Odell, was commanding, pushing, aggressive. Platt did not understand the arts of publicity, but Quigg was known as an 'accelerator of public opinion.' " As to his power of uniting contending men and conflicting interests, of bringing men to work together with a common purpose for mutual benefit, he himself says in his *Autobiography* that his power was not "possessed in like degree by any other politician in America."[2]

[2] Harold F. Gosnell, *Boss Platt and His New York Machine*, p. 334.

Or recall the career of Mark Hanna. Enterprising, dominating as he was, essentially the pushing, pioneer type, yet his success as a business man was due chiefly to a thorough knowledge of every detail of his business, his success in the Senate as much to his fullness of understanding of the measures he advocated as to the confidence he inspired or his position in his party. As to his success as party leader, while many personal qualities contributed to that, and while it was indeed due above all to his mastery and use of machine politics—no one could play politics better—yet what stood out in any mind after reading his biography was that he had mastered every task he ever undertook. His biographer, Herbert Croly, after quoting what Bishop Potter said of Hanna in regard to his management of the Civic Federation —that he had grown up to the size of his job—adds: "That comment supplies the clue to all the success of his career. He had grown up to one job after another."

The courses in "applied psychology" which are now advertised everywhere belong really to the era of the old theory that one man was to impose his will on others, but the wiser teachers say to their students: "Don't exploit your personality. *Learn your job.*"

I am not saying that certain personal qualities do not play a large part, a very large part, in leadership. I am merely suggesting further study of those possessed of such qualities in order to see whether these men or women have not also had an unusually large knowledge of the business in hand, and to consider whether history has made a wholly valid estimate of the balance between knowledge and "personality." Take even Joan of Arc—her leadership was obviously and pre-eminently due to the ardour of her conviction and her power to make others share that conviction—yet we are told that no trained artillery captain could excel Joan of Arc in the placement of guns.

Standard Practice versus "Orders"

Now let us look at business practice and see what we find there that is not in accord with the stereotype of leader as the aggressive man carrying all before him by the sheer force of his personal will. We find many things. Consider first the matter of giving orders. The word "order" is being used less and less. One man told me that the word had not been used in his factory for twenty-two years. In scientifically managed plants indeed, where the right "order" is found by research, few orders are given in the old sense of that word, that of arbitrary command—we have method sheets, instruction cards. What is called the "work-order" is given in some plants by the dispatch clerk. This makes it clear to all that it is an essential part of factory planning, not anything arbitrary on the part of the foreman. The best answer to the conception of an autocratic leader issuing arbitrary commands is to say: Look at business as it is being carried on to-day and watch where the orders come from. What is their origin? Heaven does not privately convey them to the top executives. They rise out of the work itself, and in many cases subordinates may have contributed to the order.

Take the analysis of executive jobs that is being made in some plants. This can be done in two ways. You can get in an expert to do it, or you can, as they have done in some places, get each man to make an analysis of his own job. Out of that analysis, rules for the job, or orders, are formulated. Orders are the outcome of daily activity. Orders come from action, not action from orders.

The same is true in the case of operating jobs. That is, a certain way of doing things has been found to be the most effective, and therefore that way is standardized until a better way is found. Hence the expression now used in many plants is not orders, but standard practice. Men follow standard practice rather than obey arbitrary commands.

In some of the preliminary studies made to determine standard practice, the workers often take a part. If new methods are devised by the Research and Planning Departments, still in many instances they are not adopted without a shop try-out, and the workers are sometimes given the chance in this shop try-out to make objections. In plants where there are shop committees, explicit approval is obtained from the shop committees.

But if there is in scientifically managed plants little order-giving left for the foreman in the old sense of that word, still the foreman is not only *as* important but more important than formerly, not only is he not less of a leader, but he has more opportunities for leadership in the meaning which is now coming to be accepted by many for that word. This is because his time is freed for more constructive work. He has, with the more explicitly defined requirements made upon him—requirements in regard to time, quality of work, and methods—a greater responsibility for group accomplishment. In order to meet the standards set for group accomplishment, he is developing a technique very different from the old foreman technique.

The foreman to-day does not merely deal with trouble, he forestalls trouble. In fact, we don't think much of a foreman who is always dealing with trouble; we feel that if he is doing his job properly, there won't be so much trouble. The job of the head of any unit—foreman or head of department —is to see that conditions (machines, materials, etc.) are right, to see that instructions are understood, and to see that workers are trained to carry out the instructions, trained to use the methods which have been decided on as best. The test of a foreman now is not how good he is at bossing, but how little bossing he has to do because of the training of his men and the organization of their work. The job of a foreman thus conceived, we have, as has been pointed out by an able head of department himself, a leader not ordering his men, but serving his man.

The arbitrary foreman may indeed get hoist with his own petard. I knew a case where a workman, reacting against such a foreman, deliberately carried out a wrong order instead of taking it back to the foreman and asking about it, and wasted a large amount of material in order that his foreman should be blamed for this waste. Thus the man who demands a blind obedience may have it react on himself.

Our conception of leadership is everywhere restricted by

the persistence of the fallacy in the old idea of obedience, namely, that obedience is necessarily passive. There is an active principle in obedience. Obedience is a moment in a process. The one who obeys and the one obeyed both contribute to that moment. There is, as a rule, a very elaborate and complex process going on. At one moment in that process something happens which we *call* obedience, but it depends on everything else that is happening.

Can we not see then the fallacy in the idea that an order gets its validity through consent? Consent interweaves with all the other factors in the process, and the validity of the leadership situation depends never on consent but must be tested by the basis of consent.

The men on a fishing smack are all good fellows together, call each other by their first names, yet one is captain and the others obey him, but it is an intelligent, alert, self-willed obedience.

Yet there are many who think, as I saw it stated, that "obedience is inconsistent with individuality and self-expression." On the contrary, obedience and self-expression, or even self-direction, are reciprocally involved. Group activity, organized group activity, should aim: to incorporate and express the desires, the experience, the ideals of the individual members of the group: also to raise the ideals, broaden the experience, deepen the desires of the individual members of the group. Obedience in relation to leadership can be discussed only in terms of these two aspects of the group process. From a study of this process we see that leadership rightly understood increases freedom as it heightens individuality.

Perhaps the greatest difference between theory and practice in regard to orders is that the old theory envisaged the leader as one who could get orders obeyed—any order—while in the best modern practice the leader is the man who can show that the order is integral to the situation. And an order of this kind carries weight because it *is* the demand of the situation.

I found something a few weeks ago in a recent novel which

recognizes and expresses this point. The hero of the novel, Richard Hague, was a large-scale farmer in England. And he was a very successful farmer. The author after telling how Hague got the most out of all his materials down to the very spark with which he lighted a fire, went on to say: "And he was the same with people. He got *use* out of them, though not through . . . being personally exigent in any way. It was always the force of circumstances that seemed to make the demand, not himself. He merely made it clear to them what it was that needed doing. . . . So little did it seem an affair personal to him that the sheep needed driving off the corn, or a message carried into the hay-field, that he hardly intervened. He might just call somebody's attention to what was needed, but it was the corn, the cattle, the world that required the service, not he." And later the author tells us: "Hague evidently considered that the task itself made some claim on anybody who happened to come across it, made itself the most interesting and necessary thing in the world, so that no one could resist it."

In a recent article on Adult Education in the *New Republic*, Harold Laski said: "For the business of any educational system is simply to breed scepticism of authority. . . ." I do not agree with that statement. Every situation in life has its own inner authority. To that we submit. *By* that submission we gain our freedom. What educational systems should do is to show us how to join with our leaders in finding that inner authority.

To sum up this section: In the more progressively managed businesses, orders are coming to be considered as the outcome of the requirements of the situation, as information in regard to standards, as training in methods. The leader gets an order followed first, because *men do really want to do things in the right way* and he can show them that way, and secondly, because he too is obeying. Sincerity more than aggressiveness is a quality of leadership.

If one blow at the old theory of leadership is the increasing disappearance of arbitrary commands and a truer understanding of the real meaning and basis of obedience—an understanding that commands and obedience are two aspects of exactly the same thing—another blow at the theory that "followers" should merely follow is that in looking at almost any business we see many suggestions coming up from below. We find sub-executives trying to get upper executives to install mechanical improvements, to try a new chemical process, to adopt a plan for increasing incentives for workers, and so on. The upper executives try to persuade the general manager, and the general manager the board of directors.

The Leadership of Function versus the Leadership of Personality

Moreover, there is a growing recognition among business men that there are many different degrees of leadership, that many people have *some* capacity for leadership even although it be of the smallest. And the men who recognize this are trying to work out a form of organization and methods of management which will make the most effective use of such leadership capacity. It is also recognized that there are different types of leadership. I mean not only that there are different leadership qualities possessed by different men, but also that different situations require different kinds of knowledge, and the man possessing the knowledge demanded by a certain situation tends in the best managed businesses, and other things being equal, to become the leader at that moment.

We may say that we have in scientifically managed plants a leadership of function as well as the leadership of personality and the leadership of position. We have people giving what are practically orders to those of higher rank. The balance of stores clerk, as he is called in some places, will tell the man in charge of purchasing when to act. The dispatch clerk can give "orders" even to the superintendent. The leadership of function is inherent in the job and as such is respected by the president of the plant.

Consider the influence which it is possible for the cost accountant to exercise because of his special knowledge. Where there is cost-accounting and unit budgeting, the cost accountant is in a position to know more about the effect of a change in price than anyone else. His analyses and his interpretations may dictate policy to the chief executive.

We have in industry many examples of men who lead in particular situations because they know the technique of their particular jobs. The chairman of a committee may not occupy a high official position or be a man of forceful personality, but he may know how to guide discussion effectively, that is, he may know the technique of *his* job. Or consider the industrial relations man or "impartial chairman" now maintained in so many industries. This man is an adept at conciliation. He has a large and elaborate technique for this at his command.

When it is a case of instruction, the teacher is the leader. Yet a good instructor may be a very poor foreman. Again, some men can make people produce, and some are good at following up quality who could never make people produce.

The leadership of function and the leadership of personality are of course by no means separate; but if we have to separate them for the purposes of discussion, we may say that in business the leadership of function is tending to become more important than the leadership of personality. And we may say also that the success of a business depends partly upon its organization being sufficiently flexible to allow the leadership of function to operate freely—to allow the men with the knowledge and the technique to control the situation. We have often seen this done, seen the president defer to one of his executives when that man had a larger knowledge and wider experience of the matter in hand.

We have a very interesting example of the leadership of function in the power wielded by the under-secretaries in England. The members of the Cabinet—Home Secretary, Secretary for Foreign Affairs, and so on—each has, as you know, an under-secretary who is a permanent official holding office through the party changes in administration. These permanent secretaries, because of their large knowledge of and continuing connection with the matters relating to their office, often exert a more decisive influence on affairs than the members of the Cabinet. It is they often who determine important decisions.

In speaking, however, of the leadership of function in industry, we must not forget how often we hear an employer say, "I hire executive material, not technical ability; almost anyone can acquire that," or, "I don't hire a mechanical engineer, I hire a *man*." In regard to this attitude, with which we must, of course, completely sympathize, I would say that whatever the motives of selection, by the time a man does become a leader in any business, he has also learned the technique of his particular job. Secondly, that certain changes both in organization and methods of management and also in the attitude of employers are an acknowledgment that in many cases control should go to special knowledge. And, thirdly, let me point out that what is meant by "executive material" and "a man" is not covered by the phrase "ascendancy traits."

You may have the promise of good "executive material" fulfilled in one to whom neither personality nor position, circumstance nor publicity, has given prominence. You have probably, for instance, all noticed how often leadership goes to the man, whatever his official position or personal force, who can grasp the essentials of an experience and, as we say, see it whole. This man sees the relational significance of the data at hand. In getting the facts for the solving of a business problem, the man who collects them may present them to the head of his department in their relational significance or in their literal order. If the latter, it may then be the head of the department who sees the essential unity of the data and presents his report to the president in such a way as to show that. Or it may be that the president does this for the board of directors. But wherever this process takes place, there tends to be control of the situation. Leadership tends to go to him to whom the total inter-relatedness is most clear, that is, if he has the power of using that insight.

And the most successful leader of all is one who sees another picture not yet actualized. He sees the things which belong in his present picture but which are not yet there.

Indeed, the kind of insight which is also foresight is essential to leadership. This does not mean that only the president needs it. Foresight is necessary for foreman or head of department; the only difference is that in their case the range about which foresight is necessary is narrower. But no leader of however small a group can forget, without disastrous consequences, that the activities of each group have to be fitted into a whole which is constantly changing.

I was very much struck in a certain firm in England with the fact that one man among the heads of departments seemed to be doing more guiding.than any other one man. I sought the reason first in his position, but decided that that gave him no more power than several other positions gave the men who held them. I came to the conclusion in the end that he got his power through an almost uncanny appreciation of the complexity of his relation to the organization—that is, he understood that he had both a direct relation and through others, and utilized the latter to the full—and also that he was thinking of his relation both to the organization that they had and to that toward which they were working. Please note the last clause, for I think it important. He seemed, as I say, to have an extraordinarily vivid appreciation of the challenges that were being made to him by the organization toward which they were working.

Yet with all this I am aware how often leadership does not go to the man with the largest knowledge, grasp of essentials or foresight, and that this should be so is a pregnant cause of dissatisfaction to many an executive. Over and over again a situation is controlled by a man either because his position gives him the whiphand and he uses it, or because he knows how to play politics, or for other reasons. There is not time to make anything approaching an exhaustive study of the way in which all the different aspects of leadership may play against one another—or combine with one another. My only thesis in this paper is that in the more progressively managed businesses—I realize that they are greatly in the minority—in these we see a tendency, only a tendency but one which seems to me very encouraging, for the control of a particular situation to go to the man with the largest knowledge of that situation, to him who can grasp and organize its essential elements, who understands its total significance, who can see it through—who can see length as well as breadth—rather than to one with merely a dominating personality or in virtue of his official position.

Discovering and Co-ordinating Leadership of Varying Types and Varying Degrees

In saying this, however, I do not want you for a moment to think that I minimize the job of upper or chief executives. These men should hold their positions because of their greater ability. And their task is far more difficult to-day than ever before and demands higher qualifications. If others have at times a more complete understanding of the relational significances involved in some particular situation, *they* should have this understanding for much larger situations. Theirs is the responsibility of solving the problems of to-day, of anticipating the problems of to-morrow. And these problems are complex, intricate, far-reaching. They not only require many kinds of specialized knowledge; but many types and degrees of leadership must be utilized. The chief executive discovers leaders and trains leaders. He does not want men of the submissive type but men themselves with mastery, and such men will give his own leadership worth and power.

We have a good illustration of the training and development of leaders among under executives, and also of the point I mentioned above—obedience to the law of the situation rather than to arbitrary commands—in the use of budget control. For several years I have been very much interested in budget control, for nowhere can we get a better idea of the type of leadership I am presenting to you than in the relation between upper executives and heads of departments where the budget is understood as a tool of control. Suppose an upper executive is dissatisfied with the work of a department. When this happens it is either because quality is too poor or costs too high. The old method of procedure was for the upper executive simply to blame the head of the department. But in a plant where the departments are budgeted, an upper executive can ask the head of a department to sit down with him and consider the matter. The budget objectifies the whole situation. It is possible for an upper executive to get the head of the department to *find out* himself where the difficulty lies, to make him give himself the necessary orders to meet a situation.

You have already had a lecture on budgeting as a method of executive control in which what I have just said was brought out, and Mr. Williams adds that while some may not call this leadership, in his opinion it is the very essence of leadership—teaching and training your subordinates how to control a situation themselves, helping your subordinates to develop their own ideas rather than exploiting your own. The job of the man higher up is not to make decisions for his subordinates, but to teach them how to handle their problems themselves, how to make their own decisions.

If this is the essence of leadership, we have a conception very far removed from that of the autocratic leader. The leader in scientifically managed plants tends not to persuade men to follow *his* will. He shows them what it is necessary for them to do in order to meet *their responsibility*, a responsibility that has been explicitly defined to them.

If the best leader takes all the means in his power to develop leadership among his subordinates and gives them opportunity to exercise it, he has then, his supreme task, to unite all the different degrees and different types of leadership that come to the surface in the ramifications of a modern business. Since power is now beginning to be thought of by many not as inhering in one person but as the combined capacities of a group, we are beginning to think of the leader not as the man who is able to assert his individual will and get others to follow him, but as the one who knows how to relate the different wills in a group so that they will have driving force. It is recognized by many that the most successful president of a business is not usually the one who can force his ideas on his executives, but the one who can make them do the best kind of team work. The heads of production, of sales, of finance, of personnel—each has a valuable contribution to make, but much interplay and adjusting correlation has to take place before these contributions can be welded into a force for the progress of the business.

In theory the president is usually supposed to arbitrate between his executives; but I know presidents who see the weakness of this theory and who try, not to "decide between," but to bring their executives into co-operating agreement by combining the best which each can offer with the best which he himself has to give. Or he may go even beyond this and do what it seems to me is done by the ablest presidents I have known, namely, make it possible for his executives to have the kind of practice, and train them thereto by his own conferences with them individually, which will enable them to learn the way themselves to combine their experience and judgment. Thus he gets them so that they habitually integrate.

But whatever the method, it is the president's responsibility to see that all possible contributions are utilized and made into an organized, significant whole subordinated to a common purpose. This is pre-eminently the leadership quality—the ability to organize all the forces there are in an enterprise. Men with this ability create a group power rather than express a personal power. They penetrate to the subtlest connections of the forces at their command, and make all these forces available, and most effectively available, for the accomplishment of their purpose.

We see the same thing in political leadership. The *theory* has been of personal domination, but *study* the political leaders, the party bosses, and notice how often they have gained their position by their ability to bring into harmonious relation men of antagonistic temperaments, their ability to reconcile conflicting interests, their ability to make a working unit out of many diverse elements. I spoke to you above of Mark Hanna. He was pre-eminently an organizer. The different aspects of his policy formed a unity which inevitably broke down opposition.

For several years I was doing a piece of work which brought me into close connection with a Tammany organization. I knew the head of the organization, the ward boss, and several of his lieutenants. The ward boss was not the domineering type. His lieutenants were. The boss, however, was an adept in organization, in using the power of his henchmen and in focusing it, in turning it toward certain ends.

In the complications of modern business everything tends to give the lead to organizing ability rather than to ascendancy traits because one man seldom knows enough about the matter in hand to impose his will on others. Consider retail selling. How much is the advertising department going to spend on advertising? Certainly the president cannot tell offhand. If this particular line of goods is meeting a popular demand, it will not need much advertising. If, however, an attempt is to be made to *create* a popular demand, much more will have to be spent to advertise the goods. Or if there are reasons for the price being forced up, increased advertising will be necessary. And so on; of course many more considerations than these would enter into the question. I give the illustration merely to show that a question of this kind requires the reciprocally modified judgment of several heads of departments, and the task of the president then becomes that of securing such a judgment.

But even if one man did know enough to make all the decisions, you cannot get any profitable "following" unless your followers are convinced, and you convince them in only one way—by allowing them to share in your experience. Men in business are seeing more and more clearly every day something which is wholly in accord with recent psychology, although not recognized in the older theory of leadership, and that is that habits, attitudes, are changed only by experience, are *built up*, not assumed at will. The capable leader knows that in order to secure any lasting agreement between himself and the rest of his group, they must be made to share in his experience. This insight alone changes our whole conception of leadership. The leader knows also that any lasting agreement among the members of the group can come only by their sharing each other's experience. He must see that his organization is such as to make this possible.

This is one of the reasons for the spread of committees as a part of business management. In spite of the time they take, in spite of the fact that they often seem only one extra burden, still their value is being more and more recognized, not as a method of democracy—the plea we once heard made for committees—but as a way of taking our co-workers along with us step by step in the acquiring of information, in comparing that information with past experience, in the whole process by which judgments are reached and decisions made.[3]

I read this paper to an upper executive a few nights ago, and when I got to this point he said: "Don't forget to say that the leader must also share *their* experience." We certainly must remember that, since the need for a unifying of experience, an identifying of purpose, has contributed largely to our present conception of leadership. The leader is neither the arbiter of his group nor, on the other hand, the spokesman of his group—the expression so often used. That is, he is neither mere representative nor dictator.[4]

Perhaps the feature of business practice which most sharply opposes the old theory of leadership, we can find in those cross-relations between departments given us by functional management. Here we have explicitly a co-ordinating and co-operating leadership. Where we need help from the psychologists is not to find aggressive men for

[3] Mr. Ordway Tead has brought out this point better than anyone else. (M. P. F.)

[4] *Cf. The New State*, pp. 229–30: "The leader guides the group and at the same time is himself guided by the group, is always a part of the group. No one can truly lead except from within. . . . The power of leadership is the power of integrating. This is the power which creates community. . . . The skilful leader does not rely on personal force; he controls his group not by dominating but by expressing it. He stimulates what is best in us; he unifies and concentrates what we feel only gropingly and scatteringly. But he never gets away from the current of which we and he are both an integral part. He is a leader who gives form to the inchoate energy in every man. The person who influences me most is not he who does great deeds, but he who makes me feel that I can do great deeds."

us, but to find those who do *not* tend toward "ascendancy," those who try, on the basis of a common purpose, to find the methods best suited to the accomplishment of that purpose. In the more progressively managed businesses to-day, where each man is responsible for a given set of duties and where the tendency is to give a man leadership up to his capacity for leadership, there is less and less hierarchical authority, above and below, over and under. One man is over another in some things and under him in others.

I heard a story the other day which perhaps has a moral for us. A teacher went into a new school. There were certain rules in regard to the disposal of small pieces of chalk, of erasers that needed cleaning, etc. But she carelessly disregarded these, as she had come from a school where there were no such rules. In a little while she was taken to task by the custodian of the building, who said to her: "You evidently haven't been used to working under a janitor."

It is clear to-day that the president in a plant where there is functional management has to co-ordinate leaderships of varying types and varying degrees. And among these leaderships must be included in many instances employee representatives, shop stewards, or the officials who come to the fore where this is union-management co-operation.

If then functional management gives to the chief executive a task which cannot be expressed by the old charts showing only a hierarchical authority, there is another point in regard to the chief executive equally important. It is that, as in the best forms of modern organization each man tends to have the leadership which his particular job gives him, so this is true also of the president as well as of all the others. One indication of our progress away from the old idea of leadership is the tendency of chief executives to think of their jobs more and more in specific terms.

Consider the president of a large bank. While he has given up much of the influence on every day questions still retained by the heads of small banks, he has *his* particular job. He must have a large knowledge of world conditions, he must be able to foresee the forces which may make for or against the success of large plans, and so on and so on. Or the head of a flourishing manufactory may spend much of his time in the East, South Africa, etc., opening up new markets or establishing branch factories. Others may be "leading", in the home plant.

Leadership in a Common Purpose

In speaking of multiple leadership, in considering the organization of such leadership to serve well-defined ends, it should be noted how many are coming to think that these ends should be known and understood by all. There are leaders to-day who, far from keeping their purposes from their subordinates, think that the greatest aid to leadership consists in uniting one's followers, executives or manual workers, in a common purpose. They think that back of all giving of orders and following of orders there should be a shared knowledge of the purposes of store or bank or factory. I believe this is going to be a large factor in our future industrial success.

Summer before last at the Rowntree chocolate factory in York, I listened to one of the best speeches I have ever heard. When a group of new girls is taken into this factory—they take in thirty at a time—Mr. Rowntree, the president, gives a talk to these girls. He tells them what their work is all about, he shows them how one person being careless in dipping chocolates may make the young man who takes a box of chocolates to his best girl on Saturday night say that he won't get Rowntree's chocolates next time. And then Mr. Rowntree shows how this affects far more than Rowntree profits, how in time reduced sales will mean less employment in York for girls and boys, for men and women. And then he goes on, from such simple illustrations, to show them their place in the industry of England. I don't believe it is possible for those who hear these talks not to feel a close connection with, a certain degree of identification with, the Rowntree Company. While leadership depends on depth of conviction and the power coming therefrom, there must also be the ability to share that conviction with others. Mr. Rowntree, by his vivid statement of purpose, has found a way of making all his employees share in a common purpose. That common purpose rather than Mr. Rowntree himself is their leader. And I believe that to-day we are coming more and more to act, whatever our theories, on our faith in this power of what Dr. Cabot calls "the invisible leader." Loyalty to the invisible leader gives us the strongest possible bond of union, establishes a sympathy which is not a sentimental but a dynamic sympathy.

And this purpose should be a common purpose not only in the sense of being shared by all, but it should be a purpose evolved by all the interweaving activities of the enterprise. The best type of leader does not seek *his* ends, but the ends disclosed by an evolving process in which each has his special part. And when I speak thus, please don't think that I am Utopian, for one of the most practical business men I know, the head of a factory in the West, always comes out with this as the first article of his creed. And he is not talking ethics either when he says this, he is talking of what makes for business success. Moreover, we find another blow to the conception of the leader as seeking individual ends in the fact that leaders of the highest type do not conceive their task merely as that of *fulfilling* purpose, but as also that of finding ever larger purposes to fulfil, more fundamental values to be reached.

I have spoken several times of the conception we are now acquiring of a multiple leadership. Our present historians and biographers are strengthening this conception by showing us that in order to understand any epoch we must take into account many lesser leaders. They tell us also that the number of these lesser leaders has been so steadily increasing that one of the most outstanding facts of our life to-day is a widely diffused leadership. Some go further and think that our hope for the future depends on a still more widely diffused leadership.

A few weeks ago I read H. G. Wells' last novel, which is not so much a novel as an arraignment of our present civilization, and in the last chapter he gives his hope for the future. That hope is based on the expectation that it will come to be universally realized that everyone must take part in the regeneration of society. In the past, he says, we depended on single great leaders—Buddha, Mohammed and so on. To-day many men and women must help to lead. In the past Aristotle led the world in science. To-day thousands of scientists are adding each his contribution. Our future depends on two things, Wells tells us: first, that countless men and women wake to the necessity of the *great* part each has to play, and secondly, that we have the completest confidence in the possibility of control.

The Part of the Led in the Leadership Situation

I want now to speak to you of something which seems to me of the utmost importance, but which has been little considered, and that is the part of the led in the leadership situation. Mr. Wells urges the need of a wider leadership. I wish to emphasize something else in addition to that, namely, that even as those led we have a share in the control of a situation, and that our leader must know how to give us that share and we to take it. Those led have not merely a passive part, they have not merely to follow and obey, they have to help keep the leader in control of the situation. Let us not think that we are either leaders or—nothing of much importance. As one of those led, we have a part in leadership.

In no aspect of our subject do we see a greater discrepancy between theory and practice than here. The definition given over and over again of leader is one who can induce others to follow him. Or that meaning is taken for granted and the question is asked: "What is the technique by which a leader keeps his followers in line?"

A very able political scientist writing of leadership treats it as a tropism and discusses why men obey or do not obey, why they tend to lead or follow, as if leading and following were the essence of leadership. Yet this very man has made valuable studies in leadership and the whole trend of his thinking on this subject seems away from this stereotype, yet at that moment, when talking directly of leadership, he reverts to the old idea and speaks of the leadership situation as one of command and obedience.

Again, listen to this quotation from a recent book: "People are more readily persuaded to follow as one of a crowd under a leader than to labour separately . . . for some social end." That is true, but these are not the only alternatives. You need neither be lost in the crowd nor labour separately, you can labour *with* your leader.

The technique of that process is, I believe, the most important thing for industry to learn. We want leaders? We want psychologists to discover leaders for us? Of course. But still more, we want worked out a relation between leaders and led which will give to each the opportunity to make creative contributions to the situation. This is a growing demand to-day. I have been asked once this winter to speak on the relation between college faculties and students, and at another time to speak on the relation between deans of colleges and student government councils. In the latter request it was stated that they wished to discuss how to make a "creative experience" between deans and the student body.

Part of the task of the leader is to make others participate in his leadership. The best leader knows how to make his followers actually feel power themselves, not merely acknowledge his power.

But if the followers must partake in leadership, it is also true that we must have followship on the part of leaders. There must be a partnership of following. The basis of industrial leadership is creating a partnership in a common task, a joint responsibility.

Have I taken away anything from the prestige of leadership? It seems to me that I am adding to that prestige, that those with this conception, and with the ability to embody it in organization and management, are the only ones who can play a large part in the forward movement of our civilization. One of the tragedies of history is that Woodrow Wilson did not understand leadership.

An indication of the change that is going on in our ideas in regard to leadership, we can find in the fact that while a few years ago there was much talk in colleges about training for leadership, many colleges even stating that leadership was the ultimate aim of their instruction, this is not so to-day. Dr. Charles R. Mann has told us that a search through some 250 college catalogues has revealed only eight that mention leadership as one of their aims. And Mr. Mann tells us also that President Hopkins, in addressing the student body at the opening of Dartmouth last autumn, said: "I have come to distrust the validity of much of what has been said, including much which I have said myself, in regard to its being the function of higher education to train for leadership. I ask permission to revise this statement to say that the first function of the college is to educate men for usefulness."

While the college catalogues and speech of President Hopkins show an advance in one direction, namely, that it is no longer considered desirable to gain an ascendancy over our fellows, yet the mistake is still made, it seems to me, of identifying leadership with ascendancy. For with the conception of leadership which I have been trying to present to you, there is no reason why leadership should not be put in college catalogues as a desirable aim of education. Moreover, with this conception of leadership, President Hopkins' wish to educate men for usefulness could not be fulfilled unless they are educated for leadership.

I have sometimes wondered whether it would be better to give up the word "leader," since to so many it suggests merely the leader-follower relation. But it is far too good a word to abandon; moreover, the leader in one way at least does and should lead in that very sense. He should lead by the force of example. If those led obey the law of the situation, they must realize that he is doing the same. If they are to follow the invisible leader, the common purpose, so must he. If everyone must work overtime, the president should be willing to do the same. In every way he must show that he is doing what he urges upon others.

One winter I went yachting with some friends in the inland waterways of the South. On one occasion our pilot led us astray and we found ourselves one night aground in a

Carolina swamp. Obviously the only thing to do was to try to push the boat off, but the crew refused, saying that the swamps in that region were infested with rattlesnakes. The owner of the yacht offered not a word of remonstrance, but turned instantly and jumped overboard. Every member of the crew followed.

Do you remember the story of the man with a new religion to preach who went to Tallyrand all on fire with enthusiasm and told him that he was going to travel throughout France preaching this new gospel. After a few months he came back to Tallyrand much discouraged. He had not been able to get disciples and he wanted advice as to what he should do. "Oh, it's quite simple," said Tallyrand. "All you have to do is to die and rise again in three days." He who for 2,000 years has been our greatest leader expressed in all His life the doctrine He preached.

Before closing, let me remind you that the title of this paper has not been leadership in general, but refers only to some of those aspects of leadership in which there is a discrepancy between theory and practice, and this title has guided all I have said. There are many qualifications for leadership therefore of which I have not spoken. There is the necessity for initiative, for the ability to seize opportunity, for that high integrity which inspires confidence, for the power of communicating enthusiasm, for the power to liberate and make articulate the impulses of one's group, as indeed also the power to liberate and make articulate one's own impulses. I have not spoken of these and a hundred other characteristics of leadership because in regard to these there is no dispute.

Moreover, we have not considered the qualifications necessary for elected leaders. For instance, when I spoke of the influence exercised by the under-secretaries in England in virtue of their function, we did not stop to consider that many of these men could probably not have been elected to their positions. No one can be elected to any position of prominence in England who is not a good public speaker.

My subject in this paper has been restricting, but some

time we must show how the leadership of function, the leadership of personality and of example, the leadership of position, and still another leadership—perhaps, after all, the most important—that of the man who expresses most fully the spirit of his age, some time we must show the relation of all these to one another, and study different examples of leadership where these have been combined in varying degrees.

In conclusion: if the industrial leader is a man of large understanding, of clear vision, of steadiness of purpose, if he knows how to organize all the forces available in order to accomplish that purpose, we must remember also that he not only organizes the forces at his command at the moment, but that the great leader has the power to *draw forth* the forces, which are to be used co-operatively and constructively for a given end.

William James tried to show us the relation between what he called the inmost nature of reality and our own powers. He tried to show us that there is a significant correspondence here, that my capacities are related to the demands of the universe. I believe that the great leader can show me this correspondence, can arouse my latent possibilities, can reveal to me new powers in myself, can quicken and give direction to some force within me. There is energy, passion, unawakened life in us—those who call it forth are our leaders.

"What," says James,[5] "caused the wild-fire influence of Rousseau but the assurance he gave that man's nature was in harmony with the nature of things, if only the paralysing corruptions of custom would stand from between? How did Kant and Fichte and Goethe and Schiller inspire their time with cheer except by saying, 'Use all your powers; that is the only obedience which the Universe exacts?' And Carlyle with his gospel of Work, of Fact, of Veracity, how does he move us except by saying that the universe imposes no tasks upon us but such as we can perform?"

I read recently: "It does not matter how able a man is . . .

[5] William James, *Principles of Psychology*, II, p. 315.

he cannot be a first-class leader unless he rubs people the right way." What do you suppose was meant by the phrase "rubs people the right way"? To "butter them up"? To "make them feel good"? There are leaders who do not appeal to man's complacency but to all their best impulses, their greatest capacities, their deepest desires. I think it was Emerson who told us of those who supply us with new powers out of the recesses of the spirit and urge us to new and unattempted performance. This is far more than imitating your leader. In this conception of Emerson's, what you receive from your leader does not come from him, but from the "recesses of the spirit." Whoever connects me with the hidden springs of all life, whoever increases the sense of life in me, he is my leader.

XIV

INDIVIDUALISM IN A PLANNED SOCIETY[1]

THE economic interdependence of men is a fact which is to-day generally recognized. This recognition makes imperative, as the only alternative to our present chaos, collective planning on a national or even international scale.

Fundamental Principles of Collective Planning on a National Scale

There are people, however, who are opposed to national planning. Their opposition rests fundamentally, I believe, on a fear of the word "control," on a fear that the rights of the individual are to be invaded. But this word control is to-day taking on new meanings. If those planning for a national economic control would base their schemes on this newer understanding, no one need fear them as the foes of individualism.

Consider this matter of control in some of our best-managed industries. We notice two points: (1) control is coming more and more to mean fact-control rather than man-control; (2) central control is coming more and more to mean the correlation of many controls rather than a super-imposed control.

In regard to the first point, notice how often the word control is used in the sense of fact-control. We hear, for instance, of budgeting control. This means that where you have cost-accounting and unit-budgeting, the president and the head of a department are both subject to an impersonal control. The head of the department does not receive an arbitrary order from the president, but both study the

[1] This paper, the last one prepared by Miss Follett for the Bureau of Personnel Administration annual conferences, was presented in the series entitled *Economic and Social Planning* on April 14th, 1932. These papers were duplicated by the Bureau, but have not been published in a volume.

analyses and interpretations which cost-accounting and unit-budgeting have made possible.

We hear also, less often, of inventory control. It is now customary in some plants to keep card records of raw materials, goods in process and finished stock. In some companies this is done by a stores department, in some by special committees, but what I am interested in here is simply the use of the word "control." Formerly the top executives, if they had such records, would have considered that these records helped them in *their* control. Now, we hear the expression "inventory control" because it is recognized that the facts disclosed constitute in themselves a control. Control is becoming less and less personal in the old-fashioned sense; control and fact-control are becoming synonymous.

My second point was the correlation of controls. The authority of the chief executive is not, in the best managed businesses, an arbitrary authority imposed from above, but the gathering up of many authorities found at different points in the organization.

These two principles—fact-control and collective control—are now accepted by many as sound principles of business management. They should, I believe, be the foundation of any scheme for national planning. But one pamphlet on *National Planning*, recently issued, uses the words "force," "coerce" over and over again. We shall not, I am sure, submit to an arbitrary Planning Board. Some of these writers are making the fatal mistake of thinking that coercion is the opposite of *laissez-faire*. It is not. The opposite of *laissez-faire* is co-ordination. The imperative need of the moment is a search for the best methods of co-ordination, of adjustment. But the process of adjusting is not one which can be imposed from outside—it is essentially, basically, by its very nature, a process of auto-controlled activity. No one can issue a fiat by which I am adjusted, I can only be helped to adjust myself. National planning should be a scheme for the self-adjusting of our various and varying interests. It should plan for the self-co-ordinating of industries and for the self-co-ordinating of plants within an industry. Beyond this it should,

I think, include union-management co-operation within each plant, thus giving the workers a share from the beginning.

Have we any principles for such a process of self-adjusting by which to test any schemes for national planning which may be proposed to us, by which to test whether such schemes threaten individual freedom?

Four fundamental principles of organization are:

1. Co-ordination by direct contact of the responsible people concerned.
2. Co-ordination in the early stages.
3. Co-ordination as the reciprocal relating of all the factors in a situation.
4. Co-ordination as a continuing process.

Let me speak briefly of these four. I find these principles at work in some of our best managed industrial plants. The same principles governed some of the Allied co-operation during the War. That we should find these principles in such different fields seems to me a matter of great significance. It means that our ablest thinkers, men who are at the same time thinkers and doers, have found a way of making collective control collective *self*-control.

In regard to the first principle, co-ordination by direct contact of the responsible people concerned, we find in some industries that control is coming more and more to be effected through cross-relations between heads of departments instead of up and down the line through the chief executive.

In the case of international relations, we find Sir Arthur Salter, one of our soundest thinkers on that subject, advocating, in his *Allied Shipping Control*, this method of "direct contact"—I have taken that expression from him. This means that he thinks that adjustments between nations should be made, not through their Foreign Offices, but between those who exercise responsible authority in the matters concerned, that is, between the departmental ministers.

Schemes for national planning should, to follow this principle, provide for direct contact between the responsible heads of industry. The heads of industry would thus form their own control—and individual freedom would be safely guarded.

My second principle was co-ordination in the early stages. This means that the direct contact must begin in the earliest stages of the process. We see how this works in the correlation of policies in a business. If the head of the production department meets the heads of the sales and finance and personnel departments with a finished policy, and is confronted by them each with a finished policy, agreement will be found difficult. Of course, they then begin to "play politics," or that is often the tendency—a deplorable form of coercion. But if the head of the production department, *while* he is forming his policy, meets and discusses with the other heads the questions involved, a successful co-ordination is far more likely to be reached. That is, you cannot, with the greatest degree of success for your undertaking, make policy-forming and policy-adjusting two separate processes. Policy-adjusting cannot begin after the separate policies have been completed.[2]

We have a corroboration of this principle also from the international field. In *Allied Shipping Control* we are shown most convincingly that a genuine international policy cannot be evolved by first formulating your national policy and then presenting it as a finished product to confront the completed policies of other nations. For the only process by which completed policies can be adjusted is that of bargaining and compromise; if you want integration, we are told, the process of the interpenetration of policies must begin before they are completed, while they are still in the formative stage.

This vitally necessary principle seems to be largely ignored in the schemes for national planning. Yet again it is obvious that this is a way of securing the freedom of the individual.

---

[2] *Cf. Creative Experience*, pp. 224–5: "The most essential thing to remember about government is that control must be generated by the activity which is to be controlled. Therefore in industry, in co-operative undertakings, in government, control must begin as far back in the process as possible, else—to use the language of an earlier chapter—we shall have power-over instead of power-with. Joint action must know its source."

In the union-management plan of the Baltimore and Ohio Railroad, the adjustment of unions and management begins down in the lowest shop committees, and this has very largely helped the workers to feel that they are not governed arbitrarily. A study of the history of the Amalgamated Clothing Workers of America also teaches us much on this point.

The third principle, co-ordination as the reciprocal relating of all the factors in a situation, shows us just what this process of co-ordination actually is. Think for a moment what happens between the heads of departments in a business. You cannot envisage the process accurately by thinking of A as adjusting himself to B and to C and to D. A adjusts himself to B and *also* to a B influenced by C and to a B influenced by D and to a B influenced by A himself. Again he adjusts himself to C and *also* to a C influenced by B and to a C influenced by D and to a C influenced by A himself—and so on and so on. One could work it out mathematically. This sort of reciprocal relating, this interpenetration of every part by every other part, and again by every other part as it has been permeated by all, should be the goal of all attempts at co-ordination, a goal, of course, never wholly reached.

But I do not want this to sound either abstruse or fantastic. I want you to recognize this process as one you often see and one, I hope, you want to see more of. You see it in the factory not only in the correlation of departmental policies, but in many minor adjustments, as when the employment manager, the psychologist and the foreman come to some agreement in a case of hiring, or dismissing, or promoting. I think you cannot read your daily paper without seeing that this process must be the solution of international problems.

Or, again, if anyone finds this principle difficult to accept, I would suggest that it is a principle which he has already accepted in regard to facts. Any fact gains its significance through its relation to all the other facts pertaining to the situation. For instance, if you have increased sales, you are not too pleased until you find out whether there has been an increased sales cost. If there has been, or one out of proportion to sales, your satisfaction disappears. Merchandising shows you this principle at work. For merchandising is not merely a bringing together of designing, engineering, manufacturing and sales departments, it is these in their total relativity. This is not a good phrase, but I am trying to express a total which shall include all the factors of a situation not as an additional total but as a relational total. That is, I am in this case trying to show that a merchandising policy is brought about by the interpenetration of the parts of the business concerned, and not by putting those parts alongside one of the other.

If then the process of co-ordination is one of interpenetration, it is obvious that it cannot be enforced by an outside body. That is why I have very grave doubts whether "central" planning, as at present conceived by many, will bring us any appreciable degree of co-ordination. I am not saying that a National Planning Board *ought not* to arrogate to itself the task of co-ordinating, I am saying that it *cannot*, because co-ordination is by its very nature a process of auto-governed activity.

An economist has recently written of "a system of responsible commissioners with some public authority capable of co-ordinating their activities." This is more than undesirable, it is impossible. The president of a large business, a practical and successful business man, not in any respect a theorist, said to me once: "If my heads of departments tell me that Department D and Department E are co-ordinated, and then I find that Department D and Department E are exactly the same as they were before, then I know that what I have been told is not true, they are not co-ordinated. Co-ordination means change in the parts co-ordinated."[3] In the same way the policies of our different industrial and economic organizations will have to be adjusted to one another by changes in each voluntarily undertaken, no, not exactly undertaken, but spontaneously brought about

---

[3] Co-ordination in its stricter meaning does not imply change in the parts, but co-ordination is now being used, somewhat inaccurately perhaps, as synonymous with correlation. Correlation is probably the better word because correlation implies interpenetration of the parts while co-ordination implies only an harmonious ordering of parts. (M. P. F.)

by the process of interpenetration—a planning scheme which provides the machinery by which this process can take place will not crush the individual, individual men or individual industries.

We can never reconcile planning and individualism until we understand individualism not as an apartness from the whole, but as a contribution to the whole. In some of the businesses I have studied, I have been told that the head of a department should subordinate the good of his department to the good of the whole undertaking. But of course he should do no such thing. His departmental point of view is needed in the whole. It must indeed be reconciled with all the other points of view in the business, but it must not be abandoned. Just as we have been told that men should not denationalize but internationalize themselves, so I should say to the heads of departments that they should not de-departmentalize themselves but inter-departmentalize themselves. In other words, departmental policy should be an integral part of what is known as "general policy."

If this principle were applied in national planning to the industrial organizations of a country, these organizations would not be asked to give up their own points of view for the sake of an imaginary "whole," for an air-plane view, a *deracine* view; they would be expected to learn how to interweave their points of view, their various policies. And thus we give the fullest possible scope to individualism.

It is now becoming more and more apparent every day that some such correlation between our industries is imperative. The regularization of any one industry always involves what is being done in certain others. Steel stabilized its prices, but when the depression came there was nevertheless severe unemployment in the steel industry, for the success of that industry, of course, depends on the success of certain other industries.

These three principles of direct contact, early stages and self-adjusting, applied to national planning would give us control as a horizontal not a vertical process—a horizontal control between the industries of a country, the same kind of control between the different plants of an industry, and again the same kind of control between the different departments of a single plant. As an example of the last—we could find many—we can take the New England Telephone Company. When I made some inquiries into the management of that company, I found the four departments—traffic, engineering, plant and commercial—conferring with one another in the early stages. The district traffic manager asks the wire chief from the plant department to talk a matter over with him, or if it is a commercial matter he calls in the commercial manager of that district, or if it is a question of blue prints or costs he asks the engineering department if they will send a man over. They settle it among themselves. If not, the traffic manager puts it up to the division superintendent of traffic and he may consult the division superintendents of plant and commercial departments—again a cross-relation.

We find the same principle, we are told in a recent study, in the relation between the different units of the American Telephone and Telegraph Company. Plans for future developments originate in the need of some particular locality. But the need must be correlated with the needs of other localities, hence the plan proceeds horizontally throughout the whole organization involving ultimately all the related departments. Thus planning remains an integral part of the management of the self-governing units.[4]

We have here then planning as a horizontal process between the units of a company and planning as a horizontal process between the departments of a single unit. This is what we should aim at between the different industries, a natural, continuous co-ordinating inherent in the form of co-operation agreed upon. And this does not preclude a Central Planning Department which has *its* functions, as the American Telephone and Telegraph Company has, of course, its headquarters staff. We need a Central Planning Board closely related, probably by representation, to the Planning Boards of each industry; its work should be linked up with the work of the separate boards, and also it should

[4] *Survey-Graphic*, March, 1932, "Telephones," by E. C. Lindeman.

have power itself to initiate certain forms of planning recognized as belonging peculiarly to it.

To summarize the three principles of organization so far given. In our highly complex economic society there are many points of control. The organized relating of these should constitute the central control. A co-ordinating process active throughout our whole economic society should *be* the control. A National Planning Board should express the reciprocal relating of the co-ordinating process, but if it tries to take the place of that process, it will be giving us the shadow for the substance. Any National Planning Board which proceeds from the top down is, I am sure, doomed to failure.

My fourth principle was co-ordination as a continuing process.

I am claiming that a Planning Board if rightly conceived can make for the greater freedom of individual men or individual industries. One reason for this is that the machinery for co-ordination would be continuous, not set up for special occasions. If a board is set up to consider a special problem the tendency is naturally to think only of the question under discussion; the incentive to discuss the principles which can serve as guides for future similar cases is not so great. But if we had a permanent Planning Board, and it should make some classification of problems, then when a fresh problem arose it would be able to see the points in which that resembled a certain class of problems and it could ask, "Have we evolved any principles for dealing with problems of that kind?" This is what our Supreme Court is doing. And one of the interesting things about the League of Nations, as one watches its work at Geneva, is the influence of the permanent character of the organization upon its work. A member of the political section of the Secretariat said to me: "Our treatment of every question is twofold: (1) an attempt to solve the immediate problem, (2) the attempt to discover root causes to help our work in the future." And there is a conscious attempt on the part of a number of those working in the League to secure decisions resting on certain fundamental principles in order that these principles can be taken as precedents in similar cases arising later.

Now continuous machinery for working out the principles of relation, whether it be in factory or nation or internationally, is of the very essence of freedom. For it tends toward freedom when the rest of our world is following certain principles; we are bound when someone's action toward us may be of one kind to-day and another to-morrow. The latter is the relation of slave and master, but the slave relation exists in many other places, not only when a nation uses its greater power arbitrarily, or an employer his, but it may exist between two people. *Collectively* to discover and follow certain principles of action makes for *individual* freedom. Continuous machinery for this purpose is an essential factor in the only kind of control we can contemplate.

Another advantage of a permanent Planning Board is that then the circle, or spiral, is not broken in the transition from planning to activity and from activity to further planning. A mistake we often tend to make is that the world stands still while we are going through the process of a given adjustment. And it doesn't. Facts change, we must keep up with the facts; keeping up with the facts changes the facts. In other words, the process of adjustment changes the things to be adjusted. If you want an illustration of this, consider the financial and economic adjustments between nations.

Until we look on control as a continuing activity, we shall not get out of the fallacy that we can solve problems. The belief that we can is a drag upon our thinking. What we need is some process for meeting problems. When we think we have *solved* a problem, well, by the very process of solving, new elements or forces come into the situation and you have a new problem on your hands to be solved. When this happens, men are often discouraged. I wonder why; it is our strength and our hope. We don't want any system that holds us enmeshed within itself.

In order, however, to get the fullest benefit of a permanent Planning Board, in order to utilize our experience, get the advantage of precedents, be able to formulate principles, we must learn how to classify our experience. I do not think any wholly satisfactory method for that has yet been worked out. I was present once at a meeting of the heads of departments in a large store, and heard one of these heads say in regard to a case they were discussing, "We had a problem like this two or three years ago. Does anyone remember how we treated that?" No one did! We talk much about learning from experience, but we cannot do that unless we (1) observe our experience, (2) keep records of our experience, and (3) organize our experience, that is, relate the parts. Unrelated experience is of little use to us; we can never make wise decisions from isolated bits, only as we see the parts in relation to one another.

I have given four principles of organization. The underpinning of these is information based on research. A National Planning Board should collect and publish data in respect to each industry—on raw materials, productive capacity, sales, prices, new capital investment and so on and so on. This information of itself would be a form of control, for there would be a tendency to act in accordance with information given if it were accepted as accurate. Moreover, we might even hope perhaps that each industry, basing its plans on the same information as all others, might tend to fit its activity into what might more or less automatically become a general scheme.

Ignorance always binds. Knowledge always frees. Collective research must be the basis of all planning. The knowledge thereby obtained will help much toward the release and the freeing without which business prosperity cannot be secured.

One fact gives me much hope for the future, and that is what has been accomplished in certain businesses of recent years by research in regard to all the processes and functions of the business, and by the co-ordination of selling, finance and production. There seems little reason to doubt that the same methods pursued on a larger scale would also have some measure of success.

Freedom through Organized Relation

I have given four principles of organization which I think should be applied to collective planning. But it isn't only a National Planning Board that people fear as an enemy of freedom. There are many who think that merely by joining with others, our liberty becomes thereby curtailed. This is a wholly false idea of freedom, yet it is a fallacy which unfortunately we still find in many places. Consider the illusion of the American farmer on this point. The problem of agricultural depression in America can be solved only through large-scale joint action, but here we come up against the myth of "the independent farmer." While it seems obvious that farm relief can come only through co-ordinated marketing which should include efficient merchandising, shipping, selling, price stabilization, yet not enough farmers can be made to see this to make it possible to set going and keep going a machinery of co-operative marketing. They cannot give up their "freedom," they do not see that it is a way of getting out of their present slavery, a way of becoming free.

This fear of losing a purely mythical freedom has over and over again been proved to have no basis in reality. In the case of the Canadian National Railway, at the time of the introduction of union-management co-operation the foremen were afraid that their freedom would be curtailed by the committees set up. But in the end they found that their freedom in any real sense of the word was increased.

I saw recently a statement that when employers admit the right of workers to a share in management, they deliberately give up a part of their freedom. But employers are not "free" who face strikes, sabotage, dissatisfaction, indifference—all the evils of a condition of struggle between capital and labour. Those employers are the freest who have worked out the means of preventing these evils, and who have found the way of getting from their workers all the possible contributions which they can make to management.

Again, co-operation between competitors has often been

found to pave the way for a greater freedom for all concerned. Success is not now understood as getting the better of someone in trade. As competing firms join in research, it is seen that all gain from the results. As they join in conference, they often find that they gain more by the discussion of mutual problems than they lose by the possible disclosure of "secrets." In short, we are less and less to-day at the mercy of our competitors as we are learning the advantage of cooperation between competitors.

Consider another illustration of the fear of the loss of freedom. The foreman in many industrial plants has been afraid that his freedom was about to be curtailed when a psychologist has been introduced into the plant. Yet he finds, on the contrary, that with the help of the psychologist he can accomplish more of his purposes and more easily.

Again, are our young people "free" who drift into their first job and get imprisoned for life in some job for which they are totally unsuited and in which they take no interest? Vocational guidance has helped to free many individuals, as has also job analysis and improved methods of selection and promotion.

One of the truths which the twentieth century is to give the world is, I believe, freedom not from relation, but through relation, through organized relation. How much freedom are men and women feeling to-day? Is not almost everyone at present restricted in a hundred ways as the result of the present economic depression? Such restrictions can be permanently removed only by national and international planning.

I have not space to speak of international planning, but the whole world is being made aware to-day of the interdependence of nations, of the inter-relations of economic activities. Take, for illustration, the question of markets. Nations cannot be "free" while struggling for markets. What we want to-day as much as any one thing in the economic sphere is the organization of markets. The research necessary for that, the steps to be taken to make effective the results of that research, the support of governments or actual legislation, international agreements—all that has yet to be worked out, but we are fast learning that nations cannot go their own competitive, self-seeking way and feel free. No nation to-day feels free. We can gain our freedom only through some form of international co-operation.

In trying to show that planning need not be opposed to freedom, to individualism, it is obvious that I am taking individualism in its "good" sense, but this word is also used in a "bad" sense. So-called individualistic tendencies are often spoken of as the most deplorable aspect of our present civilization. We read often of "cut-throat individualism." National planning is certainly opposed to this kind of individualism, the kind that has sought preferential legislation and every kind of monopolistic advantage, the kind that has talked of the rights of the individual, meaning by that phrase the protection of one class of individuals against others.

But even in regard to individualism in its "good" meaning there are, it seems to me, two misconceptions. One is that of which I have been speaking throughout this paper, a fear that individualism is threatened by any talk of planning and a determination to fight all such encroachments on liberty. The other misconception is also based on the belief that our freedom is now assailed, but in this case that belief is accompanied by the inculcation of self-sacrifice as what the world is requiring of us to-day, a willing sacrifice of a portion of our freedom. It is clear, I hope, that I think such sacrifice as unnecessary as it is undesirable. Some of us are hoping for co-operation among the various interests of our country, believing it to be to our self-interest, to the self-interest of all. And we want international co-operation for the same reason, because we see that it is to the self-interest of nations, because we see that only thereby can nations live and prosper.

The title of my paper is *Individualism in a Planned Society.* I hope many will agree with me that the synthesis of individualism and collective control is collective *self*-control— a phrase I have borrowed from Sir Arthur Salter. The following words in *Allied Shipping Control* could be applied to the industrial organizations within a country: "Thus the new Allied principle did not override and replace the national organizations . . . it linked them together from inside. The Allied authority consisted of the national authorities themselves . . . it was the national organizations linked together for international work and themselves forming the instrument of that work."

In the same way, a National Planning Board should not be a new seat of power, it should be, to paraphrase the above quotation, the organizations of a country linked together for national work and themselves forming the instrument of that work.

With this principle left out—the principle of the interpenetration of authority instead of a super-authority—these schemes *are* a foe to individualism. With this principle embodied in a scheme for national planning, individualism gets its chance for its fullest expression. National planning need not override individual initiative. It could stimulate and give scope to individual initiative, and give it the possibility of coming to its full fruition by showing it the way to combine effectively with other individual initiatives. It is possible for individual initiatives to cancel each other out, to fight on indefinitely or—the only fruitful way—to combine by a process not of compromise but of integration.

The Purpose of Planning

There is one subject, however, very much affecting the question of individualism, which is unfortunately too large a subject to add to this paper. That is the *purpose* of the planning. What is to give it its direction? The forces of life are something far greater than we can ever learn from either the addition or the multiplication table, from either adding our activities or relating our activities. Little drops of water, little grains of sand—that is a philosophy we have long outgrown. Count the grains, count the drops, count all men and all their activities, and the sum is not life. We may make our researches, tabulate our activities, relate our activities—and that is not all. I may talk of adjusting myself to A or B.

yet a greater adjustment is always thereby served. But the development of purpose, the unification of purpose—we cannot begin on that at the end of a paper. When we come to consider this question, however, we may find that we want another word than planning. That may seem too completely the engineer's word, express too exclusively the engineer's point of view. In a short paper one tends to become too dogmatic, also tends to use the words and phrases of the moment—"research" is almost slang now. I deplore both these tendencies, for all that I have really wished to urge in this paper is that man's freedom is not necessarily incompatible with that co-ordination of our activities the necessity for which every event to-day is pressing upon our attention.

Large-scale planning is, I think, imperative. I have been speaking chiefly of the co-ordination of industries, as that is what my own experience permits me to speak more particularly of, but of course industrial planning, land planning, and financial planning—planning for investments, credits and money policies generally—will have to be linked together. Such planning, it is conceded by many, is necessary. At the same time many of the problems connected with it need much further study. And I am sure that we have not as yet sufficiently considered the number of inter-locking factors there are in every one of these problems.

For instance, we are told that a planning board will tell us where workers are required, where capital is needed, enormously valuable information, yet even so, capital and workers may not move automatically to their prescribed stations. Can this be controlled without coercion? A very good example of the integration of coercion and freedom can be found in our marketing co-operatives, where the farmers are free to sign the contract or not, but when once they have signed, they are expected to keep the contract, and pressure is brought upon them to do so. There is much food for thought here, for I fear that there are many people, and nations too, who think that keeping your word is a form of coercion. And I might add that perhaps it is in some cases!

I am putting the matter like this deliberately in order to show that these problems are not easy, that they are tremendously complicated and require much further thinking. This thinking, is, I believe, the most pressing need of the moment.

Problems Requiring Study

The following list gives some of the problems urgently requiring our study. The list is not exhaustive, the problems mentioned sometimes overlap, moreover they are not given in any order. Indeed to give them at all is really outside the scope of this paper. I do so for one reason: in order to show that I believe in national planning *only* if we can to some extent solve these problems. If we can do so we need not fear that individualism will suffer in a planned society.

1. The process of co-operative research: how to begin in the early stages before conclusions have become crystallized.

2. The process of the correlation of policies—begun in the early stages.

This includes much: at what stage shall problems be brought to the central planning board, how can we ensure that they shall be brought at that stage, etc., etc. Indeed every problem connected with Conference procedure is here involved as well as what precedes and leads up to the conferring.

3. How to provide the flow both ways: (1) information from industries or the public to the planning board; (2) understanding of the policies of the planning board back to the industries and to the public.

4. How to make the intelligent opinion of a country, in support, in criticism, in suggestion or counter-suggestion, contribute to our collective life—to politics, to economic planning, to international agreements.

5. How the policies of the planning board can secure the necessary legislation. Is there any way by which tariffs, administration of credit, etc., can be based on sound policy rather than on log-rolling?

6. How the flexibility of the organization for national planning can be attained and maintained so that experiments

in all industries, a most urgent need, shall be encouraged and the results shown for the enlightenment of all.

7. How to classify experience. We have hardly begun to tackle this very important problem.

8. The relation of control to competition.

9. The relation of the functions of planning and administration.

10. How collective control and decentralized responsibility, the latter always desirable, can be made compatible.

11. The delimitation of the scope of a planning board: what lies within its province and what does not.

12. How to ensure that planning does not mean uniformity, which seems to be the bugbear of some people, nor centralization. National planning is quite compatible with devolution to local authorities.

13. The relation of central planning to the planning which must be taking place in all the separate units. Some of the schemes for national planning sound as if planning were to be forbidden in the separate units!

14. What changes, if any, will have to be made in the organization of the separate plants of an industry if there should be, first, some union of these plants, and secondly, a union of the industries?

I am assuming, in a planned society, a federation of industries and also some union of the separate plants of an industry with probably between the plants a cross-relation of functions.

15. Is it possible to have a federation of industries without an economic congress or parliament? If so, and I believe it is, what would be the relation of the council of federated industries to congress or parliament?

16. What should be the relation of expert and administrative officials? This involves a consideration of what the advisory function really is, and I have never seen that satisfactorily defined.

17. How can the expert principle and the representative principle be combined in a national planning board?

The last is a good example of the difficulties of economic

planning. A "central board of experts," of which we hear so often nowadays, may sound well, but our industries will never consent to be coerced by "experts." Is the alternative then to have industries represented on the central board? But this will of course mean log-rolling.

Some of the writers on planning seem not to realize that if their central planning board is given power to force things on industry, the pressure that is going to be brought on that board by the industries will be enormous. They seem to ignore all that we know of the play of industrial forces on politics.

I believe that it is possible to solve this problem, that the expert principle and representative principle can be satisfactorily combined in a scheme for national planning, and surely an attempt to solve this problem should be one of the first steps in a study of a planned society.

18. What changes will have to be made in government and administration, in addition to those already implied, to make economic planning effective?

What doctrines should govern our thinking as we try to work out these changes? Neither "regulation," our nineteenth-century panacea, nor "coercion," the socialist remedy, would be in accord with the thought I am trying to present in this paper. Central planning must not be a more extended "regulation"; it must be something quite different. Indeed, I do not like that phrase so commonly used, "central planning"; I much prefer "collective planning." As for "coercion," no policy will be whole-heartedly carried out, which is the same as saying that no policy will be wholly successful, unless it is the result of conference and agreement. I do not mean to say that policies decided on will not have to be binding on reluctant individuals, I mean only that the plan made should reduce as far as possible the coercive element. Yet "voluntary planning national in scope" is not enough, nor "supervision of voluntary trade associations by a government commission," remedies being proposed to us. I do not believe our thinking can any longer stay within the limits of large-scale voluntary collaboration (although that may well be the next step), but the best form of collective control remains to be discovered. There is much consensus of opinion to-day that the supply of raw materials, flow of labour, and allocation of capital as well as methods of financing, should be controlled; the problem is the form of organization by which that shall be done.

Those who are giving their time and thought to national planning are performing one of the most needed services in the world at the present moment, but I think that in their preoccupation with *what* needs to be done, they are not always giving enough attention to *how* it shall be done. Yet these thinkers occupy the foremost place in our esteem to-day, for they are devoting themselves to that most difficult task, the task of building. I cannot do better than to end with some words written by Wells long ago, in the first chapter of *The New Machiavelli*. "It is," he says, "the old appeal indeed for the unification of human effort and the ending of confusion. . . . The last written dedication of all those I burnt last night was to no single man, but to the socially constructive passion—in any man."

National planning must surely appeal to the socially constructive passion in any man—in every man.

We have talked of our rights. We have guarded our freedom. Our highest virtues have been service and sacrifice. Are we not now thinking of these virtues somewhat differently? The spirit of a new age is fast gripping every one of us. The appeal which life makes to us to-day is to the socially constructive passion in every man. This is something to which the whole of me can respond. This is a great affirmative. Sacrifice sometimes seems too negative, dwells on what I give up. Service sometimes seems to emphasize the *fact* of service rather than the *value* of the service. Yet service and sacrifice are noble ideals. We cannot do without them. Let them, however, be the handmaids of the great purpose of our life, namely, our contribution to that new world we wish to see rise out of our present chaos, that age which shall bring us individual freedom through collective control.

APPENDIX I

BIBLIOGRAPHY: THE KNOWN PUBLICATIONS AND PAPERS OF MARY PARKER FOLLETT

I. Books

The Speaker of the House of Representatives, Longmans, Green, 1909.
The New State, Longmans, Green, 1920.
Creative Experience, Longmans, Green, 1924.

II. Articles, Pamphlets and Papers on Political and Social Science

"Henry Clay as Speaker of the United States House of Representatives." Published in the Annual Report of the American Historical Association, 1891; reprinted by the Government Printing Office, Washington, 1892.

"Evening Centres." A paper given to Managers and Leaders of the Evening Centres of the Boston Public School System, January, 1913; reprinted by the City of Boston Printing Department, 1913.

"The Social Centre and the Democratic Ideal." A paper given at Ford Hall, December, 1913 (occasion and place of publication, if any, unknown).

"Community is a Process." Published in the *Philosophical Review*, November, 1919.

"The Nature of Community." A paper to the American Philosophical Association, December, 1919, (not published).

III. Papers on Business Organization and Administration

A. Given in the United States
   1. *Under the Auspices of the Bureau of Personnel Administration*
"Constructive Conflict."
"The Giving of Orders."
"Business as an Integrative Unity.
"Power."
   Published in *Scientific Foundations of Business Administration*, Henry C. Metcalf, *Ed.* (Williams and Wilkins, Baltimore, 1925).

315

"How must Business Management Develop in Order to Become a Profession?"

"How must Business Management Develop in Order to Possess the Essentials of a Profession?"

"The Meaning of Responsibility in Business Management."

"How is the Employee Representation Movement Remoulding the Accepted Type of Business Manager?"

"What Type of Central Administrative Leadership is Essential to Business Management as Defined in this Course?"

Published in *Business Management as a Profession*, Henry C. Metcalf, *Ed*. (A. W. Shaw & Co., now McGraw Hill, 1927).

"The Psychology of Control."

"The Psychology of Consent and Participation."

"The Psychology of Conciliation and Arbitration."

"Leader and Expert."

Published in *Psychological Foundations of Business Administration*, Henry C. Metcalf, *Ed*. (A. W. Shaw & Co., now McGraw Hill, 1927).

"Some Discrepancies in Leadership Theory and Practice."

"Leader and Expert" (reprinted).

Published in *Business Leadership*, Henry C. Metcalf, *Ed*. (Pitman, 1931).

"Individualism in a Planned Society." A paper given in the conference series on "Economic and Social Planning," 1932. Not previously published.

2. *Under the Auspices of the Taylor Society (now called the Society for the Advance of Management)*

"The Illusion of Final Authority."

Published in the Society's *Bulletin*, December, 1926.

B. *Given in England*

Under the Auspices of the National Institute of Industrial Psychology:

"The Basis of Control in Business Management."

Published in the Institute's *Journal*, January, 1927.

For the Rowntree Lecture Conferences at Oxford:

"Some Methods of Executive Efficiency—in the Use of Conflict, in the Giving of Orders, in Salesmanship, in Co-ordinating Departments", October, 1926.

"The Illusion of Final Responsibility", October, 1926.

"Leadership," October, 1928.

Published in the *Proceedings* of the Conferences.

For the Department of Business Administration at the London School of Economics (University of London), January, 1933:

A Series of Lectures under the general title "Problems of Organization and Co-ordination in Business":

"The Basis of Order Giving."

"The Basis of Authority."

"Business Leadership."

"Co-ordination."

"Basic Principles of Organization."

These lectures have not been published, with the exception of the fifth, which appeared under the title "The Process of Control" in *Papers on the Science of Administration*, edited by L. Gulick and L. Urwick, published by the Institute of Public Administration, New York, 1937.

IV. OTHER PAPERS

"The Opportunities for Leadership for the Nurse in Industry," given to the Twelfth Annual Conference of the American Association of Industrial Nurses, May, 1928, and published in the *Proceedings*.

"The Psychiatrist in Industry."

(Date and place of exposition unknown; probably about 1928.)

"The Teacher-Student Relation."

(Date and place of exposition unknown; probably about 1928, and preceded by a Paper on "Leadership.")

APPENDIX II

NOTES ON THE ENGLISH PAPERS

MARY FOLLETT gave Papers in England on four occasions. Broadly speaking, in substance as well as in illustration, the English papers differ but little from those given in America. There are certain adaptations and modifications to meet the specific occasions of the English conferences, and in some instances additional illustrations drawn from Mary Follett's own current experiences in England and with English problems are included. In the main, however, the subject matter of the English papers can be paralleled with that of the American, as follows:

1. "The Basis of Control in Business Management."
    Paper given to the National Institute of Industrial Psychology, London, September, 1926; published in the Institute's *Journal*, January, 1927.
    Equivalent to the Paper on "The Giving of Orders" (No. II), with additional sections on the value of the psychological approach to the problems of business management, and the need for organized co-operation between psychological institutes and business executives who are willing to try experiments.

2. "Some Methods of Executive Efficiency—in the Use of Conflict, in the Giving of Orders, in Salesmanship, in Co-ordinating Departments."
    Paper given to the Rowntree Lecture Conference, Oxford, October, 1926; reproduced in the Conference *Proceedings*.
    Equivalent to the Paper on "Constructive Conflict" (No. I), with some items from "The Giving of Orders" (No. II). This Paper contains the first of the two quotations made earlier (p. 17) giving Mary Follett's own version of how her interest in business organization came to be roused.

3. "The Illusion of Final Responsibility."
    Paper given to the Rowntree Lecture Conference, Oxford, October, 1926; published in the Conference *Proceedings*.
    A close reproduction of "The Meaning of Responsibility in Business Management" (No. VII).

4. "Leadership."
Paper given to the Rowntree Lecture Conference, Oxford, September, 1928; published in the Conference *Proceedings*.
Mainly built up from "Some Discrepancies in Leadership Theory and Practice" (No. XIII), with an additional concluding section dealing with the League of Nations as "a striking example of the emergence of a leadership of function, indicating the significant fact that the same trends are being found in widely different fields."

5. "The Problem of Organization and Co-ordination in Business."
A series of five Papers given to the Department of Business Administration at the London School of Economics (University of London), January–February, 1933: these have never been published, with the exception of the fifth, which appeared under the title "The Process of Control" in *Papers on the Science of Administration*, edited by L. Gulick and L. Urwick, published by the Institute of Public Administration, New York, 1937.

The details of the five Papers are as follows:

a. "The Basis of Order Giving."
Virtually reproducing the American Paper of similar name (No. II). This Paper contains the second quotation made earlier (p. 18), giving Mary Follett's own version of how her interest in business organization came to be roused.

b. "The Basis of Authority."
Built up on the American Paper on "The Meaning of Responsibility in Business Management" (No. VII), but with a somewhat different presentation.

c. "Business Leadership."
Built up on the American Papers on "Some Discrepancies in Leadership Theory and Practice" and "Leader and Expert" (Nos. XIII and XII in this volume), but with a somewhat different presentation.

d. "Co-ordination."
This Paper does not parallel any of the American Papers, though it is built up in the main from the thought of "Constructive Conflict" and "Business as an Integrative Unity (Nos. I and III in this volume), with certain items from "The Psychology of Control" and "The Psychology of Consent and Participation" (Nos. IX and X in this volume).

e. "Basic Principles of Organization."

The summarizing Paper of the series; it parallels the American paper, "Individualism in a Planned Society" (No. XIV in this volume), in developing the four fundamental principles of organization. The English exposition, though in major substance the same, differs somewhat from that of the American Paper, since the latter was given in a Conference on Economic and Social Planning, and consequently was more specifically concerned with organization interpreted within the framework of planning. The English Paper was the last of a series specifically on organization, and, although the application of the principles of organization within a framework of national planning was discussed, that aspect was not a major theme.

N.B.—These five Papers, given at the London School of Economics, though, as has been shown, based on lines of thought expressed in the earlier American papers and often repeating sections of them verbatim, in general have a rather different presentation. They were, of course, specially written for the occasion, and cover in one series of talks lines of thought that were, on the earlier occasions, developed over two or three years. Being concerned with one generic subject, "The Process of Control," they formed a more homogeneous unit, and thus have a closer continuity and a more concise mode of presentation, while not departing from or modifying in any way the fundamental principles already propounded.

Lightning Source UK Ltd.
Milton Keynes UK
UKOW04f2019231117

313253UK00002B/397/P